S0-CFE-738

Unfinished Business

The first comprehensive study of U.S. policy toward Cuba in the post–Cold War era, *Unfinished Business: America and Cuba After the Cold War, 1989–2001*, draws on interviews with Bush and Clinton policymakers, congressional participants in the policy debate, and leaders of the antisanctions business community, and makes an important original contribution to our knowledge of the evolution of American policy during this period.

This study argues that Bush and Clinton operated within the same Cold War framework that shaped the Cuba policy of their predecessors, but also demonstrates that U.S. policy after 1989 was driven principally by the imperatives of domestic politics. The authors show how Bush and Clinton corrupted the policy-making process by subordinating rational decision making in the national interest to narrow political calculations. The result was the pursuit of a policy that had nothing to do with its stated objectives of promoting reforms in Cuba and everything to do with getting rid of Fidel Castro's regime and the institutional structures of the Cuban Revolution.

Morris Morley is Associate Professor of Politics at Macquarie University in Australia. He is the author of *Imperial State and Revolution* (Cambridge, 1987) and *Washington, Somoza and the Sandinistas* (Cambridge, 1994) and has published extensively on U.S.–Latin American relations in numerous journals, including *Political Science Quarterly, The Journal of Latin American Studies*, and *The Canadian Journal of Political Science*.

Chris McGillion is Senior Lecturer in Journalism at the Charles Sturt University in Australia. He is a former editorial page editor of the *Sydney Morning Herald* and has written for newspapers and magazines in Australia, the United Kingdom, and the United States.

The authors are senior research fellows at the Council on Hemispheric Affairs in Washington, D.C.

Unfinished Business

America and Cuba After the Cold War, 1989–2001

MORRIS MORLEY

Macquarie University

CHRIS McGILLION

Charles Sturt University

CAMBRIDGE
UNIVERSITY PRESS

PUBLISHED BY THE PRESS SYNDICATE OF THE UNIVERSITY OF CAMBRIDGE
The Pitt Building, Trumpington Street, Cambridge, United Kingdom

CAMBRIDGE UNIVERSITY PRESS
The Edinburgh Building, Cambridge CB2 2RU, UK
40 West 20th Street, New York, NY 10011-4211, USA
477 Williamstown Road, Port Melbourne, VIC 3207, Australia
Ruiz de Alarcón 13, 28014 Madrid, Spain
Dock House, The Waterfront, Cape Town 8001, South Africa

http://www.cambridge.org

© Morris Morley and Chris McGillion 2002

This book is in copyright. Subject to statutory exception
and to the provisions of relevant collective licensing agreements,
no reproduction of any part may take place without
the written permission of Cambridge University Press.

First published 2002

Printed in the United States of America

Typeface Times New Roman 10/13 pt.   *System* LATEX 2$_\varepsilon$ [TB]

A catalog record for this book is available from the British Library.

Library of Congress Cataloging in Publication Data
Morley, Morris H.
Unfinished business : America and Cuba after the Cold War, 1989–2001 /
Morris Morley, Chris McGillion.
p.   cm.
Includes bibliographical references and index.
ISBN 0-521-81716-1 – ISBN 0-521-52040-1 (pbk.)
1. United States – Foreign relations – Cuba.   2. Cuba – Foreign relations – United
States.   3. United States – Foreign relations – 1989–1993.   4. United States –
Foreign relations – 1993–2001.   I. McGillion, Chris, 1954–   II. Title.
E183.8.C9 M75   2002
327.7307291′09′049 – dc21   2002017405

ISBN 0 521 81716 1 hardback
ISBN 0 521 52040 1 paperback

E
183.8
.C9
m75
202

070703-52801 8

For Adriane and Cathryn

"... I have bent over backwards to try to reach out to them, and to try to provide more opportunities for people-to-people contacts, to get better transfer of medicine into Cuba and all kinds of other things. And every time we do something, Castro shoots planes down and kills people illegally or puts people in jail because they say something he doesn't like."

Bill Clinton, Speech,
November 1999

"... when [he] heard that the three top U.S. television networks were pulling out their anchors because of breaking news about a White House intern named Monica Lewinsky 'Fidel was furious,' he said, 'Those damned Yanquis always fuck up everything.' "

Gabriel Garcia Marquez,
quoting Fidel Castro
during the Pope's visit
to Cuba in January 1998

Contents

Acknowledgments

We particularly thank William LeoGrande for his incisive comments on the manuscript. Barry Carr and Steve Niblo also read individual chapters and provided helpful suggestions. Mark Sullivan, Nina Serafino, and Larry Storrs at the Congressional Research Service of the Library of Congress gave us valuable assistance during our research in Washington, D.C. The research for this book was partly funded by a Macquarie University Research Grant.

Introduction

THE Cuban Revolution was a watershed in United States–Latin American relations, posing the most serious challenge to U.S. regional hegemony in the previous 100 years. Washington poured billions of dollars into an initially successful effort to politically isolate the revolutionary regime and restabilize the hemisphere in a manner conducive to U.S. interests, and mobilized resources and personnel on a global scale to sever the island's economic ties with the rest of the capitalist world. In the process, U.S. policymakers sought to foreclose the possibilities that the new Cuban socioeconomic "model" might be viewed by the rest of the Third World, especially Latin America, as a viable noncapitalist path to development. Over four decades, American presidents, whether Democrat or Republican, liberal or conservative, exhibited a marked reluctance to accommodate themselves to the permanence of Cuba's symbol of resistance to U.S. imperial ambitions. At minimum, each has maintained the core economic and political sanctions put in place in the early 1960s while searching for the right mix of coercion and diplomacy to achieve the consensus goal: the demise of Castro's government and its institutional structures.

The changing global context that followed the end of the Cold War, however, eliminated the key security concerns that were presumed to underpin U.S. policy in the early 1960s through the late 1980s. Although Cuba took measures Washington had repeatedly argued were necessary conditions for any move toward normalized relations – withdrawing its troops from Africa, halting the export of revolution to Latin America, and drastically reducing its military security ties with the former Soviet Union – the White House in the 1990s failed to respond in a measured and reciprocal fashion. George Bush and Bill Clinton refused to contemplate any reassessment of the fundamental premises undergirding America's Cuba policy, or any resolution of outstanding differences, in the absence of major changes in Cuba's political economy. In fact, neither shifts in Cuba's foreign policy nor the end of U.S.–Soviet rivalry lessened

1

Washington's order of priorities: first, to achieve a political transition on the island; then, to talk about reengagement.

At least three major arguments have been advanced by U.S. policymakers to justify this continued hardline stance. First is the Castro regime's alleged intransigence and refusal to change in response to White House overtures. The impasse in relations is exclusively of Cuba's making. Havana's foreign policy shifts and its selective opening to market forces – initiatives Cubans were forced to make as a result of events (principally the collapse of the Soviet Union) over which they had no control – did not alter the essential nature of the regime. Economically, the reform process is deemed inadequate or irrelevant; politically, Cuba remained a country where democratic rights are absent, dissidents are imprisoned and harrassed, and foreign terrorists are harbored. The Castro leadership manipulates issues of concern to the United States, such as unregulated migration flows, for internal political advantage and revealed its true colors when it ordered the 1996 shootdown of unarmed aircraft over international waters in a callous disregard for basic norms of international behavior. Throughout the post–Cold War era, Fidel Castro has retained sufficient authority to be able to orchestrate confrontations with Washington and/or other provocative acts whenever relations across the Florida Straits show signs of thawing. In so doing, he constantly undermined the position of Clinton administration moderates. Whenever they proposed a policy review or discrete changes, Castro would impose new constraints on the island's dissident community or resort to some other act of sabotage, thus strengthening the hand of the executive and congressional hardliners.

Second, Bush and Clinton policymakers argued that the U.S. demand for democracy in Cuba was perfectly consistent with the rise of democracy-promotion (and human rights concerns) as a cornerstone of America's post–Cold War policy. This explicitly ideological component of U.S. foreign policy, they contended, was never limited to relations with Cuba, but was a global policy that Washington viewed as a key determinant of its relations with authoritarian and dictatorial rulers throughout the Third World. The Castro regime was denounced as an unreconstructed Cold War relic that resisted the kinds of political (and economic) liberalizing measures being embraced by the rest of the world, and this indictment legitimated a "no-change" White House policy.

The third major justification for keeping up the pressure for change in Cuba is the supposed failure of the "constructive engagement" approach adopted by the Europeans, the Canadians, and the Latin Americans to produce the desired results. The Castro regime, Bush and Clinton officials declared time and again, resisted democratic political changes, continued to intimidate political dissidents and human rights activists, and refused to move to a full-blown free market economy irrespective of the attraction of closer ties with America's allies. Constructive engagement, U.S. policymakers argued, achieved nothing beyond the promotion of short-term economic ties to the benefit of those advocating this approach – and, of course, the revolutionary government in Havana.

What our study reveals is that each of these arguments purporting to explain the immobility of U.S. policy is fundamentally flawed. Setting aside the Castro regime's own attribution of its behavior to the problem of dealing with a hostile superpower that is unresponsive to shifts in Cuban policy, U.S. policymakers' mantra of "Cuban intransigence," and the cavalier dismissal of reforms that have taken place as inadequate, leave unanswered a basic question: Why, if all administrations from Kennedy to Reagan linked substantive bilateral negotiations to changes in Cuba's *external* behavior, was neither Bush nor Clinton prepared to open substantive discussions with Havana once these long-demanded shifts in Cuba's foreign policy had taken place? Instead of reciprocity, the White House added new conditions – changes in Cuba's *internal* political and economic arrangements – as the basis for any move toward normalized ties. Washington insisted that the limited nature of Cuba's economic reforms as compared with the more extensive opening to market forces undertaken by other socialist states, notably China and Vietnam, was a major obstacle to rapprochement. However, this argument was disingenuous in the extreme because neither administration responded to *any* of Cuba's economic reforms. Also, after passage of the 1996 Helms–Burton Act, U.S. policymakers never ceased to emphasize that political rather than economic reforms were paramount for any change in U.S. Cuba policy to take place.

"Moving the goalposts" profoundly undermined any notion of reciprocity in U.S. policy and testified to a broader, overarching reality: the demise of Castro's rule and the end of the revolution were the actual preconditions for U.S. rapprochement with Cuba. Changes in American policy were not conditioned on Cuban actions or, as one senior Clinton policymaker so evocatively put it, Washington was not engaged in a duet with Havana. Thus, it was not surprising that the Castro regime could never implement the kinds of changes that would set in train the much vaunted "calibrated response" to reforms. Each Cuban shift was followed by demands for more concessions or taken to confirm the fact that the embargo was working and that it was important to keep the pressure on. Instead of viewing the reforms that did take place as a basis for negotiations, Bush and Clinton officials minimized their significance, dismissed them as window dressing, interpreted them as confirmation of the effectiveness of U.S. policy, or argued that talking to Havana would only delay more reforms rather than hasten them. Washington's starting point for compromise was the demise of the regime.

The demonstrated refusal to respond to Cuban policy shifts and the Bush–Clinton commitment to achieving the historic goal that eluded seven presidents before them also cast serious doubt on the argument that Cuba policy liberals consistently had the ground cut out from under them by Castro's actions. Indeed, what our study shows is that the basic White House stance between 1989 and 2000 provides little or no reason to believe that, if the Cubans had behaved themselves, these liberals could have gone beyond the kinds of limited modifications that took place. The obstacles were always formidable, not least including the view from the White House, where the domestic political calculus was overriding. The liberals' room for maneuvering was extremely limited, and became even more so after the 1994 midterm congressional elections when Republicans assumed control of the House and Senate, and hardline anti-Castroists took over the running of the key foreign policy committees in both chambers.

Asserting that democracy-promotion was an integral feature of Bush–Clinton global policy is one thing; the practical application, however, was something else altogether – especially when it came to Cuba. Certainly by 1996, Washington was demanding arguably the most thorough and intrusive political reorganization that any state has required of another: a change of Cuba's government, constitution, and political and economic systems. Not even Saddam Hussein's Iraq was presented with these kinds of stringent conditions as a quid pro quo for improving ties after the Gulf War. The more appropriate comparisons, of course, were the socialist states of Vietnam and China. In both cases, the Clinton administration placed no political conditions on its relations with these countries remotely comparable to those it insisted Cuba must meet. On the contrary, although issues of human rights and economic reform were basic agenda items in discussion between U.S. officials and these governments, American demands for political democratization were not allowed to impede closer diplomatic and trade ties.

Far from exhibiting a sustained and principled commitment to democracy-promotion (and human rights), Bush and Clinton maintained the practice of pursuing these goals in a highly selective fashion, dictated by U.S. interests. Clinton policy toward China or, closer to home, to Haiti were instructive in this regard. Notwithstanding China's well-documented record as a major human rights abuser and the manifest absence of democratic politics, economic and strategic factors were always accorded priority status in dictating relations between Washington and Beijing. Indeed, Clinton considered the congressional passage of legislation granting China permanent normal trading status as one of his major foreign policy successes. In the case of Haiti, the decision to intervene to oust the brutal rule of the generals in mid-1994 followed more than two years of procrastination and attempted compromise, and was ultimately dictated by the latter's intransigent refusal to relinquish power (amid rising White House concerns about the electoral consequences of an unregulated refugee outflow) rather than by any principled commitment to democracy.

Finally, the concerted effort by Clinton officials to discredit constructive engagement by labelling allied governments that promoted this idea as mere economic mercenaries totally contradicted the approach the United States itself pursued in dealing with countries such as China and Vietnam. Although constructive engagement did not produce democratic change on the island, gaining access to the Cuban market for their traders and investors was not the only result achieved by those European, Canadian, and Latin American governments who championed this strategy. Expanding relations with Castro's Cuba permitted America's allies to engage in a dialog about reforms and negotiate outstanding bilateral issues such as compensation for nationalized properties. In the process they also developed contacts with mid-level Cuban officials, who are far more likely than the small and fragmented dissident community to play a crucial role in the post-Castro era. As far as these governments were concerned, engagement along these lines ultimately promised the best results, especially when contrasted with the blunt instruments preferred by U.S. policymakers over the previous forty years that had failed so dismally to show *any* signs of success. Hence, they were not discouraged by short-term setbacks for which they blamed Havana.

The central argument of this study is that although the rationale for a hostile posture no longer existed at the beginning of 1989, Washington's policy toward Havana remained consistent in the transition from the "Old World Order" to the "New World Order." Bush and Clinton policy operated within the same Cold War conceptual framework that shaped the policies of their predecessors: heightened economic warfare and a refusal to consider normalized ties in the absence of a regime change. The result was the pursuit of a policy that had nothing to do with promoting reforms in Cuba and everything to do with getting rid of Fidel Castro's regime and the institutional structures of the Cuban Revolution.

In the course of our discussion, a number of issues are highlighted that have a broader relevance to post–Cold War American foreign policy beyond Washington's relationship with Havana. The first is the unilateral nature of U.S. policy, most graphically reflected in the Bush–Clinton attachment to the doctrine of extraterritoriality. European and other allied governments were urged to fall into line behind Washington's approach – and pushed to do so by the global application of U.S. sanctions laws. A second issue is the way in which the White House sets the parameters for profit making by America's overseas capitalist class. Where the U.S. government designates a political regime like Cuba's as fundamentally hostile to American interests, however defined, it is prepared to subordinate profits to foreign policy imperatives. Clinton officials simply dismissed the pleas of U.S. agricultural producers, for example, that they could do business in revolutionary Cuba under the economic reforms that had taken place.

A third issue, never more salient than during the Clinton administration, was the triumph of politics over policy. Although U.S. policy toward Cuba remained a complex mix of historic ideological concerns and domestic politics during the 1990s, decision making was increasingly shaped by the latter. The White House was constantly sensitive to the interests of, and pressures exerted by, the anti-Castro forces in Miami and Washington. In those few cases where it pursued face-to-face negotiations with Havana, the justification was invariably couched in terms of the need to solve a discrete problem that threatened potentially negative electoral consequences beyond the Cuban-American community. On these occasions, however, U.S. officials went to extraordinary lengths to discount suggestions that any bilateral talks were the precursor of a major policy overhaul, or a response to anything Castro had done.

Privately, a number of past and present administration officials conceded that Bush–Clinton policy was anachronistic, even absurd, and on occasion publicly canvassed the need for a more rational approach similar to the increasingly businesslike manner the United States adopted toward most other governments with which it had disagreements, including even North Korea. The major obstacle remained the absence of political will in the White House to challenge entrenched interests in the Cuban-American community and, more importantly during the latter half of the 1990s, its champions in Congress. Staying tough on Cuba was the line of least resistance, no matter that it benefited European and Canadian foreign investors, denied cash-strapped American farmers a small but potentially lucrative export market, complicated a range of bilateral issues from immigration to trade to drugs to telecommunications, and maintained an unnecessarily stormy political climate across the Florida Straits.

Chapter One analyzes Bush administration policy toward Cuba in a period of shifting international alignments and the return to the world of a single superpower. It examines the reasons why the White House declined to take advantage of the collapse of the Soviet Union and the fading Cuban security threat to contemplate a new policy direction in relations with the Caribbean island. The Cold War may have been in its death throes in January 1989, and the revolution about to confront its worst economic crisis, but Washington's historic strategic goal remained basically unchanged. Indeed, Cuba's new external vulnerability was seen as an opportunity to apply increased pressure in the hope of toppling the Castro leadership from power. This took the form principally of urging the Soviet Union to terminate all economic ties with its longtime ally and tightened

U.S. economic sanctions. The decision to link any kind of reciprocity to major changes inside Cuba was partly ideological (a desire to simply get rid of the regime), but also a response to Cuban-American hardliners who wielded considerable influence over the administration's Cuba policy deliberations.

Chapter Two examines American policy toward Cuba from the beginning of the Clinton presidency until the February 1996 shootdown. The strategic goal of terminating Castro's revolution remained unchanged, as did the extreme reluctance to explore some new approaches or engage Havana. The electoral commitment to a rigorous application of the Cuban Democracy Act and other punitive measures to "bring the hammer down on Cuba" – contrary to the approach taken by America's allies – was the hallmark of Clinton's new policy, accompanied by limited, marginal changes in pursuit not of improved bilateral ties with the Castro government but its dissolution. The administration's failure to bring this objective any closer to fulfillment during its first term, however, triggered increasing frustration among the exile leadership in Miami and its Capitol Hill allies. The result was an attempt by both groups to seize the initiative from the executive branch and assert greater control over Cuba policymaking. During this period, no single issue preoccupied Clinton officials more than the Cuban rafter problem and how to solve it. Domestic political concerns dictated the method of settlement – direct negotiations – and established the limits of Washington's interest in engaging Cuba.

Chapter Three illustrates Clinton's even greater willingness than his predecessors to allow pragmatic political considerations to dictate Cuba policy decisions at crucial moments and on critical issues. The decision to sign the extraterritorial Helms–Burton legislation into law after Cuban fighter jets shot down unarmed planes piloted by Miami exiles off the coast of Havana in February 1996 provides the most striking example: even though his senior foreign policy advisers retained profound misgivings about the legislation, fearing that it would likely create major problems with America's trade allies, Clinton was prepared to take that risk. Helms–Burton (like the Cuban Democracy Act) did, indeed, trigger widespread condemnation among Washington's allies around the world who judged it unlikely to achieve its objective of destabilizing the Castro regime and, more importantly, defined the law as a threat to global free trade. Europe, Canada, and most of Latin America argued that economic pressures and political confrontation were much less likely to induce the revolutionary regime to implement desired changes in Cuba's political economy than an approach based on constructive engagement. By signing Helms–Burton, Clinton not only rejected this argument, but also ceded unprecedented power to Congress over the terms for lifting the embargo and normalizing relations with Havana.

Chapter Four examines the rising domestic opposition to the Cuba sanctions policy, driven principally by influential sectors of the U.S. business community (notably agricultural producers) whose hostility toward Clinton's proliferating global sanctions regime had reached a breaking point. This occurred against the backdrop of a number of developments during the president's second term that could have been used to justify a major reassessment of Cuba policy: a relative weakening of the Cuban-American hardliners' claims to speak for the community as a whole; a growing mood in Congress sympathetic to an easing of Cuba trade and travel restrictions without posing any threat to Helms–Burton or the Cuban Democracy Acts; the 1998 visit of Pope John Paul II to the island; bipartisan support within the Washington political establishment for a comprehensive review of Cuba policy; and the Elián Gonzalez custody dispute, which severely tarnished the popular image of the Miami exile community. The White House greeted each of these developments as either a test of its resolve to stay tough on Castro or as an unwelcome challenge to the historic goal of forcing a regime change in Cuba. Nor was it prepared to use up any valuable political capital with the Congress by confronting the still formidable "Cuba lobby," for whom even the most miniscule policy shift was unacceptable.

In summary, what occurred during this twelve-year period was a corruption of the policy-making process by the Bush and Clinton administrations in the service of the erratic demands of increasingly unrepresentative hardliners in the Cuban-American community and their unreconstructed anti-Castroist allies in the Congress. Each strained to contort an intellectual defense for maintaining a confrontational approach in a changed global and regional environment and, having settled on democracy and human rights, proceeded to apply standards of good behavior to Cuba that they eschewed in dealings with other authoritarian and equally, if not more, repressive Third World regimes. Internal reports critical of the policy approach (e.g., over the effectiveness of TV Martí) or at variance with its underlying assumptions (e.g., the Pentagon assessment of Cuba's regional threat) were shelved or returned to the originating agency for reassessment. Bush and Clinton undermined their own, admittedly shifting, initiatives to encourage the growth of civil society in Cuba by pandering to domestic pressures for an ever-tightening embargo. They rebuffed Havana's overtures for cooperation in the war on drugs and placed at risk agreements already reached (e.g., migration) in order to be seen as tough on Castro. They sacrificed the long-term interests of the American agricultural sector for short-term political kudos or to avoid a struggle with the Congress, and ultimately surrendered to the legislature much of the executive branch's prerogative to make decisions regarding the normalization of U.S.–Cuban relations. Finally, they were prepared to brook no opposition from allies, subjecting them to the extraterritorial application of national laws and demonstrating a willingness to caverlierly put in danger the operations of global free trade instrumentalities and understandings.

As the Clinton presidency drew to an end, there was no foreign policy issue over which Washington was more isolated than Cuba. In October 1998, after 157 members of the U.N. General Assembly voted in favor of its annual nonbinding resolution calling on the United States to end its economic embargo of Cuba, with a mere 12 abstentions and only Israel lining up with the dominant hegemon, Cuban Foreign Minister Roberto Robaina called the White House "blind and deaf."[1] Two years later, the "yes" vote jumped to 167 with only 4 abstentions, the White House managing to entice only the tiny Pacific Island microstate of the Marshall Islands to join it and Israel in voting against the resolution. Worldwide, American policy was seen as anarchronistic and irrational, and beholden to domestic interests that cared little for the responsible conduct of foreign affairs or respect for international law.

Ever since the first strains began to appear in the Soviet Union's hold on superpower status during the Gorbachev era, the United States seemed intent on recreating a world of uncontested American power, in the process subordinating the ambitions of competitor allies to its interests. George Bush declared that American leadership and power were prerequisites for a stable international order; that "American leadership [means] economic, political and, yes, military"; and that, in all three areas, it embodied "a hard nosed sense of American self-interest."[2] Bill Clinton and his senior foreign policy advisors also stressed the importance of continued U.S. global leadership, or what National Security Council (NSC) Adviser Anthony Lake termed "enlargement." In a major September 1993 policy speech, Lake spelled out the administration's global strategy: "Only one overriding factor can determine whether the U.S. should act multilaterally or unilaterally, and that is America's interests. We should act unilaterally when that will serve our purpose."[3] Yet what was new about this approach the United States would take in the New World Order was the fact that America's key allies were much less willing to subordinate their economic interests in particular to American policy objectives and dictates. The conflict over Cuba was perhaps the outstanding example. When George W. Bush Jr. took up residency in the White House in January 2001, few issues more starkly revealed the degree to which U.S. policymakers had exhibited a striking lack of realism – about the U.S. national interest broadly defined or about America's capacity to impose its will globally despite the return to the world of a single superpower.

1

The Bush Administration and Cuba: From Cold War to Deep Freeze

> I'm looking forward to being the first president of the United States
> to set foot on the free soil of post-Castro Cuba.
>
> George Bush

UNITED STATES policymakers' perceptions of the Cuban threat had diminished markedly as the 1980s drew to a close. The collapse of the Soviet Union and the ensuing crisis in the Cuban economy had forced the Castro government to take a number of foreign policy decisions that effectively marked its retreat – materially (with some exceptions) if not rhetorically – from the world revolutionary stage. The termination of Cuban military activities on the African continent – the withdrawal of troops from Ethiopia beginning in 1984–5 and Angola following Castro's decision to support a negotiated political settlement in December 1988 – signaled a fundamental shift in the broad thrust of Havana's international relations, from a foreign policy based on revolutionary politics to one increasingly determined by market possibilities and thus government-to-government relations. At the same time, Cuba's ability to challenge U.S. regional interests had waned considerably. Latin America had managed temporarily to ride out the debt crisis of the early 1980s without a political explosion and to contain the social costs of austerity measures and economic restructuring demanded by the United States, the International Monetary Fund (IMF), and other external creditors in return for new aid packages and lines of credit. By the end of the decade, Washington arguably never had an alignment of regimes so favorable to its economic agenda or so desirous of establishing stronger links with the region's hegemonic power – an outcome it could certainly take some credit for bringing about.

Yet, although Cuba no longer preoccupied Washington as it did in the early Reagan years, when George Bush entered the White House in January 1989 it was still perceived as a significant foreign policy problem in need of a solution. The incoming policymakers refused to reciprocate Cuba's foreign policy shifts or support and encourage its efforts to establish greater links with the capitalist marketplace. Like every predecessor since Eisenhower, Bush harbored the dream of toppling the Castro regime on his watch and was encouraged to believe that possibility may have been enhanced by the changing international landscape that resulted from the disintegrating Soviet Union and the return to the world of a single superpower. Even as a backburner issue, Fidel Castro's Cuba remained a potent symbol of unfinished business for those inside the White House and the highest echelons of the foreign policy bureaucracy. It was also similarly viewed by influential forces in American society at large.

THE DOMESTIC IMPERATIVES OF CUBA POLICY

Nowhere was opposition to Castro's revolution stronger than among the Cuban-American community. Fifteen years after the revolutionary regime came to power in Havana, anti-Castro extremists in the United States continued to wage a terrorist war against both the island government and those Cuban-Americans who dared take a soft public position on Cuba. During 1974 and 1975, Miami police accused Cuban exiles of responsibility for fifty bombings around the city; in March 1975, Mayor Maurice Ferré was forced to take the drastic step of requesting the help of federal law enforcement agencies to "combat the violence."[1] At the same time, thoughts of "going home" had become a thing of the past for the overwhelming majority of exiles. Although their support for Castro's ouster remained as strong as ever, their energies were now focused on climbing the socioeconomic ladder, becoming naturalized U.S. citizens, and getting on the voting rolls.[2] Cuban-Americans in Florida and New Jersey, two key presidential electoral college states, transformed themselves into politically important constituencies that no aspirant for local, statewide, or even national office could ignore. This fact was not lost on Cuban-American leaders, themselves now wealthy and respectable businessmen, who viewed political gangsterism as a threat to their own personal interests as well as to their public anti-Castro agenda. By 1980, a consensus had developed within the conservative exile leadership that ways must be found to better harness the community's potential influence as a force in mainstream politics. The timing could not have been more propitious, coinciding as it did with the election of a Republican president extremely sympathetic to the community's anti-Castro message and willing to provide resources as well as ideological support in pursuit of a common goal.

11

In the midst of the election campaign, Ronald Reagan's soon-to-be National Security Council (NSC) Adviser, Richard Allen, established contact with prominent Cuban-American businessmen, seeking their support for the Republican Party in Florida. He urged them to "create an organization that would speak with one voice or appear to speak with one voice" if they wanted to maximize political influence. Cuban-Americans, Allen said, should "take a chapter from the very successful history of organizations like AIPAC [American Israel Public Affairs Committee]."[3] In early 1981, one of the newly appointed NSC staff members, Mario Elgarresta, a Cuban-American hardliner who had notions of his own about setting up a political action committee to raise funds and channel them to candidates who were sympathetic to the anti-Castro cause, proposed the idea to Jorge Mas Canosa, a charismatic businessman with impeccable anti-Castroist credentials. Mas Canosa had fled Cuba in 1960, set out on an aborted mission during the failed Bay of Pigs invasion, and had cultivated links with rightist political and paramilitary groups in the exile community. Elgarresta's words found a receptive audience. "We had to stop commando raids," Mas later recalled, "and concentrate on influencing public opinion and governments."[4] Having decided to make the Cuban-American community a player in shaping U.S. policy toward Cuba, AIPAC became his model for constructing a successful lobby: "We realized pretty soon that to influence the U.S. political system, we must copy . . . the Jewish model, and we became very close-allied with the Jewish lobby and the Jewish movement in Washington."[5] Soon after, the Cuban American National Foundation (CANF) was established as a tax-exempt research and educational organization. Its first chairman was Jorge Mas Canosa.

CANF's ambitions dovetailed with the Reagan administration's global anti-communist crusade and, in particular, its Central American policy, which was based on a refusal to accept the permanence of established revolutionary regimes (Nicaragua, Cuba, Grenada) and an equal determination to ensure the survival of allied governments (El Salvador, Guatemala, Honduras) irrespective of their methods of rule. In pursuit of these subregional goals, Reagan officials devised a "public diplomacy" program charged with responsibility for "sell[ing] the policy to a reluctant Congress and public."[6] New domestic organizations would be established for the express purpose of contesting or neutralizing opponents of the policy, forging contacts with pro-American operatives in Central America, and lobbying Congress to support the policy approach with generous appropriations. CANF was a perfect candidate for the kind of Faustian deal the "public diplomacy" program demanded. In return for funds, legitimacy, and access to senior policymakers, it would publicly back the White House covert wars against real and imagined communists and target individual members of Congress to support administration policies using a mixture of vigorous lobbying and inducements in the form of Free Cuba Political Action Committee (PAC) financial contributions to election campaigns.

CANF quickly became indistinguishable from its chairman, who, with the strong backing of the Reagan White House, wielded increasing influence over U.S. policy toward the revolutionary government in Havana. In 1982, for instance, Mas Canosa complained so loudly when a Cuban stowaway who had landed in South Florida was deported back to Cuba that the White House Chief of Staff, James Baker, sacked the head of the State Department's Office of Cuban Affairs over the objections of senior agency officials.[7] One of Mas's first anti-Castro proposals was to establish a radio station to beam programs specifically into Cuba. With strong administration backing, Congress passed the Radio Broadcasting to Cuba Act in September 1983, setting up Radio Martí with a brief to transmit "news, commentary and other information about events in Cuba and elsewhere to promote the cause of freedom in Cuba."[8] Mas Canosa was appointed to head its Presidential Advisory Board, which managed the station's approximately $12 million annual budget. As the first programs went to air in 1985, CANF was celebrating another victory, having successfully lobbied Congress to approve funding to study the feasibility of establishing a complementary television service to Cuba to increase the flow of information and so "[further] promote the cause of freedom."[9] Three years later, the legislature authorized funding for the startup and testing of TV Martí.

CANF's outlays were more than offset by what it received from the administration. The Foundation, for instance, was a major recipient of funds from the National Endowment for Democracy (NED). Established by Congress in 1983 on the recommendation of a bipartisan study group, NED's ostensible purpose was to promote democracy worldwide; no federal grants awarded under the program could be used for "lobbying or propaganda which is directed at influencing public policy decisions of the Government of the United States." To circumvent this prohibition, CANF applied for, and received, NED grants totaling $390,000 between 1983 and 1988 to establish and fund a Madrid-based front organization, the European Coalition for Human Rights in Cuba, to spread information about human rights abuses in Cuba.[10]

Just as important as funding was the influence Mas Canosa could trade through his access to senior Reagan policymakers and Republican Party officials. The CANF chairman became a regular visitor to the White House, and the president in turn frequently appeared at CANF-sponsored gatherings in Miami. George Bush was also a target of Mas's strategy. According to a brother, Mas's personal relationship with the then vice president began in the early 1980s with a meeting in Miami, attended by NSC aide Oliver North, presumably to discuss what role CANF might play in furthering the administration's

Central American policy goals.[11] Other Reagan officials also warmed to the exile leader. United Nations Ambassador Jeane Kirkpatrick participated in a $130 million property deal with Mas, unconcerned about any possible conflict of interest, and NSC staff member Jacqueline Tillman became so close to CANF that in 1989 she was appointed to head its Washington office.[12] Among the powerful connections Mas cultivated within the Republican Party organization was the vice president's son Jeb Bush, a politically active Miami businessman who worked closely with CANF and managed the successful 1988 campaign of Ileana Ros-Lehtinen, the first Cuban-American to win a seat in the House of Representatives. Toward the end of Reagan's second term, Mas leveraged former Cuban political prisoner Armando Valladares into the job of chief U.S. delegate to the United Nations Human Rights Commission (UNHRC) in 1987 and played a role in the appointment of Georgetown University professor and one-time CANF director José Sorzano to the NSC with responsibility for Latin America.[13]

Reagan's patronage had facilitated CANF's emergence as a powerful political lobby wielding a formidable influence over Cuba policy through its well-developed base of support within the executive branch. The transition from Reagan to Bush promised that the exile leadership in Miami would remain an important reference point for dealing with Fidel Castro's regime. The new president had an additional reason for cementing the best possible relations with Mas and his Cuban-American allies. Influential sections of the Republican Party were skeptical about Bush's conservative credentials. Getting tough with Cuba and stressing the CANF link provided Bush with one means of neutralizing such criticism.

During the Bush presidency, CANF began to expand and deepen its influence on Capitol Hill. Although it had supported and funded a number of anti-Castro legislators throughout the Reagan years, its lobbying reputation had derived primarily from its ties to the executive branch. Over the next four years, however, CANF "devoted most of its energies," as one involved Senate foreign affairs specialist put it,[14] to acquiring an equally formidable, if not stronger, power base among the nation's elected officials. "It certainly lobbied the administration," a State Department Cuba official during the Bush years remembered, "but its real clout was with the Congress."[15] CANF wielded its financial power in an entirely self-serving but uncomplicated fashion. Mas Canosa played no favorites with respect to party affiliation; what was important was the support a candidate was willing to lend to the effort to isolate and undermine the Castro regime. "I always suspected that Mas Canosa preferred the republicans," said Michael Skol, principal deputy secretary of state for Inter-American Affairs during the first Clinton administration, "but this was not true. He supported those who

14

supported him on Cuba."[16] In the decade ending in December 1992, CANF provided more than $670,000 in campaign contributions to members of Congress on both sides of the aisle. In the House, the major beneficiaries were Florida republicans Ileana Ros-Lehtinen, Dante Fascell, and Lincoln Díaz-Balart, as well as New Jersey democrat Robert Torricelli. The leading Senate recipients were spread across four states: Ernest Hollings (D–South Carolina), Robert Graham (D–Florida), Joseph Lieberman (D–Connecticut); Connie Mack (D–Florida); and Orrin Hatch (R–Utah).[17]

Mas also employed his formidable personal lobbying skills and was not averse to exploiting the reelection or other political obstacles confronting members of Congress to bolster the core group of anti-Castro legislators. In 1989, for instance, California Representative Mervyn Dymally, a liberal Democrat and chair of the House Foreign Affairs subcommittee debating the TV Martí legislation, announced that he would not vote against the proposal even though he had opposed its sister project, Radio Martí, in 1983. This time around, however, he did not want to provoke any kind of serious rift with CANF ally and Foreign Affairs Committee chairman Dante Fascell as mid-term elections approached. A pro-CANF PAC showed its gratitude by donating $7,000 to Dymally's reelection campaign.[18]

However, Dymally's turnabout was dwarfed by Mas's 1990 coup in persuading two influential democrats, the chairman of the Senate Foreign Relations Committee, Claiborne Pell (D–Rhode Island), and the chairman of the House Foreign Affairs Subcommittee on the Western Hemisphere, Robert Torricelli, to switch sides on the Cuba issue. A longtime staunch proponent of negotiations with Castro and critic of the trade embargo, Pell, in the midst of a difficult reelection campaign, announced he would vote in favor of legislation (the Mack amendment) to tighten economic sanctions. The decision was made public soon after a Miami meeting with CANF's boss. The Foundation's political and financial support was his reward.[19]

If Pell's shift dealt a major blow to the already small band of congressional moderates on Cuba, Robert Torricelli's defection had a similar impact. Since entering the House in 1983, the New Jersey legislator had positioned himself on the liberal wing of his party in both domestic and foreign policy. He was a critic of Reagan's Central American policies and an advocate of dialog with Havana. In 1989, Torricelli dismissed a Cuba policy "based upon the idea that we wish the revolution didn't happen, that [Castro would] go away [as] foolish going into a fourth decade" and cosponsored legislation to permit the shipment of medical equipment and supplies to the island.[20] Torricelli's backflip on Cuba policy was initially the result of a sustained lobbying effort by Mas Canosa himself. As to why Torricelli and CANF "eventually became very, very close," his staff adviser on Cuba policy at the time attributed it partly to "the fact that CANF gave him a lot of financial support" but also to the "almost father–son relationship" that developed between Mas and the congressman.[21]

Although CANF expanded the scope of its influence on Capitol Hill during the Bush years, it still remained a lobby to be reckoned with in the executive branch and continued to benefit from this special relationship in a number of ways. In 1991, for instance, the NED funded seven CANF anti-Cuba projects with grants totaling more than $462,000, whereas the State Department earmarked a $1.7 million grant for the Foundation's Cuban refugee resettlement program, which was established on the basis of a "highly unusual arrangement" struck with the Immigration and Naturalization Service (INS) to make federal funds available to sponsor Cubans from third countries seeking to migrate to the United States.[22] Discussing CANF's influence as the Bush presidency moved into its final months, one administration official was in no doubt that "the Foundation has had a chilling effect on the debate. Any time anyone starts to think creatively about Cuba we're told: What do you want to do, lose South Florida for us?"[23]

Unsurprisingly then, despite shifts in Cuba's foreign and domestic policies, there was little incentive and certainly no mood among Bush policymakers to pursue any normalization of relations with the Castro regime. Havana's recent decision to withdraw its 50,000 troops from southern Africa, said one official, "has no bearing on our relations."[24] A member of the U.S. delegation that negotiated with the Angolans, South Africans, and Cubans was just as categorical: "The Cubans wanted out of southern Africa and we wanted them out. However, it was made clear to the Cubans that cooperation in this one area did not affect bilateral relations."[25] Castro's release of forty-four political prisoners in November 1988 as a goodwill gesture toward the president-elect was similarly ignored. The same was true of Cuban overtures to the Bush transition team about Havana's readiness to participate in bilateral negotiations on similar terms to those that had proved so successful in arriving at a solution to the Angolan conflict. Not only were these messages ignored by senior personnel in the White House and State Department, but some of the U.S. officials who conveyed them were also reprimanded for their efforts.[26] Intended or otherwise, this treatment sent a signal throughout the Washington bureaucracy – as well as to Cuban officials – that any discussion about opening talks with Havana, let alone serious consideration of a new direction in Cuba policy, was off limits. Bush seemed to confirm as much when he told supporters in January 1989 that there would be no softening of the Reagan administration's approach to Cuba for the forseeable future. One state official provided a concise explanation: "There's no U.S. political cost in keeping things the way they are."[27]

In March 1989, whatever hopes the Cubans may have harbored about a more conciliatory stance were summarily dashed. To counter speculation about an impending thaw in U.S.–Cuban relations, Secretary of State James Baker sent a confidential memo to all U.S. diplomatic posts categorically denying that any such move was being entertained "because Cuban behavior has not changed *sufficiently* to warrant a change in U.S. attitudes." Although noting the positive role Havana had played in the recent multilateral negotiations over southern Africa, Baker wrote that Cuba "has steadfastly failed to offer any concrete proposals of its own to satisfy long-standing and well-known U.S. concerns." Among these, he listed the fact that "Cuba provides the U.S.S.R. major political, strategic and intelligence benefits that it otherwise would not have," that Havana "continues to engage in military adventurism abroad and to support subversive movements in the Western hemisphere," and that the Castro regime "persists in its internal repression and violation of the basic human rights of its citizens." In short, the secretary concluded, "Cuba has not changed its basic policies" and an end to the trade embargo would be "premature."[28] At this juncture, reaffirming the Cuban security threat could not be explained simply in terms of domestic pressures or the phantom imaginings of Bush policymakers: the Havana–Moscow alliance was still intact; Soviet troops were resident on the island; Cuba still had some troops deployed overseas; and it continued to provide limited material support for revolutionary movements, most notably the Farabundo Martí Liberation Front (FMLN) in El Salvador.

The timing of Baker's memo had a twofold purpose: to shore up support within the Cuban-American community and signal to its allies in Congress that there would be no backsliding on Cuba policy; and to send a message to Mikhail Gorbachev as the Soviet president prepared for his upcoming visit to Cuba. By posting in advance the administration's clear and uncompromising demands on Cuba, it was hoped that Gorbachev, anxious to curry favor with the White House, might be willing to bring added pressure to bear on his Caribbean ally.

In the event, the messages Gorbachev brought to Havana in April 1989 were mixed. He praised Castro as an "outstanding revolutionary of the 20th century," assured him that Soviet solidarity with Cuba "is not subject to circumstantial fluctuations," and signed a treaty of friendship and cooperation affirming support for negotiated political solutions to regional conflicts.[29] All of this was consistent with Cuba's continuing value to Moscow. The island remained an important ally symbolically, it was a source of raw materials (principally sugar and nickel) to the Soviet Union that could be purchased without hard currency, its prestige within the Non-Aligned Movement gave the Soviets an advantage in forums like the United Nations, and it allowed Soviet intelligence agencies an invaluable opportunity to monitor U.S. compliance with weapons agreements through the electronic listening facility at Lourdes.

Yet Gorbachev's visit also revealed strains in the Soviet–Cuban relationship, the portents of which were hardly favorable to Havana. In 1986, the Soviet president undertook to arrest the country's worsening economic performance with a program of far-reaching reform. Internally, Gorbachev simultaneously introduced a degree of political liberalization (*glasnost*) intended to unleash new ideas and energies behind a program of measured economic restructuring (*perestroika*). Externally, he sought to end superpower competition in order to release scarce resources for domestic needs and facilitate Moscow's access to Western markets and financial assistance – the key to any hope of reviving and modernizing the stagnant Soviet economy. Integral to this new thinking was the retrenchment of Soviet geostrategic investments abroad. Cutting back on the costs of empire had dictated the unilateral withdrawal of Soviet troops from Afghanistan in 1988; it now translated into the phasing out of military and economic aid programs to other Third World allies, and encouraging the latter to replicate Moscow's policy innovations at home and abroad. This was one message Gorbachev hoped to impress on Fidel Castro.

The dramatic shifts in Soviet domestic and foreign policies coincided with the transition in Cuba from an era of dynamic growth (1970–85) to a new period of economic stagnation and austerity. Persistent structural rigidities in the island economy – the absence of new export industries, excessive dependence on volatile primary commodity exports and oil reexports, the failure to pursue market diversification – converged with shifts in the international environment to produce a marked downturn in the Cuban economy: prices for sugar and oil declined precipitously, the Socialist bloc countries began to reallocate their external financial resources toward internal modernization and to look toward greater integration with Western markets, Cuba's hard-currency balance-of-payments account deficits widened, debt payments to Japanese and West European bankers increased pressure on hard currency reserves and export earnings, and the inability to negotiate new loans produced shortages of key imports.[30]

Cuba's economic crisis precipitated a major internal policy debate over whether to shift to a strategy more closely approximating the new Soviet model. Fidel Castro successfully argued that to combine political openness with economic austerity could provoke serious political polarization and the consequent weakening of the revolutionary leadership. Although the Cuban leader proposed an economic restructuring based on increased labor discipline, rising productivity, greater export competitiveness, and management accountability, as well as a deeper insertion into the capitalist marketplace, it could not be at the expense of social cohesion and political order. Given Cuba's proximity to the United States and the latter's continued belligerence, replicating Gorbachev's political opening was a high-risk strategy that might result in deep cleavages and the rapid escalation of opposition (in part funded by external sources).[31]

Nonetheless, during his visit the Soviet leader sought to counsel Castro about the "task of renovation" to improve "the prestige of socialism" and the worth of "self-criticism" – a none-too-subtle suggestion on the need for a Cuban-style perestroika and glasnost.[32] Through foreign ministry spokesman Gennadi Gerasimov, he also let it be known that Moscow would seek a "gradual balance of our economic ties." In line with this shift, Gorbachev pointedly refused to write off Cuba's debt to the Soviet Union despite American speculation to the contrary. Gerasimov also flagged Soviet concern over Cuba's continuing support for radical regimes and guerrilla movements in the Third World as an obstacle to better relations between Washington and Moscow, adding that the Soviet government was unequivocally "against export of revolution."[33] Gorbachev himself was far less candid about the Soviet position on this issue in discussions with his Cuban hosts. In a speech to the Cuban National Assembly, he termed Washington's announcement of a new $40 million nonmilitary aid package to the Nicaraguan contras "regrettable," and emphasized that Moscow would halt military aid to the Sandinistas only if the United States stopped funding the rebels.[34] However, he had already struck a deal with U.S. officials to end Soviet arms supplies to the Sandinistas. On his return to the Kremlin, Gorbachev sent a confidential note to Bush informing him that the Soviet Union was complying with that agreement.[35] As far as the Soviets were concerned, close allies in Central America now warranted rhetorical support, but nothing more.

Castro's response to this coaxing to adopt the Soviet internal reform model was blunt and combative: political liberalization at a time of painful economic restructuring was a recipe for regime disintegration. To the suggestion that he seek improved ties with Washington, he responded: "We have no assurances that the imperialists have assimilated the new political mentality like the Soviet Union and we have many reasons to be skeptical about their conduct."[36] Even if both comments were prescient, Castro's failure to embrace Gorbachev's new thinking only reinforced Washington's belief that the Cuban leader was a communist dinosaur who would only moderate his policies under extreme pressure from outside.

Yet Castro had already begun the painful process of adapting to new realities inside and outside the country long before Gorbachev set foot on Cuban soil. Externally, moves were well underway to streamline the economy, seek new export markets, and diversify trading partners. Between 1985 and 1988, Cuba's trade with Latin America climbed from $359 million to $1.3 billion; the value of

China–Cuba trade reached $500 million in 1990; total exports to the advanced industrialized world were projected to rise to $4 billion by 1992; U.S. subsidiary trade tripled in value between 1988 and 1990 to $705 million; and, attracted by new majority foreign-ownership laws, hundreds of millions of dollars were pouring into the tourist sector from off-shore investors. In this fastest growing economic sector, hard currency earnings jumped from $125 million in 1988 to $250 million in 1990.[37] Internally, the regime began to renovate the bureaucracy in ways that would make it more efficient and accountable, reform other state and party organizations, and crack down on corruption and drug-trafficking among top officials. Efforts were also underway to improve relations with the local Catholic church, and thus blunt the one persistent and significant internal critic. These initiatives, however, were dismissed by U.S. policymakers as mere tinkering on the margins while the regime's stepped-up intimidation of human rights activists and other dissidents (in an attempt to keep a tight rein on what was and was not permitted during a difficult period of adjustment, and in no small measure because of fears that Washington would exploit any signs of social cleavage) was used as proof that nothing of any consequence had changed in terms of Castro's behavior.

Cuba's foreign policy shifts were treated with similar disdain by senior Bush officials. In congressional testimony in August 1989, Deputy Assistant Secretary of State for Inter-American Affairs Michael Kozak echoed Baker's March memorandum declaring that as long as Cuba "continues to support violent insurgencies in other countries in the region, to provide the Soviet Union strategic advantages at the expense of the United States, and to suppress the human rights and political rights of its own people, we can't consider any fundamental improvement in our relationship with Cuba." Kozak downplayed the withdrawal of Cuban troops from southern Africa, an insistent Reagan demand for any move to unfreeze bilateral relations. Compliance should be sufficient reward because "nobody will be complaining about their being in Africa anymore," he insisted.[38] There was no acknowledgment of the repatriation of the last Cuban troops from Ethiopia in early 1989, or the Castro government's support for a multilateral approach to solve the interrelated Central American conflicts.

Kozak even added a new precondition for normalized relations: Havana's cooperation in the war on drugs. At the same time, department officials were skeptical that Castro would carry out any agreement reached between the two governments. "Cuba has some things to do to improve its genuineness in the effort to fight against drugs," Kozak told the legislators. "We put a high priority on that." The primary objective was "to avoid [getting] into a situation where we seem to be endorsing the bona fides of another regime in the drug area without being confident of the level of that commitment."[39] This may have explained the earlier rejection of a Cuban offer to share information about drug operations obtained during the July 1989 narco-trafficking trial of General Arnaldo Ochoa and other senior officials.[40]

Kozak also defended the administration's refusal to scale down the U.S. economic embargo. Although never likely to topple the revolutionary regime the embargo continued to serve the basic policy goal of "reduc[ing] the amount of hard currency available to the Cuban government to finance mischief [abroad]." The hallmark of the Bush approach was "constancy"[41]; thus the lack of enthusiasm for congressional initiatives, led by Florida Republicans, Connie Mack in the Senate and Lawrence Smith in the House, to tighten the embargo by prohibiting U.S. subsidiaries in third countries from trading with Cuba. Passage of the Mack–Smith amendments would have revived a similar measure on the books until 1975, when it was jettisoned by President Gerald Ford and Secretary of State Henry Kissinger to remove "a recurrent source of friction" between Washington and key European and Canadian allies who were trading with Cuba.[42] Although the Bush White House "support[ed] in principle anything that can be done to tighten up loopholes in the embargo," it did not want to lend support to "something that backfires."[43]

Two weeks after Kozak's appearance on the Hill, however, the president himself proceeded to undermine this support for "constancy" in U.S policy toward Cuba. During a speech at a Miami fundraiser for Republican congressional candidate Ileana Ros-Lehtinen, Bush expressed his desire for normalized relations with Cuba but insisted that this could not happen "as long as Castro violates the human rights of his own people; as long as he, almost alone in the entire world now, swims against the tide that is bringing sweeping change, democracy and freedom, to closed societies around the world."[44] These sentiments prefigured an entirely new rationale for Washington's hardline stance on improved bilateral ties that would bear little resemblance to the original justification for this policy of confrontation, and eventually put paid to any realistic possibility of a compromise solution leading to the eventual renewal of diplomatic relations.

Bush's comments, however, delighted his audience. They signaled the White House shared its belief that whatever debate was underway in Cuba about the direction of the revolution, and whatever adjustments this might produce at home and abroad, was not a reason to rethink the basic thrust of U.S. policy, but rather signs of the increased weakness and vulnerability of the Castro regime. Hardliners such as Mas Canosa and the CANF leadership wanted to go for the jugular: the influence they wielded through the exile community ensured that they would take an important domestic constituency with them. Bush, too, was prepared to move in the same direction – the only question was how best to do it.

AMERICA ASCENDANT: PRESSURING THE SOVIETS

During the Bush presidency, Cuba's economic free fall showed no signs of bottoming out. Among the several formidable challenges that Havana faced in shifting to a new export-oriented strategy was Washington's determination to exploit the worst economic crisis in the revolution's history to bring about its demise. Taking advantage of its dominant global status and the Soviet Union's wholehearted turn to the market under Gorbachev were perceived as integral to the success of this destabilizing strategy. The White House seems to have concluded that Moscow's policy shift held an important key to softening up the Cuban economy, thus making Castro more amenable to the economic and political changes the Bush administration desired. To hasten the process, U.S. policymakers targeted the Soviet Union's most vulnerable pressure point: its desperate need for U.S. economic assistance.

For the moment, however, Washington's attention was riveted on Europe. On November 9, the Berlin Wall was breached and, in the following weeks, torn down. Gorbachev's response was to do nothing to support Moscow's satellite regimes. He renounced the Brezhnev Doctrine, by which the Soviets claimed the right to intervene militarily in Eastern Europe to ensure the unity of the Socialist bloc, lent his support to the reunification of Germany, and agreed to its membership in NATO. The Cold War in Europe was over. In Central America, by contrast, it was heating up in the closing months of 1989. As the Berlin Wall came down, the civil war in El Salvador exploded. Leftist guerrillas of the FMLN mounted their biggest military offensive in a decade, with well-orchestrated attacks throughout the countryside and in the capital, San Salvador, that came close to toppling the right-wing military-controlled ARENA government.

Newly appointed Secretary of State James Baker's only interest in Central America was to get this "bleeding sore" off the national agenda[45] so that the Bush administration could concentrate on the far more historic (and politically rewarding) changes underway in Eastern Europe. From the outset, a consensus emerged that this goal could not be achieved without Moscow's active support. Assistant Secretary of State for Inter-American Affairs Bernard Aronson initiated the process with a secret memo to Baker proposing that this be made the litmus test for future relations with the United States. Gorbachev and the Soviet leadership, he wrote, must see "tangible signs that they will pay a real price in bilateral relations if they obstruct our Central American diplomacy." The secretary concurred and recommended to the president that they employ the "Chinese water torture" approach: "We'll just keep telling them over and over – drop, drip, drop – that they've got to be part of the solution in Central America, or else they'll find lots of other problems harder to deal with."[46]

Although the Soviets had for some years been encouraging their allies in El Salvador and Nicaragua to pursue negotiated settlements, U.S. officials remained skeptical about Moscow's commitment to these solutions. In late March, as Gorbachev prepared for his upcoming visit to Cuba, a letter arrived from Bush that did not mince words: "It is hard to reconcile your slogans ... with continuing high levels of Soviet and Cuban [military] assistance to Nicaragua. ... A continuation of [this] practice in this region of vital interest to the U.S. will ... inevitably affect the nature of the [American–Soviet] relationship."[47] Cuba's refusal to end its military involvement in the subregion, particularly its publicly acknowledged material support for the Salvadoran guerrillas, incensed the White House. For this, it held the Soviets principally responsible. Gorbachev failed to make much headway when he raised the issue with Castro during their April meeting, which senior State Department officials attributed to an absence of sufficient pressure on his part or, in more charitable moments, to the Cuban leader's intransigence. Either way, the omens were not good for Soviet access to U.S. economic aid.

On May 4, just days before an official visit to Moscow, Secretary Baker received a staff memo which read in part: "The bottom line is this: Soviet reduction in aid and Soviet pressure on its clients are necessary to make up for the leverage we lost in Central America when military aid to the contras was ended." Gorbachev's letter to Bush two days later stating that "the U.S.S.R has not been sending weapons to [Nicaragua] since 1988" did not assuage Washington's concerns. In his talks with Foreign Minister Eduard Shevardnadze, Baker "asked the Soviet Union to use its influence to convince Cuba and Nicaragua to halt their assistance to subversion within the region."[48] Although conceding that Castro was a difficult ally, the predominant view among Bush policymakers was that Moscow could apply greater pressure if it wished. Assistant Secretary Aronson refused to believe that Moscow could not force Castro to withdraw militarily from Central America when his Soviet counterpart Yuri Pavlov said that the Cuban leader was responsible for the ongoing supply of Eastern Bloc weapons to the Sandinista government. Whether Castro, as Pavlov insisted, "doesn't take orders from anyone"[49] was of little consequence.

Consequently, when Bush met Gorbachev off the coast of Malta in the first week of December, principally to discuss the situation in Europe, Cuba was one of the few other issues on the U.S. president's agenda. In his opening presentation, Bush called Soviet–Cuban activities in Central America the "single most disruptive element" in the bilateral relationship and "a gigantic thorn in your shoe as you try to walk smoothly along." Then he turned specifically to Moscow's continued willingness to put up with the aging revolutionary in Havana: "Castro is embarrassing you. He's detracting from your credibility, violating everything you stand for."[50] That Cuba's military activities in Nicaragua and El Salvador was the "most contentious issue" could not simply be attributed to opposition from "the rightwing in the United States," Bush said. "Concerns run deeper than that." Some Americans ask: "How can [the Soviets] put all this money into Cuba and still want [agricultural] credits?" This was Bush's trump card: Western countries' economic assistance to the Soviet Union would largely depend on decisions made in Washington.[51]

Gorbachev could only respond that he had done his best to convince Castro that he was "out of step with us," and should implement domestic reforms similar to those being carried out in Eastern Europe. But the Cuban leader remained "his own man" and could not be "dictate[d] to on policy issues."[52] Gorbachev urged the U.S. president to meet with Castro. Bush gave that suggestion the thumbs down, revisiting the theme of his speech in August 1990, when he excoriated the Cuban leader for being hopelessly out of step with the rest of world. "Castro is like a sea anchor," he told Gorbachev, "as you move forward and as the Western Hemisphere moves toward democracy."[53]

Meanwhile, in Nicaragua, the decision to throw Washington's support behind the peace process and elections appeared to be paying dividends. Having shifted away from the contra insurgency option, James Baker and Bernard Aronson persuaded Congress to authorize a nonmilitary aid package to facilitate the relocation of thousands of contra troops and their families from bases inside Honduras. State Department officials had gambled that the Sandinistas would be more likely to hold elections if external military pressure was ended and that the return of the exiles would improve the chances of the U.S-backed slate of parties removing the Sandinistas from office in scheduled February 1990 elections.[54] The gamble paid off; the candidate of the anti-Sandinista UNO coalition, Violetta Chamorro, won a surprisingly clear-cut victory. As news of the election outcome filtered back to Washington, department spokesperson Margaret Tutwiler told assembled media: "Two down and one to go."[55] In a speech to the National Convention of the Veterans of Foreign Wars, Vice President Dan Quayle proffered that change in Cuba, the one outstanding agenda problem, may only come about with the help of a resistance movement modeled on the Nicaraguan contras.[56] This idea seemed to have originated with Aronson. "Bernie's thought at the time," recalled one of his aides, "was that somehow what happened in Nicaragua could be replicated in Cuba, if given the right incentives."[57] Such a strategy was little more than a pipe dream, at least in the absence of the kind of political opening in Cuba that might allow U.S. policymakers to exercise some leverage over events on the island.

SHIFTING THE GOALPOSTS

Having played a key role in the electoral defeat of the Sandinistas, the White House turned its attention to Cuba. "Now [that] they've lost their most closely aligned partner in Nicaragua," said a senior administration official, "our primary pressure is to keep Cuba economically and politically isolated until it changes."[58] Initially, Bush policymakers launched a ferocious rhetorical attack, describing the Castro regime as the "last holdout," operating in "splendid isolation" from global political and economic trends.[59] Then, in a marked policy departure, Bush spelled out his conditions for any future normalization of bilateral relations: the holding of free elections, the establishment of a market economy, and a reduction in the country's armed forces.[60] Whereas for Carter and Reagan, changes in Cuba's foreign policy had been the litmus test of Castro's seriousness about engaging Washington, with these demands in the process of or having been met, Bush now shifted the quid pro quo for any major diplomatic initiative to changes in Cuba's domestic political economy. The ante had been sharply raised.

The broader regional developments within which this policy change took place were dominated by the electoral transitions that swept Latin America during the 1980s and Washington's decision to shift from supporting authoritarian military rulers against totalitarian threats to brokering redemocratization processes. In most cases, the reason for this policy shift was a fear that these regimes, weakened by economic crises, the loss of elite support, and a growing popular social mobilization with a resurgent left often playing a leading role, would collapse and be replaced by mass-based civilian governments opposed to the free market economic model that was a symbol of dictatorial rule or simply reluctant to do the automatic bidding of foreign bankers and governments. The experience of the early transitions in Peru (1980) and Argentina (1983) confirmed a perception that it was not only possible, but also politically advantageous, to promote a return to civilian rule based on a given set of assumptions that preserved the existing state institutions and socioeconomic systems. By 1989, the process of redemocratization and free markets had spread across most of the continent, and significantly now included all three of the powerful ABC countries (Argentina, Brazil, Chile).

What had originated as Washington's adaptation to practical demands for political and social change in Latin America was soon transformed into a new political strategy for preserving the status quo. U.S. policymakers argued that free trade and democracy were interlinked such that any regime resisting the demands of external creditors and foreign multinationals could be accused of undermining democracy, and thus deserving of rebuke or worse. This argument conveniently overlooked the fact that the free market experiments originated with the dictatorships and had been sustained by restricted electoral regimes over which the armed forces, although having formally surrendered power to the civilians, more often than not still retained a substantial veto regarding the nature and scope of changes that were permissible under the redemocratization process.

Once the formula (democracy and free markets) was in place and the rules for electoral transitions firmly established, U.S. policymakers proceeded to encourage, promote, and support democratization as the most effective lever for breaking down hemispheric barriers to markets, privatizing public enterprises, and attacking one-party collectivist states. Washington looked askance at any competitive regional alternative to its highly polarizing free market prescriptions and exploited the moral authority derived from its support of electoral transitions to legitimate its hostile posture toward Cuba. The island was the exception – a nonelected regime clinging to a heterodox, market-welfare system in a hemisphere now dominated by neoliberal governments.

Irrespective of Havana's shift toward a complex array of relations with Latin America, the Bush White House clung to its predecessor's increasingly tattered policy of "keep[ing] Havana's [regional] options limited" and refusing to contemplate any *modus vivendi* prior to the demise of the Castro leadership.[61] Bernard Aronson said this was an administration in the business of "promoting democracy in Latin America and trying to isolate dictatorships, and the effort was to maintain a consistent policy on democracy."[62] There was little consistency, however, in Washington's readiness to engage with, and indeed on occasion offer aid to, the military rulers in Peru, Guatemala, and Haiti and its steadfast refusal to even open a dialog with Havana. Moreover, under preconditions attached to normalized ties, Castro was being asked, in return for no prior guarantees, to implement steps that would effectively amount to an end to the Cuban Communist party's monopoly on power, the abolition of the socialist system, and a weakening of the country's ability to defend itself. For Havana, the defense question had assumed a new importance in the wake of the December 1989 U.S. invasion of Panama to remove a recalcitrant General Manuel Noriega from power and extradite him for trial in the United States on charges of drug trafficking, a January 1990 incident in international waters off the coast of Mexico when a U.S. Coast Guard vessel fired hundreds of rounds into a Cuban cargo ship wrongly suspected of transporting drugs, and Vice President Quayle's bellicose statement in March 1990 to the Veterans of Foreign Wars.

If Havana was dismayed and angered by this decision to comprehensively move the normalization goalposts, CANF headquarters in Miami celebrated. Negotiating with Castro was anathema to conservative Cuban-Americans; now

26

the administration had all but ruled out that option by insisting on internal changes so profound that they would have portended the revolution's demise. These new U.S. policy diktats carried with them important domestic and foreign policy implications. By effectively ruling out any possibility of serious negotiations, Bush further undercut and marginalized those moderate groups within the exile community such as the Cuban-American Committee for Family Rights, which had been calling for talks between Washington and Havana to assist with family reunions, thereby making it easier for CANF to portray alternative community voices as at best pursuing an impossible agenda and at worst acting as surrogates of Fidel Castro.

Inside Cuba, the impact of the Bush statement on those pushing for reforms promised to be no less counterproductive. It threatened the limited political space that had opened up for dissidents and human rights organizations, leaving them with no room to maneuver. Many dissidents had been urging the United States to lift the embargo and tone down the level of its anti-Castro rhetoric on the grounds that such a move would create space in which a political opposition could develop. Ricardo Alvarez San Pedro of the Cuban Commission on Human Rights and National Reconciliation explained the internal dynamic: "The formula is simple. When we have a more rigid economic and social [situation], the government tries to maintain a hard line toward any nongovernmental organization. . . . If there were a relaxation of relations with the U.S. and no talk of war or blockade or invasion or aggression or TV Martí, there'd be no arguments left for the Cuban government."[63] Although the new White House demands effectively rendered the dissidents' proposed strategies moot, they did lend a certain twisted logic to the June outburst by U.S. Ambassador to the United Nations, Armando Valladares, when he accused Cuban dissident Gustavo Arcos of "treason" for suggesting a dialog with Castro. American diplomats in Havana told Arcos that Valladares's statement did not reflect administration policy,[64] but no amount of State Department assurances could totally undo the impression created by this CANF-backed official that the United States cared little for the fate of a prominent Cuban dissident.

In practice, the Bush White House kept the internal opposition to Castro's regime very much at arm's length. "We had no relationship, or a distant relationship, with the dissidents in Cuba," said Vicki Huddleston, the deputy coordinator in State's Office of Cuban Affairs. Apart from "a couple of small groups in New Jersey and Florida the bulk of our [attention] was basically someplace around CANF's line."[65] The White House had effectively hitched its Cuba policy to the conservative Miami exile community rather than the island's anti-regime groups, which was at least consistent with an administration view that Castro did not face any immediate challenge akin to the one that had brought down communist regimes in Eastern Europe. "We don't see any of the indications of the type of dissatisfaction in Eastern Europe in Cuba," a State Department official told the *Miami Herald* in late January. "There aren't the mass demonstrations or the surge in defections. There isn't even graffiti on the walls."[66] Another observed that "Castro was not a Ceausescu, not a Jaruzelski, not a foreign import."[67] It was therefore not all that surprising that Washington subordinated an insider dissident strategy in favor of an outsider exile approach, even if this meant ignoring what insights the dissidents might offer U.S. policymakers and further encouraging the expectations of the Cuban-American lobby.

Indeed, the White House stance intensified the view that Castro's fall was imminent. Florida Governor Bob Martínez established a Commission on a Free Cuba, chaired by Jorge Mas Canosa, to study the impact on that state of the Cuban leader's demise. Testifying before the Commission, INS officials revealed an emergency plan, involving the Coast Guard and the Border Patrol, to cope with the likely flood of Cubans attempting to enter the United States, while the Miami Police Department indicated that contingency planning was underway for the expected celebrations that would mark the collapse of the regime.[68] This kind of talk only fueled the demands that the Bush administration somehow achieve CANF's anticipated result, and sooner rather than later.

Having linked the prospect of any future negotiations to a set of unrealistic preconditions tantamount to the demise of the revolutionary government and, in the process, shown itself unresponsive to the pleadings of Cuban dissident groups, the Bush White House settled on a multitrack approach to extract the kinds of concessions that would terminate once and for all this problem ninety miles off the coast of Florida: stepped-up psychological warfare taking the form of U.S. military exercises and naval maneuvers in the Caribbean–Central American region; more funds and resources to increase the effectiveness of the propaganda offensive; and a new round of political and economic measures that was perceived likely to force Castro to embrace democratization and the neoliberal economic model – and ultimately bring down his regime.

As part of this strategic objective, the administration clung to the tattered regional isolation strategy, notwithstanding Havana's deliberate efforts to promote greater trade and investment ties with Latin America and its success in reestablishing diplomatic and economic relations with most hemisphere governments. In the absence of Cuba's shift to a foreign policy based on ideological pluralism and to a greater market pragmatism, it is inconceivable that all Latin countries would have backed, as they did, Cuba's successful candidacy for a United Nations Security Council seat in 1989.

"Diplomatic demarches" protesting new bilateral ties between Latin American governments and the Castro regime became fairly routine in the early months of 1989, according to one State Department official: "We didn't like Cuba strengthening its relations with the hemisphere because it was counterproductive to our major policy goals and because it might mean strengthened influence among governments in the Western Hemisphere, and this might lead to eventual Cuban membership in the OAS [Organization of American States]." At the same time, given the strength of the tide running in favor of relations with Cuba, the administration was not prepared to expend a great deal of political capital in an effort to obstruct these moves: "It was not something we were prepared to go to the mat about."[69] A much higher priority was placed on ensuring Cuba did not return to the OAS and contesting future invitations to Havana to join other regional groupings. "The bilateral isolation was eroding," recalled Vicki Huddleston, the deputy coordinator in the State Department's Office of Cuban Affairs, "so you tried to hold the line where you could hold the line."[70] Her superior, Bernard Aronson, was even more emphatic about the "fundamental" importance of resisting Latin attempts to reconsider Cuba's OAS membership on the grounds that readmission "would have undermined the OAS as a defender of democracy."[71]

Latin Americans, however, had a different perspective. Even Argentina's President Carlos Menem, one of the region's least hostile opponents of Washington's policy, was willing to abide by a broad consensus in support of Cuba's return to the OAS because, as he told an October 1990 Washington press conference, such a move could facilitate the process of change: "[it] would give us the opportunity to dialogue with the Cubans and achieve some democratic reforms in that country."[72] Yet the White House would have none of it. Following a statement by Mexico's Foreign Minister Fernando Solana in mid-1991 supporting Cuba's readmission, U.S. Ambassador to the OAS Lawrence Eagleburger responded tartly that his government "has a very clear position on Cuba and it will maintain it."[73]

The changing regional context did have an impact on the way in which American policymakers assessed the approach to be taken toward Cuba, however. "With the end of the Soviet Union and the Cold War, changes in Cuba behavior in the hemisphere, democratic governments getting elected who were not rightwing so they could isolate Cuba," recalled an executive branch participant in the Cuba policy debate, "the question for us was whether we try keeping Cuba isolated or try to develop a new strategy toward Latin Americans who wanted to develop ties with Cuba."[74] The result was a strange cohabitation of ritualistic denunciation and diplomatic realism: a yearly cable was transmitted from the State Department to American embassies around the world, "particularly in Latin American and the Caribbean, saying 'be sure to go in and tell the Foreign Ministry how bad Cuba is and that you shouldn't renew diplomatic ties with Cuba' but the aim was to deliver it to a minor official because we didn't really want to call attention to it."[75]

Cuba's human rights record was another obvious political target. Even though Amnesty International and United Nations reports in late 1989 were highly critical of the lack of political freedoms and the Castro government's legal system, both noted a decline in human rights abuses, and significant improvements in the prison system and the treatment of political prisoners.[76] Yet these relative gains were dismissed out of hand by Bush officials who urged the United Nations to increase the pressure by more closely monitoring Cuba's human rights performance. Although Secretary General Javier Pérez de Cuellar refused to bow to Washington's demands that he submit a report on alleged human rights abuses to the UNHRC following talks with Cuban officials in January, weeks later the United States did succeed in cajoling the Commission to authorize the secretary general to appoint a special representative to monitor the situation on the island.[77] In March, Secretary of State Baker cabled American diplomats around the world that one of the fundamental obstacles to any rapprochement with Cuba was the Castro regime's persistent violation of the basic rights of its citizens.

The annual State Department human rights reports produced during the Bush presidency labeled Cuba a "totalitarian state dominated by a single person" that denied its citizens "equal protection under the law, the right to freely choose government representatives, freedom of expression, freedom of peaceful assembly and association [and] freedom to travel to and from Cuba without restriction."[78] By branding the Castro regime an abusive dictatorship, the White House hoped to isolate the regime from the hemisphere's democracies, put Havana on the defensive internationally, and bolster the case for its own draconian policies. The actual intention of this campaign had little to do with a concern for the treatment of dissidents the administration had little interest in getting to know anyway. "We engaged in an effort to broaden support for our policy with regard to Cuba," the State Department's Coordinator of the Office of Cuban Affairs Robert Morley explained. "That was the major factor in switching to the human rights issue."[79]

In contrast to the highly politicized Reagan era reports on Cuba, the yearly Bush State Department studies received a much more favorable reception from the independent human rights monitoring community. Instead of resorting to "unsubstantiated allegations," "baseless claims," and "exaggerations and distortions,"[80] the New York–based Human Rights Watch now acknowledged the "increasingly reliable human rights reporting being done by the U.S. Interest Section in Havana" and "the largely accurate account of human rights violations in Cuba." At the same time, it admonished the White House for "undermin[ing]" the good work being done in this regard by its "single-minded campaign against the Cuban government at the [UNHRC]." Although Castro's regime was "fully deserving of UN criticism for its unyielding human rights repression," the obsessive anti-Cuba campaign was diminished by its "widely perceived failure to devote similar energy to comparably abusive U.S. friends."[81] In March, the UNHRC backed a U.S.-drafted resolution condemning the Castro regime's human rights record and called on the secretary general to report to the Committee on his discussions with the Cuban government during its 1991 session. Interestingly, the resolution was backed by Poland, Hungary, Czechoslovakia, and Bulgaria – all of them emerging from behind the Iron Curtain to the kind of uncertain future where a U.S. debt of gratitude would not go astray.

The ideological/propaganda war against Cuba received a significant boost in March 1990, when, over the objections of several hemispheric governments, the UNESCO Council on Broadcasting, and numerous American broadcasters, the White House embraced the Reagan-era TV Martí initiative. Declaring the test transmissions a success, it released $16 million to fund the project, and merged TV Martí and Radio Martí into the Office of Cuban Broadcasting under the direction of a favored CANF ally, Antonio Navarro.

The initial TV Martí broadcast was effectively jammed by the Castro government which then returned like for like by interfering with U.S. domestic radio frequencies. Fearful of precisely this kind of "technical" retaliation, the American radio and broadcasting industry took the lead in attacking the project. "We think TV Martí is a dumb idea," said Michael Rau, a senior vice president of the National Association of Broadcasters. "It doesn't work." He contrasted the millions of dollars spent on beaming a television reception into Cuba with the cost of jamming it, which amounts to only a "few tens of thousands."[82] After four months of transmission, President Bush himself was forced to concede that Cuba's "constant and effective" obstruction had kept the prospective audience to a minimum.[83] Although this led the White House to temporarily postpone any decision about continued funding, CANF and the anti-Castro coalition on Capitol Hill made sure the administration understood the importance they attached to this project. By mid-1991, the latter's initial concerns had clearly dissipated. Ignoring reports by a presidential task force that "the service should be terminated" unless its audience could be increased and the U.S. Advisory Commission on Public Diplomacy, which concluded that TV Martí "is not cost effective," the White House submitted its fiscal year 1992 request for TV Martí that would have increased funding for the project to $20.5 million.[84]

According to the State Department's Vicki Huddleston, while administration officials rationalized support for TV Martí on the grounds that such a communications infrastructure might "become more valuable" in the event of some future crisis situation on the island, electoral politics dictated continued support for this project even though the investment reaped minimal returns at best. Huddleston recounted:

The Cuban-Americans wanted TV Martí. The administration wanted to give them TV Martí because we could see the value of it. It really was an issue of 'we have to do it' and so it became an issue of how do we do it. I chaired a lot of working groups just trying to come to some kind of consensus and the one consensus you could never come to was that you wouldn't do it. That was not an option.[85]

Ironically, despite the clamor among anti-Castro legislators, many of their colleagues had severe doubts about the effectiveness of the two broadcast projects. "Most people on the Hill thought that Radio and TV Martí was a joke," a Senate foreign policy staffer at the time said, "but Congress kept funding it because of campaign contributions from the Cuban-American community."[86]

Economic pressure, however, was the most powerful and reliable weapon in Washington's anti-Cuba arsenal and could be used far more comprehensively to target not only American corporations and individuals, but also foreign governments and their multinational business communities doing business with Havana. During early 1990, the Bush White House showed it could be just as zealous as its predecessors in implementing what Press Secretary Marlin Fitzwater called "a total embargo against everybody and everything going to Cuba."[87] The major objective was twofold: to restrict the Castro regime's access to hard currency and to frustrate its efforts to find alternative sources of aid and trade to compensate for losses resulting from the collapse of the Soviet bloc. Citing embargo regulations, the Treasury Department refused American Telephone & Telegraph (AT&T) permission to connect its newly laid $7 million underwater telephone cable between the U.S. and Cuba because AT&T proposed to transfer $220,000 annually to the Cuban telephone company to cover repair and service costs.[88]

To minimize potential financial benefits accruing to Cuba from its staging of the 1991 Pan American Games, Washington resorted to a "full court press": ABC Television was denied a license to broadcast the games because the deal would have involved paying Havana more than $6 million for exclusive coverage rights;[89] Hewlett-Packard, the traditional supplier of drug testing equipment to regional and international sporting events under a standard arrangement whereby the equipment was later sold to the host nation's organizing committee at reduced prices, was similarly blocked; and, finally, Treasury imposed restrictions on how much money officials and athletes traveling to Cuba for the games would be allowed to spend. This hard currency crackdown also extended to individual American citizens whose activities had gone unchecked for years: Texas bass fisherman Dan Snow, for example, who had been taking groups to fish in Cuban waters for more than a decade, was suddenly charged and prosecuted in a Houston court with violating the Trading with the Enemy Act in relation to a bass-fishing expedition he led to Cuba in 1987.[90]

Bush efforts to apply pressure on the Cuban economy also targeted imports into the U.S. market containing Cuban-origin materials, Cuban purchases of goods from third countries containing "significant" American-origin materials, and potential joint venture initiatives by foreign investors. In May 1991, for instance, Washington blocked the sale of five Brazilian passenger-transport planes to Cuba because they included several American-made components.[91] That September, Brazil's VASP airlines terminated negotiations for a joint venture agreement with Cuba's state airline after U.S. officials warned VASP Chief Executive Wagner Canhedo that he "could have problems in other things" if any agreement was concluded with the Castro government.[92]

The toppling of Panama's General Noriega in December 1989 provided Washington with an opportunity to get rid of a Havana-related irritant in the bilateral relationship: the proliferation of front companies reexporting U.S.-origin technology and other capital goods to Cuba, which totaled an estimated $82 million in 1989.[93] Relations between Panama and Cuba had deteriorated steadily over Castro's nonrecognition of the new U.S-installed Endara regime and was not helped by the latter's unconditional support of Bush regional policy or the American President's March 1990 proposal that Nicaragua and Panama receive a special $800 million aid package that he pointedly described as an initiative to "increase the pressure in that marvellous island of Cuba for change."[94] In any event, Bush officials took advantage of this acceptable regime change in Panama to encourage a crackdown on front companies facilitating Havana's access to American inputs critical to its economic revival.

Important as these initiatives were, however, they paled in significance when compared to Washington's success in persuading the Soviet Union to cut, or better still eliminate, its aid and subsidized trade arrangements with Cuba. Visiting Moscow in February 1990, Secretary of State James Baker used American displeasure over the recent dispatch of six MiG-29 jet fighter aircraft to the island to question the validity of the larger Cuban–Soviet economic relationship.[95] The jet fighters did little to increase Cuba's air power and certainly posed no threat to the U.S. mainland. Indeed, neither the six MiGs nor the subsequent Soviet decision to upgrade its electronic listening facility at Lourdes caused the Pentagon to revisit an earlier assessment that Cuba was no longer the major security issue it had once been. "Cuba's military adventurism had decreased markedly," the Pentagon's Assistant Country Director for the Caribbean during the early 1990s,

John Christiansen, recalled. "The Lourdes intelligence facility was still an issue in the sense that the Soviets could be spying on us, they could presumably find out things about what we were trying to do. But the information that the Cubans were able to glean from that did not have much of a significant impact." Castro's regional ambitions were now less of a concern to the Defense Department than planning for another "outward migration" crisis. The view that Cuba had largely ceased to pose a security threat to the United States was more or less shared by the rest of the foreign policy bureaucracy dealing with Latin America: "We were all pretty much on the same sheet of music," said Christiansen. "Inter-American coordination on Cuba was pretty smooth at that time."[96]

At the political level, however, Russian jet fighter planes and its intelligence monitoring post on the island still symbolized Moscow's continued backing for Castro's revolution, and thus offered a perfect excuse for Baker to rail against military and economic cooperation with the island. In early June, Assistant Secretary of State for Inter-American Affairs Bernard Aronson told a visiting delegation of Soviet officials that "we hope the Soviet Union will see the fundamental contradiction between its new thinking and its contribution of $5 billion a year in assistance to Cuba, where human rights are being violated."[97] At Camp David, meanwhile, Gorbachev and Bush conferred about a number of Third World issues. High on the U.S. president's agenda was the aid subsidy to Cuba. On the receiving end of another lecture about the need to stop funding this troublemaker, Gorbachev finally began to give ground with the comment that "during the coming year, we're going to normalize the [aid] relationship."[98]

During a White House press conference later that month, President Bush returned to a theme first canvassed at the December 1989 Malta summit. The United States would withhold economic aid to the Soviet Union for the time being, partly because Americans would balk at "X-billions of dollars [being put] into the Soviet economy when it's not reformed, when they're spending 18 percent of their gross national product on military [*sic*] and when they're spending an estimated $5 billion in Cuba." Addressing the lack of concern among some U.S. allies about the last point, a clearly irritated Bush stressed his resoluteness on this issue: "I'm very concerned about it."[99]

Although the president and his secretary of state kept up a steady drumbeat of criticism to pressure the Soviets to cooperate over Cuba if they hoped to obtain large-scale U.S. aid to renovate their floundering domestic economy, they were also keen to involve the exile community leaders in this effort. "The Cuban-Americans have an opportunity to work with the Soviets and encourage the kind of cooperation we had on Nicaragua," a State Department official told the *Miami Herald* in June 1990. Or they can "play a very destructive role" and risk "slowing the demise of Castro."[100] CANF and Mas Canosa were apparently convinced of the benefits of playing the kind of role Washington had in mind. "We explained what we were doing vis-à-vis the Soviet Union and Central American issues," Assistant Secretary Aronson explained. "As a result, they began to see the Soviet Union under Gorbachev as a potential ally."[101] Mas Canosa appeared to take note of the point in the course of his own diplomatic efforts to isolate Cuba from its former allies. On several visits to Eastern European capitals, he urged the new democratically elected leaders to cut their aid and trade ties with Castro's regime. Hosting several visits by Soviet legislators, journalists, and academics to Miami, he gave them the same message: CANF would lobby Washington against aid to Moscow while the Soviets continued to subsidize the Cuban economy.[102]

By 1990, the debate in Moscow over Cuba aid programs revealed that a majority of Gorbachev's senior foreign policymakers still favored critical support of Cuba. That year the two countries signed a bilateral trade agreement worth $15 billion, an approximately nine percent increase over the 1989 accord. General Mikhail Moiseyev told Cuban officials that the cooperative relationship was not under threat, and that the contractual agreements signed following Gorbachev's April 1989 visit would be honored.[103] Two months later, the head of the Foreign Ministry's Latin American Department, Valery Nikolayenko, dismissed speculation that economic ties would be terminated. Moscow would continue to service Cuba's vital needs "regardless of what the Soviet Union has or doesn't have."[104]

Nonetheless, Moscow did begin the process of putting its relationship with Cuba on a more businesslike footing with a mid-year announcement that as of January 1991, all bilateral trade would shift from subsidized barter to hard currency. However, the shift would take place more slowly than would normally be the case "to avoid damaging the Cuban economy."[105] Washington was not overly impressed, given its preference for a rapid and complete rupture. U.S. officials calculated an effective loss of $1.5 to $2.5 billion in Soviet support, or around one-half of Moscow's aid program. However, perhaps $2.5 billion of the trade subsidy remained unaccounted for.[106] Addressing the Soviet parliament, President Gorbachev reportedly conveyed his unhappiness over recent Washington efforts to dictate Moscow's future relations with Havana, restated his support for normalized ties between the United States and Cuba and a willingness to mediate any such talks, and made it clear that "the ball is [now] in the U.S. court."[107]

When not focusing its energies on permanently fracturing the Soviet–Cuba axis, Bush policy gave no indication that it was prepared to contemplate any shift away from its well-worn path. In July, amid rising terrorist activities against the moderate Cuban-Americans in Miami by hardline anti-Castroists, the U.S. Justice Department approved the early prison discharge of convicted terrorist Orlando Bosch, who had specialized in attacks on Cuban embassies and consulates throughout Latin America and was believed responsible for the 1976 bombing of a Cuban airliner over Venezuela, in which seventy-three people died. Lobbying by CANF and its Florida republican allies, including the president's son Jeb Bush, was an instrumental factor in Bosch's release. Havana's protests that the decision was likely to encourage more terrorist acts against the island fell on deaf ears in Washington. At the same time, Cuban proposals for broad-ranging discussions met with the predictable rebuff, and the U.S. failure to implement the 1984 immigration agreement had resurfaced as a source of tension.

Entering 1991, however, more pressing matters consumed the energies of the Castro leadership as it struggled to survive the economic consequences of the political transformation of Eastern Europe. The cutbacks in Soviet fuel exports had totally eliminated one of Cuba's two major sources of foreign exchange – crude oil reexports, which in 1985 accounted for $620 million in hard currency – and the island faced the added burden of future purchases of Soviet crude in hard currency at world market prices. The December 1990 trade pact between the Soviet Union and Cuba, which reduced the terms of an agreement from five years to one, ended the arrangement whereby Cuba traded with a single Soviet government entity in favor of more stringent negotiations with individual Soviet Republics and state companies, and signaled a further reduction in the number of Soviet economic and technical advisors to approximately 1,000 by early 1991 (down from more than 3,000 in 1989).[108] Cuban Vice President Carlos Rafael Rodríguez predicted "five or six very difficult years ahead."[109]

The 1991 trade and economic agreements did indicate a continued willingness on Moscow's part to cushion the impact of the changes on Cuba's economy: sugar imports remained at the 1990 level; grain and flour exports to the island increased; and funding was continued for eighty development projects begun during the previous five year plan (1986–90). However, these positive expressions of support were also accompanied by more negative developments. The aid pipeline had virtually dried up; trade with the Eastern Bloc countries was now half of its 1988 level; Soviet oil exports to the island continued to plummet; falling Soviet prices for Cuban sugar, nickel, and other commodities resulted in a net loss of purchasing power of more than $1 billion in 1991 compared with 1990;[110] and midway through the year, bread rationing was introduced because Moscow could not even honor promises to deliver specified shipments of much-needed grain and flour to the island.

In July, the cumulative impact of these economic setbacks forced Castro to announce that the economy was moving to a virtual war footing, which he dubbed a "Special Period in Time of Peace." New austerity measures would be introduced to compensate for shortages and as part of an effort to reorganize the internal economy with a view toward making it more globally competitive. To attract increased foreign investment, the government proposed to create local mixed capitalist companies for joint ventures, provide tax exemptions on imported goods needed by foreign investors, and guarantee the unrestricted repatriation of profits.

Given Castro's belief about the likely destabilizing consequences of political liberalization in a time of economic austerity and sacrifice, it came as no surprise that these carefully measured openings to the market were balanced by new closures in the sphere of political activity. Arrests of dissidents became more frequent, prison sentences grew longer, and neighborhood Rapid Response Brigades were organized to harass and intimidate anyone speaking out against the regime or its policies. Castro justified the Special Period policies with reference to the need to preserve the social gains of the revolution and the island's sovereignty and independence. To Washington, however, this latest crackdown just reconfirmed a long-held belief that the Cuban leader could not be trusted and had no genuine interest in normalizing bilateral relations.

In a May 1991 Cuban Independence Day address beamed into the island on Radio and TV Martí, President Bush promised a veritable sea change in bilateral relations if Castro would only meet certain preconditions. "If Cuba holds fully free and fair elections under international supervision, respects human rights, and stops subverting its neighbors, we can expect relations between our two countries to improve significantly."[111] The statement effectively calmed fears within the Cuban-American community that the administration was about to make some new offer to Havana. In Miami, State's Bernard Aronson told exiles that the president's statement was "an effort to clear the air in U.S. policy toward Cuba. It's not a change in policy, but an open door, an important message in which we are describing the shape and size of the door." Turning to the demand for political change, he added a list of conditions that must accompany any electoral process if the outcome was to receive Washington's imprimatur. The Cuban government would have to authorize all political parties to contest the elections, allow them unfettered access to the media, and welcome supervision of the process by the Organization of American States and the United Nations. CANF welcomed the "shape and size of the [democratization] door," although Mas Canosa opposed any election in Cuba while Fidel and Raúl Castro remained in power.[112]

The White House could not have been under any illusion that the Cubans would accept this latest price for better ties. Indeed, while Bush had been delivering his Independence Day offer, senior U.S. officials confirmed that Secretary of State Baker had renewed pressure on the Soviet leadership to cut aid to Cuba if it hoped to obtain American help in solving its own domestic economic problems. Unless Moscow "abandoned its support for Castro," Baker told a visiting high-level Soviet delegation, it would be "unrealistic" to expect that either public opinion or the U.S. Congress would "endorse any steps to bolster the Soviet economy."[113] At their June summit meeting in Houston, Bush directly relayed the same domestic politics message to Gorbachev. By then, however, it was clear that the U.S. president had limited discretionary power to offer Moscow a substantial aid package and was trying to salvage domestic political capital from the appearance of being tough on Cuba.

The administration continued to accuse Havana of trying to subvert its neighbors, but the evidence was hardly overwhelming and almost exclusively related to a single country in the midst of a civil war. When Aronson was asked by House Foreign Affairs Committee member Robert Torricelli in July 1991 whether Cuba continued to supply weapons to the leftist guerillas in El Salvador, his response was excessively general and contradictory: "Let me put it this way, Congressman. The FMLN has no problems gaining weapons, ammunition or training, and the Cuban Government is the principal reason why they have no problem." He assured the committee that "every bullet will come out of a Cuban stock," but then immediately conceded that the Salvadoran guerrillas could be getting its ammunition from "elsewhere."[114] The latter may have been all the more likely given Castro's statement to Soviet Ambassador Yury Petrov that Cuba quietly ceased supplying weapons to the FMLN forces in February.[115]

Nor was there any inclination on Washington's part to give much credence to the views and suggestions by Havana-based dissidents for improving the political situation inside Cuba. Its muted response to the September decision by eight dissident organizations to form the Cuban Democratic Convergence (CDC) to work for "peace, national reconciliation and full democracy" in Cuba was not all that surprising, especially as the CDC advocated a dialog with the Castro regime.[116] The White House believed the cause of political reform in Cuba could be more rapidly advanced by such measures as doubling the amount of funds in the 1991 federal budget to be channeled through the NED for this purpose. "Cuba," announced NED President Carl Gershman, "is a priority." Nevertheless, in keeping with the administration's outsider strategy, the recipients were not internal dissidents; rather, the funds were spent publicizing human rights abuses and attacking the island's one-party socialist system. The two major beneficiaries of NED largesse were CANF and the AFL-CIO: the former received $100,000 to fund efforts of the Madrid-based European Coalition for Human Rights in Cuba to alert public opinion to repression on the island; the latter collected more than $127,000, most of which was allocated to promote the virtues of independent labor unions on Radio Martí.[117] Yet, this could only be a long-term strategy; even the Soviet card was looking uncertain of producing the desired outcome any time soon, and the anti-Castro hardliners were growing impatient for results.

CONGRESS TAKES THE INITIATIVE: THE CUBAN DEMOCRACY ACT

Amid the focus on Cuba's human rights performance and the shortcomings of its political system, the Bush administration kept its attention sharply focused on the island's most vulnerable external pressure point: the lack of hard currency. As the August 1991 Pan American Games neared, State and Treasury officials kept a watchful eye for any activity that might put U.S. dollars into the coffers of the Cuban government. In March, a cruise ship was denied permission to take relatives of participating athletes to Cuba and house them for the duration of the games. Although food, accommodation, and other costs would be paid to the company, ABC Charters, the payment of a port tariff to the regime contravened the embargo regulations. Some months later, Assistant Secretary of State Aronson linked proposed new restrictions on Cubans applying for tourist visas to the United States to the hard currency denial policy. The number of applications, he told the House Foreign Affairs Committee, had jumped appreciably in recent months due to a series of Castro government decisions to lower the age limit for its citizens to travel abroad. Because each Cuban who left the island was required to pay fees totaling at least $900 in U.S. currency for a travel permit, tightening the entry conditions would reduce the Castro government's access to this source of funds.[118] Ironically, given the exile community's traditional opposition to any restrictions of this kind and the island's worsening economic crisis, some Miami Cuban-Americans and their supporters on the Hill were not, at least in the short term, averse to the contemplated new immigration measures. As Robert Torricelli, chairman of the House Western Hemisphere Affairs subcommittee, observed: "a pause in the issuance of visas provides a chance to increase pressure on Castro and explore a change of policy that restricts his ability to export his dissenters and economic problems."[119] In other words, blocking disgruntled Cubans from leaving the island could perhaps bring an internal political upheaval that much closer.

Under Treasury regulations announced in late September, no more than $500 could be transferred to Cuba for travel fees and round-trip airline tickets; the amount that family members could send to close relatives on the island every quarter was cut from $500 to $300; and Cubans returning to the island were forbidden from taking more U.S. currency than they arrived with on the mainland. The Department's Office of Foreign Assets Control director, Richard Newcomb, summarized the objectives Washington hoped these measures would achieve: "The new regulations are designed to limit exorbitant fees imposed by the Cuban government [and] at the same time the provisions accomplish the objectives of the embargo by further limiting financial and commercial transactions with Cuba."[120]

Yet if the administration was satisfied with the measures being taken, the same could not be said for the anti-Castro lobby on Capitol Hill, where sentiment was still strong that Bush officials had failed to wage a sufficiently aggressive campaign to bring about change inside Cuba. They were particularly excised by the inability of the White House to force a complete rupture in Soviet–Cuban economic ties and its refusal to support the Mack–Smith initiatives to ban the overseas subsidiaries of American corporations from trading with the island. Torricelli spoke for his colleagues when he characterized the Bush approach as one of "allow[ing] the natural political and economic forces to work to bring change to Cuba. It is a policy of awaiting [rather than] engaging in a proactive policy.... [T]he fact remains that there are levers of power that the United States potentially has available to hasten change in Cuba which [are] not being used."[121]

Florida's Bill McCollum (R), Connie Mack, and Bob Graham (D); New Jersey's Torricelli; and North Carolina's Jesse Helms (R), the ranking minority member on the Senate Foreign Relations Committee, took it on themselves to force the issue. The House approved an amendment to the foreign operations appropriation bill conditioning future aid to the Soviet Union on an end to the latter's military support to the island. Torricelli justified the vote with a typically blunt statement: "Whatever George Bush might intend, it is not possible to give large-scale assistance to the Soviet Union as long as the Soviet Union gives large-scale assistance to Cuba."[122]

The Senate adopted an even tougher stance, approving a Helms amendment to the foreign aid bill without debate, by ninety-eight to one, requiring the White House to certify that Moscow had stopped all aid to Cuba in return for economic assistance from the United States and making an end to its Cuba alliance a *sine qua non* for supporting Soviet membership of the IMF. The Senate also gave consideration to a measure that would have tied the granting of Most Favored Nation trading status to China to a "significant" reduction in Beijing's aid to Havana. Last, but not least, CANF's closest allies signaled that they were preparing a renewed attempt to pass the Mack–Smith amendments that Bush had vetoed when they first came across his desk in October 1990 on the grounds that they could place U.S. corporations in the unenviable position of forcing them to choose between disobeying national or host-country laws.

Appearing before the House Foreign Affairs Committee in July, Mas Canosa presented his own wish list of measures to strangle the Cuban economy and force a change of regime: Washington should close the subsidiary trade loophole in the embargo; prohibit commercial ships "touching Cuban waters" from entering U.S. ports for a six-month period; ensure Castro's government received no economic benefits from the proposed North American Free Trade Agreement (NAFTA) – a veiled reference to Mexico and Canada's economic ties with Cuba and their hostility toward the U.S. embargo; eliminate the sugar quota of any nation that imports Cuban sugar and reduce U.S. aid to any country purchasing Cuban sugar by an amount equal to those purchases (a measure directed at the Soviet Union and its former Eastern European allies); and end Castro's "exploitation" of the humanitarian provisions of the embargo by limiting shipments of gifts and visits to the island for strictly humanitarian purposes (targeting the activities of church groups in both countries). CANF's chairman also aimed a broadside at foreign companies investing in Cuba, informing the legislators that a post-Castro government "will have to take over those properties and do with them the same thing that is going to be done with all the other properties that are in the hands of the government today."[123]

In Torricelli's office, the attention of his Cuba affairs adviser Richard Nuccio was focused on the issue of third country subsidiary trade with Cuba, which he was convinced had the potential to

> eventually erode the core of the embargo, that one day down the road the U.S. would wake up and discover that it had a four or five billion dollar annual [subsidiary] trade with Cuba. The only problem was it happened to go through Italy, France, Mexico, Venezuela and Panama. None of it left the United States. At this point the business community in Miami and New Orleans would say, "Why are we letting all the dock workers in Italy and France get this business, why don't we get some?"

Nuccio's concern that the White House "was mostly trying not to do anything about Cuba" was shared by his boss and other anti-Castro legislators who now set about an effort to hijack control of the policy.[124]

In February 1992, based on a draft proposal put to him by Mas Canosa, Torricelli introduced legislation – the Cuban Democracy Act (CDA) – into the House to further tighten the trade embargo while simultaneously promoting greater interaction at a people-to-people level between Americans and Cubans. Subsequently, Bob Graham and Connie Mack submitted a virtually identical proposal into the Senate. A key provision of Torricelli's bill would terminate all trade between U.S. subsidiaries abroad and Cuba. Between 1989 and 1990, the value of exports to Cuba from these firms jumped from $169 million to $533 million, while island exports to these enterprises rose marginally from $162 million to $172 million.[125] The CDA would also bar ships involved in Cuba trade from docking in U.S. ports for six months.

The explicit intention of the legislation was to advance democracy in Cuba by punishing the Castro regime while rewarding the Cuban people. It sought to combine new economic pressures (Track I) with increased bilateral contacts at a nongovernmental level (Track II). According to Torricelli, Mas's original proposal "was all sticks – sanctions, penalties, prohibitions" to which he appended the "carrots." Richard Nuccio played a key role in crafting an early draft of the legislation that would have eased restrictions on family visits to the island; furthered cultural, academic, and scientific exchanges; and "allowed U.S. companies to work with the Cubans to upgrade telecommunications between the two countries."[126] Even though this last promised to substantially increase Cuba's hard currency reserves, the belief was that this would be more than offset by the role that greater people-to-people access could play in facilitating opposition to the Castro regime.

According to Nuccio, CANF's enthusiasm for the legislation was also based "on a perception that the Bush administration was doing nothing on Cuba, or at least nothing good from their point of view and now was the time to strike."[127] Mas Canosa initially balked at Track II, but changed his mind after Torricelli convinced him that it would be difficult to gain bipartisan congressional support for the bill if this provision was deleted. However, some of his allies on Capitol Hill were not prepared to be so accommodating. Ileana Ros-Lehtinen, still the only Cuban-born legislator, "didn't like Torricelli's carrots, even after Mas had signed off on them," and was successful in getting measures to open news bureaus in Washington and Havana and to permit educational and scientific exchanges deleted from the Track II provision.[128]

When the legislation was submitted to the House it nevertheless included both sticks and carrots, although the impact of the former appeared likely to be greater and more immediate. These included an extension of the embargo to foreign-based subsidiaries of U.S. companies trading with Cuba, banning port visits by Cuba-friendly ships, fines of up to $50,000 imposed (at the president's discretion) for violations of the embargo, and a request that the White House encourage foreign countries to restrict their trade with Cuba. The Track II people-to-people carrots provided for increased communication between Cuban-Americans and the island's populace, including the donation of food directly to individual Cubans or to Cuban nongovernmental organizations, the export of medicines and medical equipment (but only on the unlikely proviso that the regime allowed on-site inspections to ensure the supplies "benefit . . . the Cuban people" and were not reexported), and the allocation of funds to designated nongovernmental bodies "for the support of individuals and organizations to promote nonviolent change in Cuba." Finally, Cuba would be rewarded if free and fair elections took place by a lifting of the embargo and the granting of U.S. aid. Mas Canosa and the powerful anti-Castro forces in Congress applauded the Torricelli Bill. Getting White House approval, however, was another matter altogether.

At least two factors explained the Bush administration's decidedly cool response to the CDA legislation. One was a desire to avoid any repetition of the conflicts with U.S. allies that erupted during the first half of the 1970s over almost identical legislation that eventually led the Ford administration to lift the executive order prohibiting American subsidiaries from trading with Cuba. Turning a blind eye to this still relatively modest level of trade was deemed preferable to a certain revival of the same conflicts, unnecessarily complicating important bilateral relations that, from the vantage point of the State Department's Seventh Floor, outweighed the uncertain benefits to be derived from passage of the bill. "[It's] not because we want more people to trade with Cuba," explained a department official, "but because we have no legal authority to tell other countries that they can't do it."[129] The other factor related to the White House assessment of internal Soviet developments that appeared ready to offer more guaranteed opportunities to increase the economic pressure on Cuba at no cost to the American business community.

The worsening economic and political crisis in the Soviet Union boded ill for allies like Cuba. In August 1991, a coup by communist hardliners who temporarily seized political power was swiftly put down, but it left Gorbachev's grip on power seriously compromised and the Soviet economy reeling on the brink of collapse. More than ever, the country's reformist leadership looked to Washington for help. When Secretary of State Baker arrived in Moscow that September for meetings with Mikhail Gorbachev and Moscow's mayor, Boris Yeltsin, who had stared down the coup plotters, he quickly reached the conclusion that the two leaders first and foremost "needed to deter another coup attempt, to prevent a complete disintegration and anarchy, and to avoid a famine." Surveying "the highly uncertain Soviet future," Baker recalled that "we were in even more of a hurry to 'lock-in' gains then and there." In the case of Cuba, this meant going for maximum advantage and pushing hard for an end to Soviet financial subsidies as well as the Soviet military presence on the island. Western governments, he told Gorbachev and Yeltsin, "would be far more willing to support them and to help them with their debt if it was clear they were no longer subsidizing Communist regimes around the world." The response was immediate, surprising even Baker: Gorbachev agreed to withdraw the 2,800-man Soviet brigade in Cuba and would announce the decision without consulting the Cubans. Baker was in no doubt that "a key motivation behind the step was to clear the way for stronger U.S. support."[130] On making the decision public, the Soviet president also revealed he had told Baker that Moscow was preparing to meet the other U.S. demand by transferring relations with Cuba "to a plane of mutually beneficial trade and economic ties."[131]

In Havana, the news was greeted with public stoicism but private anger and dismay. Not only were the Soviet troops being withdrawn without consultation, but Gorbachev was now also under intense U.S. *and* domestic pressures to forgo the strategy of cushioning the adverse effects of the Soviet bloc economic and political crisis on Cuba, and cut the island adrift. The failed August 1991 coup had led to the emergence of Boris Yeltsin as a formidable political rival to Gorbachev and one who signaled a willingness to pursue an even less accommodating approach to Cuba across a range of issues.

Following these concessions, however, senior Bush policymakers decided that Eastern European and Soviet policy objectives might be best served by a temporary halt to further demands for action against Cuba. With the Cuban economy in free-fall, buoying new hopes of Castro's possible demise, Washington settled on a "watch-and-wait strategy," one official declaring that "the ball is . . . in Fidel's court."[132] Addressing a group of Miami business leaders in October, Bush confidently predicted that the changes in the Soviet Union "soon will sweep away our hemisphere's last dictator, Fidel Castro."[133] Although some officials feared that this do-nothing approach would upset Cuban-American voters in Florida and New Jersey, the dominant administration view was that demanding more changes from Gorbachev at this time put at risk much more important Bloc gains and might generate increased sympathy for Castro in Latin America.

As the presidential year began to unfold, George Bush moved to ensure no slippage in the overwhelming support he had received from Florida's Cuban-American community in 1988. In January, for instance, the State Department revealed that, in line with normal policy in such circumstances, it had been providing Havana with information on potential terrorist attacks against the island. The outcry in Miami, however, was so loud that it forced Assistant Secretary of State Aronson to publicly deny there was any "ongoing policy of cooperating or collaborating with the Castro regime."[134] Jeb Bush, the president's reelection campaign director in Florida, also took to the air waves to reinforce Aronson's statement.

Stepping up his verbal attacks on Castro, Bush told a March rally in Hialeah, just outside of Miami, that he looked forward to being the first president of the United States to set foot on the soil of "post-Castro Cuba," compared Castro to

Stalin, and promised that "there cannot be and will not be a normal dialogue with Cuba as long as this dictatorship is in power."[135] That April, Bush complemented tough words with action. Borrowing from the CANF-inspired CDA legislation, he issued an executive order to bar ships from docking in U.S. ports within six months of their having docked at a Cuban port. One objective was to make Cuba trade unattractive to both cargo and cruise ship operators, and to curb the movement of Cuban-made goods slipping into the United States through third countries. Another was to mollify the Cuban-American lobby and its congressional supporters by further squeezing the island economy. Finally, there was the (vain) hope that the executive order might not only satisfy the anti-Castro political right, but derail the CDA as well. Bush coupled this measure with instructions to Treasury to begin issuing licenses for the direct shipment of mailed packages between Miami and Havana, a move intended to eliminate the Castro regime's access to hard currency from mail sent through Mexico at substantially higher cost. Administration officials remained convinced that specific measures of this kind would have greater impact than ever, given the end of the Cuba–Soviet economic relationship, and hence the necessity "to strike while the iron is hot."[136]

However, a potential problem loomed between the White House and CANF over the former's continuing reluctance to support key CDA provisions. On April 18, Principal Assistant Secretary of State for Inter-American Affairs Robert Gelbard told a House Foreign Affairs Committee hearing that the bill's core provision – the restoration of the ban on U.S. subsidiary trade with Cuba – was both unworkable and counterproductive. During its earlier incarnation in the 1960s and early 1970s, this ban "was found to be completely ineffective. What it ended up producing was not support for our policy but more opposition for our policy and implicitly more support for Castro."[137]

Certainly, the warning signs from key allies indicated that precisely this outcome was likely if the CDA became law. The conservative Mulroney government in Canada termed the bill's objective "unacceptable," and said that if the bill was passed it would issue a "federal blocking order" under the Foreign Extraterritorial Measures Act, making subsidiaries of overseas corporations that complied with the CDA liable for financial and prison penalties.[138] Minister of Justice Kim Campbell described the move as necessary "to protect the primacy of Canadian trade and law policy."[139] In a formal diplomatic protest to the State Department, the European Union's (EU's) executive arm – the European Commission (EC) – condemned the proposed legislation as a "violation of the general principles of international law and the sovereignty of independent nations [with] the potential to cause grave damage to the transatlantic relationship," and urged President Bush to exercise the veto if it reached his desk for signature.[140] British Trade Minister Richard Needham bluntly declared that London would not accept any attempt to "impose US laws on UK companies" and that Whitehall alone "will determine the UK's policy on trade with Cuba."[141] Several European allies announced their intention to take countermeasures to nullify the impact of the CDA if it was signed into law. Britain led the charge. The conservative Major government invoked the 1980 Protection of Trading Interests Act, which legally prevented U.S. interests from complying with extraterritorial measures such as the CDA. In the hemisphere, Mexico, like Canada, warned local subsidiaries of U.S. corporations to disregard the new law, and that measures would be implemented to block adherence if they refused to do so. Even Latin governments sympathetic to U.S. objectives in Cuba drew the line at what they perceived as a direct challenge to the principles of self-determination, national sovereignty, international law, and/or free trade.

The administration also had reservations about those CDA provisions that allegedly impinged on the constitutional powers of the president to make foreign policy and one that terminated U.S. aid to countries providing debt relief, favorable terms of trade, or economic assistance to Cuba. The latter not only jeopardized a possible free trade agreement with Mexico and Canada, said Gelbard, but the CDA's "definition of assistance is so broad that even a residual amount of trade or aid [to Cuba] could disqualify [Russia and the former Soviet bloc states] from receiving badly needed assistance from us."[142]

Throughout his testimony, Gelbard argued that the executive was committed to implementing a "tough" diplomatic and economic isolation policy, that there had been no let-up in this effort, and that it continued to be effective, pointing to the disappearance of all Soviet bloc aid subsidies to Cuba, which, he asserted, was "the result of persistent U.S. diplomacy." This precipitated a tense exchange with committee member Robert Torrricelli, who could not understand these qualms about increasing the effectiveness of a policy that the administration maintains is working or why the concerns of allies should loom so large in what was basically a U.S. foreign policy problem.

TORRICELLI: Somebody has to take on leadership on policy regarding Cuba. [Deferring to Ottawa, Paris, and London] would abrogate a principal responsibility of this administration. The Cuban problem is disproportionately an American concern internationally.
GELBARD: I think it is quite difficult to accuse this administration of being soft on Cuba. To the contrary.
TORRICELLI: Well. You may find it difficult, but I am doing it.
GELBARD: Well I just blatantly disagree. I am sorry.
TORRICELLI: The language is –

GELBARD: If I could comment –

TORRICELLI: You can, when I am finished speaking.

GELBARD: If I could finish my answers –

TORRICELLI: You can, as soon as I finish speaking. No one argues that
your language is tough. It is whether in moments of choice you are
prepared to make tough choices. [How tough is a policy that] believes
that American corporations should have tax deductability for doing
business with Cuba, even though we have an embargo, that would allow
a $400 million annual exception to the embargo to continue because
people in Ottawa or London might get upset.[143]

However, this was more a dispute over form than substance. Among those
members of Congress who took an interest in Cuba, the perception was that
White House policy had run adrift; to conservative Cuban-Americans, the president was failing to provide leadership.[144] That both groups increasingly saw
eye-to-eye on the need to get tougher with Cuba (fourteen of the twenty-two
original House cosponsors of the CDA were beneficiaries of Free Cuba PAC
donations) made matters worse for Bush. Compounding his dilemma was a
continuing problem of dealing with the likes of Mas Canosa, for whom one
concession only fuelled the desire for more. If Bush would not support the CDA,
the CANF head would go looking for a White House aspirant who would. He
found one in the person of democratic presidential candidate Bill Clinton.

The two met in Tampa, Florida, in the spring of 1992. Mas left the meeting
with the impression that Clinton would consider the need to strengthen the
embargo on Cuba; Clinton left with the notion that he could at least neutralize
Cuba as an election issue for Cuban-Americans and so concentrate their vote
in November on the social and economic policies he had to offer. The belief
that this might be a political masterstroke was not confined to Clinton. Richard
Nuccio recalled,

> I was with Torricelli, we were actually on a trip to Mexico and Guatemala
> when George Stephanopoulos called Torricelli and said, "I think I've got
> Clinton to agree to sign the CDA, to endorse it. He's going to be in Florida
> next week making some appearances. Can you help get some of your
> friends in the Cuban-American community to come to his fundraiser?"
> And the answer to all of those things was, "Are you kidding, of course."[145]

On April 23, Clinton met several hundred wealthy exiles in Miami and told
them the Bush administration had "missed a big opportunity to put the hammer
down on Fidel Castro and Cuba" by not supporting the CDA: "I have read the
Torricelli–Graham Bill and I like it." After the meeting, Mas Canosa remarked

that, "If Clinton is elected president, I don't think that we should have anything to fear." The former Arkansas governor left Miami with his campaign coffers $275,000 richer for the endorsement and with Bush suddenly outflanked in a key electoral college state.[146]

The president immediately found himself locked in a bidding war over which candidate could be tougher on Cuba policy. In negotiations with Torricelli and other congressional supporters of the CDA, the administration secured amendments that removed some of the more vexed provisions of the original draft (for instance, the prohibition on the United States entering into a free trade agreement, providing debt relief, or giving economic aid to any country providing assistance to Cuba) and clawed back some degree of presidential latitude in enforcing the bill's provisions and protecting contracts already negotiated between Cuba and overseas subsidiaries of American companies. Then, after a hastily called press conference at his Kennebunkport vacation home, Bush announced his support for the CDA. In this changed domestic political environment, invoking larger foreign policy considerations to successfully ward off earlier Capitol Hill attempts to pass extraterritorial legislation targeting Cuba (the Mack amendment) would no longer suffice.

In August, the State Department's Robert Gelbard returned to the Hill, where he put on a brave face before a Senate subcommittee, insisting that the administration's abrupt reversal on CDA was "not a change of policy." That may have come as a surprise to Washington's trade partners, who were already up in arms about this extraterritorial extension of U.S. law and to many U.S. companies who were slowly waking up to the fact that their subsidiaries stood to lose more than $700 million a year in trade with Cuba. Gelbard, however, had anticipated at least some of this reaction. "Our allies have told us that they will impose blocking legislation which could hurt U.S. companies." Yet, however much the White House continued to push for changes in the legislation, it was not about to brave domestic political reality. Despite significant reservations, Gelbard told the senators that "We will support it as it now stands."[147]

Questioned by Claiborne Pell over Castro's likely fate and whether "he should be left to stew in his own juice," Gelbard agreed that the Cuban leader's days were numbered and, in the current propitious circumstances, perhaps sooner rather than later:

GELBARD: The situation is such that we feel that the moment is opportune to try to accelerate the process which is occurring anyway.
PELL: The stewing process?
GELBARD: Yes, sir.[148]

Although the White House had decided to use the CDA to turn the heat up on Cuba, privately Gelbard was unconvinced as to the wisdom of the move. Following his testimony, he told a congressional foreign policy specialist that he had serious reservations about the new embargo tightening measures he had just endorsed: "I'm a good soldier, but my own personal feeling is that it's not very good policy."[149]

Congressional opposition to the CDA was mainly led by members representing export-oriented agricultural states hostile to economic embargoes in general or those from states where individual corporations would be hardest hit by the new rules. One of the latter was the Hartford-based United Technologies, whose elevator and air conditioning subsidiaries did an estimated $10 million business with Cuba in 1991. Connecticut's democratic Senator Chris Dodd said that Cuba would easily find alternative sources for any shortfall in imported goods while U.S.-owned companies were forced to shed workers. Yet his filibuster motion to kill the Senate bill and other anti-CDA proposals was comprehensively defeated.[150] No amount of argument that the legislation would not weaken Castro's hold on political power, have no discernable economic impact on Cuba, and only hurt American corporations could overcome the power of the anti-Castro coalition. The House approved the CDA by 276 to 135; Senate support was just as decisive.

Within the electorate at large, there was still few signs of any emerging, competitive countervailing force willing to support a change in Cuba policy. Labor, religious, and other groups opposed to current policy were small in number and politically ineffectual at either end of Pennsylvania Avenue; the Washington-based Cuban American Committee, which advocated a dialog with Havana and argued that the CDA would deprive ordinary Cubans of basic foodstuffs and medicines, was no match for CANF and its exile supporters, and those sectors of the American business community who were directly affected by the legislation or advocated an easing of the embargo were slow or reluctant to take a public stance. "We could barely get any of them to testify against the bill," said one Senate Foreign Relations Committee staffer. "Those sectors who opposed the bill weren't prepared to stick their heads out."[151] Assistant Secretary of State Aronson recalled almost no corporate sector lobbying: "They were not on the radar screen."[152]

One reason for this timidity on the part of business was the belief that no benefits would accrue from publicly opposing the CDA. "Let's say they lobby against it and win and there is no Torricelli Act," a prominent Washington consultant on U.S.–Cuba business opportunities observed. "You still have the embargo; you're no better off. You're still at ground zero. So you're offering them a reward that is nonexistent; it's an empty shell."[153] Companies were also hesitant to be seen as aligning with Castro, not least for fear of confrontation with the Cuban-American community. "Any company that had a subsidiary in Florida or New Jersey did not want to have a bunch of pickets outside their plant," a senior U.S. Chamber of Commerce official recalled. "They told me just that blunt. 'We agree with you [opposing extraterritorial sanctions], but we don't want our name out there because the next morning Jorge Mas Canosa and the CANF people will be there with a band, and they will have TV, and that's bad for business.' "[154] The business community's failure to treat the CDA as a high priority matter was reinforced by the limited importance of Cuba trade within companies' total foreign operations; the Bush administration track record of opposing legislation that hurt American trade abroad; and the widespread belief, until the CDA became a domestic political issue, that the bill was unlikely to reach a vote in Congress and if, per chance, it did reach the president's desk, he would veto it.[155]

Yet in an election year, domestic political perceptions were all that counted when it came to Cuba policy. With the contest in full swing, "both presidential candidates were now elbowing each other out of their road to be the most anti-Castro."[156] The democratic candidate, having set his sights on cutting into republican support among Cuban-Americans in Florida and New Jersey, went so far as to personally write to the House and Senate sponsors of the CDA legislation, Robert Torricelli and Bob Graham, praising their successful navigation of the bill though the Congress, denouncing Castro as "one of the world's most ruthless dictators," and emphasizing the "important opportunity to increase pressure on Castro" provided by the collapse of the Soviet Union.[157] For Clinton, the objective was to neutralize the image of the Republican Party as the only genuine anti-Castro party. "Once you strip them of that weapon," Florida Democratic Party Chairman Simon Ferro argued, "you can deal with them on other issues, like the economy."[158] At a televised New Jersey town hall meeting in late October, Clinton showed the lengths he was prepared to go in pursuit of the Cuban-American vote, acknowledging that many in the exile community still held the democrats "in general responsible for the Bay of Pigs debacle and for Castro still being in power." Yet he implored the audience to take into account his strong support for the CDA and his recent "extraordinary overtures to the Cuban community, particularly in Florida."[159]

Bush's calculations were no less self-serving. As the newly appointed NSC Staff Director on Latin America, Robert Morley, observed, although State and the NSC "were both seriously concerned about the impact of the CDA legislation on relations with friendly countries like Canada and Britain, our NATO allies," the predominant sentiment was that "it was not worth a major fight with Congress." In any event, there was a "national security" loophole in the law that allowed the president to suspend implementation of key provisions. "So, in effect, the negative consequences of the CDA were controllable."[160] Be that as it may, the critical, overriding reason for the president's policy reversal was domestic politics. "The State Department had felt that the extraterritorial provision of the CDA could create a real problem with our allies in Europe," said Aronson. "But when Bill Clinton endorsed it, the *political calculus* changed and the White House wanted us to back the bill."[161]

In his nomination acceptance speech before the Republican National Convention in September, the president said again that he looked forward "to being the first president to visit a free, democratic Cuba."[162] Some weeks later, the Dade County Bush campaign organization issued 1,000 invitations to attend a gathering on October 23 to celebrate the signing of the CDA legislation into law. The democratic sponsors of the bill, Torricelli and Graham, were not among the invitees. Speaking before the highly partisan audience, which included Mas Canosa and about 100 other Cuban-American leaders, the president's rhetoric climbed to new heights. "For freedom to rise in Cuba," he declared, "Fidel Castro must fall," and a return to democracy on the island must happen "not sometime, not someday, but now."[163] A suitably impressed CANF leadership was nonetheless beginning to hedge its bets on which candidate could best deliver on that demand.

Only days after the CDA signing ceremony, Mas Canosa and the CANF executive committee held another surprise meeting with Clinton in Tampa, Florida. The two had conferred briefly in September after Clinton had telephoned several congressional democrats and urged them to get behind the CDA legislation, which was then bogged down in the Senate and at risk of languishing there. This meeting, however, was the most productive politically for the democratic nominee. After the session, the CANF participants issued a statement praising Clinton for his support in getting passage of the CDA and virtually invited Cuban-Americans to reconsider their historic ties to the Republican Party. "Your statements on Cuba," the document said, "have demonstrated to us here in Miami, as well as to the entire Cuban-American community throughout the United States, that we need not fear a Bill Clinton administration."[164] On the surface, this seemed a major political setback to Bush and a boost to Clinton's campaign. However, its significance for Cuba policy lay elsewhere: Congress had seized the initiative on how the United States should deal with Fidel Castro, and whoever won the presidency in November had signed onto CANF's agenda for forcing a regime change on the island.

2

Clinton and Cuba, January 1993 to February 1996: Closing the Options

All of a sudden a segment of the community is starting to understand that this guy isn't as bad as they were led to believe he would be. They see that he is not going to establish relations with Castro and, in fact, that his policy is clearer and firmer than it was under Presidents Reagan and Bush.

> Simon Ferro, Florida Democratic Party chairman,
> on Bill Clinton

A S a newly elected president, Bill Clinton was well placed to regain the foreign policy initiative from Congress, to push his own ideas on issues of specific interest and to make new appointments to key bureaucratic posts through which he could seek to stamp his own mark on America's international role. An approach to Cuba more rational, if not more accommodating, than the one pursued under Reagan and Bush thus appeared at least a possibility. "The choice for President Clinton," Peter Hakim of the Inter-American Dialogue told a congressional panel in February 1993, "is whether to pursue a fresh and more activist approach, involving an effort to mobilize an international coalition and begin bargaining with Cuba, or whether to continue a policy of passively waiting for the Cuban authorities to take the first steps, or for Fidel to pass from the scene."[1] The particular choices Hakim outlined were of less immediate interest than the general thrust of his testimony: Clinton had options on Cuba that were not available to his predecessor.

Clinton's embrace of CANF's Cuba agenda as expressed in the CDA, and the subsequent increase in the Florida Cuban-American vote for the Democratic Party, convinced the president-elect that his pitch to the exile community had worked. Yet his overall percentage vote in Florida (thirty-nine percent) was the same as that achieved by democratic presidential candidate Michael Dukakis in 1988, and a mere eighteen percent of Cuban-American voters contributed to his win in the exile heartland of Dade County.[2] So, although he had established his credentials with CANF and its supporters, the election result was no reason for him to remain beholden to them in his desire to consolidate and enlarge the Democratic Party vote in Florida.

Perhaps because Havana's overtures to the Bush transition team had back-fired in 1988–9, Cuban officials were decidedly low key at first about the prospects of improved relations with the new Clinton administration. Still, although there was no expectation that Clinton would change U.S. policy overnight, Havana signaled that it was receptive to initiatives from Washington. Outgoing Foreign Minister and newly appointed president of the Cuban National Assembly Ricardo Alarcón urged Clinton to lift the embargo for a twelve-month trial period, hinting that this could pave the way for changes in the Cuban polit-ical process.[3] During early 1993, the Castro government also took a number of small practical measures to test the new climate in Washington, including the early release of several political prisoners and a decision to ease travel restric-tions on other dissidents and human rights activists.[4] Justifiably or otherwise, U.S. foreign policymakers had grown skeptical about the significance of such gestures and saw little to be gained from any response in kind. "The cycle has always been the same from Ford through Bush," explained a senior Clinton NSC staffer who monitored Cuba developments in the State Department during the Bush years. "Every time the U.S. makes a gesture, almost as if premedi-tated, there is a self-destructive action by the Cuban government which makes it difficult for the U.S. to stay the course."[5]

Even so, the opportunity presented by Clinton's election to change direction on Cuba policy was not lost on political moderates within Miami's exile com-munity or dissidents groups on the island. In January, Eloy Gutiérrez Menoyo, a veteran anti-Castro activist and head of the newly formed exile organization *Cambio Cubano*, told a Washington press conference that the CDA "creates an even more difficult position for the Cuban people, creates frustration be-tween the United States and its allies and allows Castro to claim that he's being attacked."[6] A few months later, prominent Cuban dissidents signed a letter to the White House that echoed the same judgment. They implored the president to relax the embargo, in particular the CDA, which they said "will achieve [noth-ing] other than increased tensions [and] a narrowing of the space for diplomacy and political negotiations."[7]

CANF, its congressional allies, and those groups in American society advo-cating a tough approach in dealing with Fidel Castro's government were just as cognizant that the new president had options open to him and they were determined to ensure that he chose the most draconian among them. The first test of strength came in mid-January, when Clinton announced he intended to appoint Cuban-born New York lawyer Mario Baeza as his Assistant Secretary of State for Inter-American Affairs. The proposed appointment drew the immediate wrath of CANF and the conservative Cuban-American community. At Mas Canosa's request, influential anti-Castro legislators, principally Florida's Bob Graham (D) and New Jersey's Robert Torricelli (D), lobbied the president-elect to dump the Baeza nomination. The Miami hardliners loudly opposed Clinton's choice for a number of reasons: First, although a Cuban-American who had spent part of his youth growing up on the island, Baeza was an outsider in the sense that he had no connection with the Florida exile community; and second, he was designated "soft on Cuba," primarily because he had attended a two-day June 1992 Euromoney trade and investment seminar in Havana in his capacity as an investment and privatization law specialist. Torricelli attacked Baeza on the grounds that because he had "spoken openly about promoting American investment in Cuba" while in Havana, he could not be trusted to enforce the new CDA embargo provisions.[8] Finally, Mas was visibly irked by the administration's failure to consult CANF during the course of the selection process. The signal this sent was of a White House that failed to display the appropriate sensitivity toward Miami's concerns over Cuba policy. Capitulating to this sustained attack, the White House allowed Baeza's nomination to lapse by putting it on indefinite hold. His eventual replacement, Alexander Watson, was a career diplomat with a record of defending the merits of the embargo and someone who, in the words of an approving CANF statement, had "a clear understanding of the complexities involved in U.S.–Cuban relations."[9]

With the dust barely settled on this victory, the anti-Castro legislators began to send unmistakable messages that they had a more ambitious goal in sight: to force the new administration's hand on Cuba policy itself. In February, Florida republicans Lincoln Díaz-Balart and Connie Mack introduced a concurrent resolution calling on the Clinton White House to seek a mandatory international embargo against Cuba in the United Nations Security Council (UNSC) over its human rights record. The resolution was nonbinding and easily ignored, but it was also a harbinger of things to come.

The battle over Baeza's nomination and the administration's failure to take up the call for a UNSC-sanctioned embargo did not amount to a White House working at cross purposes to CANF's Capitol Hill supporters. During these early months in office, Clinton officials took every appropriate opportunity to drive home one clear and simple message: the fundamentals of Cuba policy would remain unchanged. Support for the CDA was set in concrete; the trade embargo would not be eased or lifted; and only fundamental political and economic changes in Cuba would induce any move toward open, broad-ranging talks with Havana, or any diplomatic initiatives toward normalized ties. Secretary of State–designate Warren Christopher also told a Senate confirmation hearing that it was "very hard to envisage normal relations with Cuba with Castro still in place."[10] Once settled into the new job, his anti-Cuba rhetoric toughened: Castro remained "a relic of the past [and someone] mired in the communist ideologies of an earlier day."[11]

The president himself insisted that there would be no fundamental change in Cuban policy during his term in office. In late March, he ruled out any warming toward Castro: "I have no change in Cuba policy except to say that I supported the Cuban Democracy Act, and I hope someday that we'll all be able to travel to a democratic Cuba."[12] Meeting with the *Miami Herald*'s editorial board in early May, Vice President Al Gore explained the rationale behind this hostile U.S. approach: "Castro's chickens are coming home to roost. His policies have been an utter failure, and always have been." Somewhat indiscreetly, he then revealed the self-fulfilling prophecy behind Washington's calculations: "Let us not forget that our principal policy for hastening the departure of Castro is to convince the people of Cuba that his leadership is an abject failure."[13] The instrument for persuading "the people of Cuba" was the same blunt one that had been wielded by previous administrations: economic warfare.

Still, not everyone was convinced that these statements were the last words on the subject. Clinton's decision to break with tradition and host his Cuban Independence Day reception at the White House rather than in Miami raised the faint hope of a change in some of the old ground rules governing the politics of Cuba policy. So did the fact that CANF's representative at the gathering was Florida Democratic Party chair, Simon Ferro; Mas Canosa was conspicuous by his absence. There was also the occasional subtle change in tone, if not emphasis, in remarks senior officials were making about Cuba. In opposing legislation sponsored by Representative Charles Rangel (D–New York) to lift the trade embargo and open direct talks between Washington and Havana, the president argued that "support for democracy" was the guiding principle for policies relating "not only to Cuba, but to Haiti, Peru and to our relationship with all other countries through the hemisphere and the world."[14]

At first glance, this seemed little more than a restatement of the republicans, policy approach. "By the Bush administration the defense of democracy had become the most important political issue in Latin America itself," explained Principal Deputy Assistant Secretary of State for Inter-American Affairs Michael Skol. "So the logic of it [which continued under Clinton] was that we had to resist, to work against, the Castro regime, not because it was a threat any longer to the United States or other Latin American countries," but because consistency demanded that Washington could not promote democracy across the region and ignore its absence in Cuba.[15] The suggestion that Cuba would no longer be singled out for special attention because of the nature of its government when contrasted with the exaggerated position the island had occupied in Washington's Cold War regional perspective in itself could be seen as a positive development.

In a comparable address to the Council of the Americas in early May, Under-secretary of State Clifford Wharton declared that the "United States poses no military threat to [Cuba]," sought only a "peaceful transition" to democracy on the island and "oppose[d] attempts to bring change through violence."[16] The import of Wharton's comments revealed an administration still determined to bring down the Castro regime, but not at any cost.

The official reaction to efforts by the U.S. Attorney's Office in Miami to indict the Cuban government, armed forces commander-in-chief Raúl Castro, and fifteen other regime officials on drug-trafficking charges, for instance, contrasted sharply with the decision taken by George Bush to approve a similar indictment against General Manuel Noriega preparatory to the December 1989 invasion of Panama. When news of a draft indictment became public in April, the administration gave the whole idea a cool reception.[17] Federal authorities also began to take a harder line on curbing the activities of exile militants than was the case during the Bush years. In May, nine members of Alpha 66 were intercepted in the Florida Keys en route to Cuba to attack military targets and charged with federal explosives and weapons law violations. The State Department characterized the arrests as "positive."[18]

This was the public face of the new administration's approach to Cuba. Privately, Clinton officials understood that, as Assistant Secretary of State for Inter-American Affairs Alexander Watson explained, "If there was a driving force behind Cuba policy it was the maintenance of the status quo in such a way that it would not get anybody hurt and not cause any more difficulties and distract us from other things that we had to do."[19] During the first half of 1993, the foreign policy agenda was dominated by the need to find a political settlement in Haiti and thereby staunch the flow of refugees to American shores. Cuba was far down the list of other priorities. According to Richard Nuccio, Watson's then senior policy adviser, there were also few political or job rewards to be gained from any suggestions to improve ties with Havana: "Most of the political appointees in the State Department and the NSC were smart enough to know that this was a losing issue, that there was not some great constituency out there that is going to applaud you and, more importantly, promote your confirmation for higher office because you did the right thing on Cuba."[20] Other officials, notably Michael Skol, were personally opposed to the publicly stated policy it was their responsibility to implement. Skol completely rejected the premise behind the thinking of a group of officials newly involved with Cuba policymaking who proposed the idea of using the CDA, which allowed for a degree of flexibility with respect to travel and communications, to try to open up the island to outside influences. These "engagers" contended that the more people-to-people contact there was with the Cubans, the greater the likelihood that civil society would grow and flourish. To Skol, this was sheer fantasy: "I never believed that meant anything in a country run by Fidel Castro."[21] Even Assistant Secretary Watson had reservations about the existing policy: "I have never had a clear analytical understanding of exactly what the embargo's impact has been."[22]

Watson's limited efforts to explore new directions in Cuba policy were largely confined to informal interagency meetings he chaired with representatives from Defense, State, Justice, and the CIA to talk about "contingency planning to do with migration policy and what would we do if there were mass migrations out of Cuba and how would we handle that." Even though there was no canvassing of major policy shifts, least of all in regard to the embargo, Watson found it necessary to ensure the group "met very quietly" because of the political sensitivity attached to any indication that a policy change might be in the wind. The mere "existence of such meetings," he explained, "would be viewed by [the president's domestic policy advisers] as very provocative and very dangerous, and they would want to know immediately what's going on." The need to go to such lengths reflected, above all, the influence of the "political side of the administration." As Watson cuttingly observed: "For the United States, Cuba is not a foreign policy issue. Most of the time it's a domestic political issue."[23]

Efforts to dissuade foreign governments and their overseas investors and traders from developing new economic ties with the Castro regime intensified under Clinton. Richard Nuccio maintained that the annual State Department cable to American embassies around the world reminding them to warn host governments against forging too close a relationship with Havana was now taken far more seriously by American diplomats: "There was a kind of escalation of those kinds of demarches on other governments during '93 and '94," due partly to the efforts of the new Director of the Office of Cuban Affairs, Dennis Hays, who "took that letter seriously and, like [Michael] Skol, was of the old 'Kick' em in the nuts to get their attention' school of U.S. diplomacy. He wanted to go around and berate governments and tell them, 'Don't you know who we are, don't you know who you are messing with?' "[24] Or as Hays himself put it: "I wanted to see as tough a line as possible opposing Cuba's reentry into Latin America, bilaterally and regionally." In the absence of strong U.S. disapproval,

Hays reasoned, it would send exactly the wrong signal to hemisphere governments, that normalizing relations with Cuba was no longer an important issue for Washington, which, in turn, would simply accelerate the trend.[25]

Although not even the Pentagon any longer viewed Cuba as a destabilizing presence in the hemisphere,[26] like its predecessor, the Clinton administration made a sharp distinction between the growth in Cuba's bilateral relations with its Latin American neighbors and its membership of regional organizations and forums. If the former was still to be "discouraged whenever we got wind of it,"[27] a collective reaching out to Fidel Castro's regime struck at the very heart of Washington's isolation strategy. If the idea took hold that Cuba was just another member of the hemispheric community with which all the rest could – and should – deal with as a group, this would pose an infinitely more serious challenge to the U.S. view of Cuba as a rogue state. Above all, it would undercut U.S. attempts to force Havana to implement the kinds of political and economic changes being demanded as the quid pro quo for normalized ties.

The result was a decision to partially adapt to the new regional realities without jettisoning the basic policy approach. "We decided on a new strategy," said an NSC official, "which was to say if you establish new bilateral relations, condition those ties on Cuba making changes."[28] Reflecting on the achievements of the approach in 1999, State's Office of Cuban Affairs Coordinator Michael Ranneberger conceded that they were meager indeed:

> We have continued to say that we really don't think that's a good thing to do because it sends the wrong signal, that it reinforces the regime, that you give Castro a little more legitimacy. We have approached them. But normalizing bilateral relations has just become a way of life. So we have made our principal focus keeping them out of the OAS.[29]

However, as U.S. officials insisted that Cuba remained a problem for the hemisphere because it was mired in "the communist ideologies of an earlier day," from the perspective of Rio, Caracas, Santiago, Mexico City, and other Latin capitals, it was America's Cuba policy that appeared outdated and problematical. The solution lay not in demonizing Castro, but in mediating between Havana and Washington.

No Latin American government understated the need for political redemocratization or greater economic changes in Cuba, but most rejected Washington's argument that satisfaction of these demands was a precondition for normalized ties. At the Fourth Ibero-American Summit in Cartagena, Colombia, in June 1994, outgoing OAS Secretary-General João Baena Soares received a standing ovation when he declared the time had arrived to reexamine Cuba's January 1962 expulsion. "The nineties," he told assembled delegates, "aren't the sixties."[30]

Clinton's determination to prosecute an accelerated economic war against Cuba quickly emerged as an ongoing area of disagreement with its Canadian and European allies as well. In April 1993, on the eve of U.S.–European trade talks, the EC released its annual report on trade barriers that singled out the CDA for specific attack. What most concerned Europe, said one EC commissioner, was the White House adopting the position that "U.S. domestic concerns take precedence over U.S. trade law."[31] In Ottawa, the newly elected Chretien government put Washington on notice that it intended to actively promote improved bilateral relations with the Caribbean island. The Minister for Foreign Affairs, André Ouellet, challenged the Americans to turn the page on Cuba as they had done on Vietnam: It is "a country that . . . is no longer a threat in any way, shape or form [to the United States]."[32] That June, the Minister for Latin America and Africa, Christine Stewart, announced that the sixteen-year suspension on Cuba's eligibility for Canadian development assistance, instituted by the Trudeau government over Cuba's Angola involvement, was being revoked.

Frustrated by its inability to prevent the almost complete collapse of its policy to maintain Cuba's isolation on a regional and global scale, the Clinton administration soon gave increased attention to initiatives of a more specific kind in an attempt to bring pressure to bear on the Castro regime. Treasury continued to pursue embargo offenders in its determination to close off hard currency opportunities. In April 1993, a boat owned by a Dutch citizen residing in Seattle was seized, impounded, and the owner fined $17,000 after it returned from one of several trips to Cuba carrying boat parts and aid packages.[33] That July, at the behest of the White House, Treasury's Office of Foreign Assets Control (OFAC) directed seven companies operating through Bell Canada and providing 800-number services linking American telephone calls to Cuba to cease the practice within twenty days or risk their executives being liable to large fines and prison sentences. U.S. officials argued that the service contravened the embargo because the Cuban government was receiving hard currency from calls originating on the mainland. Later in the year, the State Department sent a "Buyer Beware" cable to American embassies and consulates around the world to "strongly urge" host governments to dissuade their nationals from investing in Cuba to avoid possible legal proceedings by former U.S. property owners on the island.[34] In searching for hard currency loopholes to close, the administration placed new travel restrictions on Cuban citizens visiting the United States and told Havana-approved charter companies in Miami that exiles visiting Cuba were not obliged to buy package deals. The latter restriction was to ensure such trips did not become "a cash-cow operation for the Castro government."[35]

The White House also signaled it was not about to decelerate the propaganda war against Cuba, requesting a combined $28 million for Radio and TV

Martí during fiscal year 1994. House and Senate conferees eventually pared the figure down to $21 million, of which $7.5 million was placed in escrow pending the report of a USIA Advisory panel established specifically to inform Congress on these Cuba-targeted broadcast operations. In testimony before the Panel, the National Association of Radio Broadcasters ridiculed TV Martí as "a Rube Goldberg operation" and a complete waste of funds given its night-time transmission hours and Cuban government jamming, which meant that the prospective audience was less than five percent of the populace.[36] However, although the Panel had recommended the "shutdown" of TV Martí on similar grounds twelve months earlier, its report concluded that "despite the obstacles, interference and shortcomings which have hampered both Radio and TV Martí, the United States interest is served by their continuing to air."[37] Secretary of State Warren Christopher concurred with the recommendation despite admitting that TV Martí "has not been very cost effective."[38]

In the meantime, senior State Department officials made sure there was no misunderstanding or confusion in Havana, Washington, or Miami about the basic policy approach. During a House appearance in August 1993, Deputy Assistant Secretary Robert Gelbard summarily dealt with recent Cuban government statements "that the Clinton administration has somehow taken up a warmer position, a more liberal position toward Castro" and with comments by Castro himself to the effect that "there has been a change in the American government's position on Cuba." An indignant Gelbard did not want his questioners to be under any illusions on this point: "Let me assure you there had not been [any change]."[39]

Dismissing similar rumors that the administration "intends to soften its [Cuba] policy," Assistant Secretary Watson told a CANF-sponsored luncheon to celebrate the first anniversary of the signing into law of the CDA that there would be no let-up in efforts to break "the hammerlock of the Castro regime." In his address, Watson said that bilateral ties "will not improve and the embargo will not be lifted until such time as there are democratic reforms and respect for human rights in Cuba." Congress received bouquets for voting continued funding of Radio and TV Martí, which provided "the kind of information" the Cuban people needed "now more than ever." However, the Cuban government was chided for refusing to allow the United Nations human rights rapporteur to visit the island, as if it was "trying to hide" something. He stressed the CDA's role as a force for bolstering anti-regime forces on the island, reaffirming support for that part of the legislation that permits private humanitarian donations to nongovernmental organizations in Cuba.[40]

Watson termed his address "probably the first comprehensive articulation of Clinton policy on Cuba."[41] That nine months had already passed since the

January inauguration partly testified to a White House whose interests were heavily skewed toward domestic concerns as well as Cuba's second-level status on Clinton's foreign policy agenda. It also reflected a consensus decision to put the onus for any shift in U.S. policy on Havana. Bush had signed the CDA into law, but after initially opposing it and only after Clinton had challenged him to do so in the heat of an election campaign. The CDA was thus an initiative the new president could claim as his own and it was enough for the time being to allow a new foreign policymaking team to explore its ramifications rather than resort to additional measures. "We're just going to have to wait," Clinton told the *Miami Herald* in September. "The ball is, to some extent, in Cuba's court if we keep the pressure up."[42] The dominant assumption behind the overall policy approach was expressed more bluntly by another U.S. official: "We ain't sinking under the waves, they are."[43]

CLEAVAGE WITHIN THE CONSENSUS

Given the depth and scope of the post-Soviet economic crisis, this assumption seemed well founded. In a rare open meeting of the Senate Select Committee on Intelligence, the CIA's National Intelligence Officer for Latin America, Brian Latell, provided a gloomy assessment of the island's economic plight. Overall, the economy had contracted by more than forty percent since 1989; export earnings had fallen from $5 billion in 1989 to $1.6 billion, due largely to the smallest sugar harvest in three decades; imports had declined by nearly seventy-five percent between 1989 and 1992, and were projected to fall another twenty to twenty-five percent during 1993. "The impact of the economic crisis on the populace," Latell contended, "has been devastating."[44] Little wonder that Washington saw no reason to alter its *sine qua non* for any move toward normalized bilateral relations.

Signs of the Castro regime's shift toward a less doctrinaire economic policy were already observable, however, well before Watson's October policy speech. In June, Cuban officials made informal contact with the International Monetary Fund (IMF) to seek advice on possible economic changes and pave the way for an IMF delegation visit to the island later in the year. The following month, Castro announced new measures to help keep the economy afloat: among them, possession of hard currency was "depenalized" to try and impose greater government control over the circulation of dollars on the black market, and foreign investment restrictions were eased. Although the impact on Cuba's centrally planned economy promised to be relatively limited, these initiatives had considerable symbolic importance. A reluctant revolutionary leadership had conceded the need for new market mechanisms;

the debate was now over what options to select and how they should be implemented.

Cuba's selective opening to the market elicited a positive response from America's allies: European, Latin American, and Canadian governments sought to encourage and accelerate the process throughout 1993 by moving to develop new economic ties with the island.[45] Yet if international opinion was moving rapidly to the view that the U.S. embargo was a Cold War relic, and that Cuba should be engaged, not isolated, the response from Washington was, if nothing else, consistent. "In our view," Robert Gelbard told a congressional committee, "the reforms which have taken place [in Cuba] so far do not constitute a fundamental change," and thus offer no basis for removing the embargo.[46] Another administration official also highlighted the lack of political reforms: "Things Cuba has done to reform its economy might have been interesting in years past [but] Castro has done nothing to liberalize politically and is so far behind the curve now, compared to what's going on in the rest of the world, we don't see a reason to change our policy."[47]

Within a foreign policy bureaucracy where, as the Director of State's Office of Cuban Affairs Dennis Hays put it, "everybody obviously thought Cuba would be better off without Castro," a debate began over what to do about the eleven million Cubans themselves. On the one side were hardliners and moderates like Skol, Watson, Nuccio, and Hays, for whom the key question was "to try to figure out ways to go around the regime" and provide assistance "directly to the Cuban people." Such an approach, said Hays, "would have been impossible five years before in the sense that the wall around Cuba was so high and so thick that you couldn't penetrate it . . . to get to these people." Yet in the aftermath of the collapse of the Soviet Union, Cuba was more economically vulnerable and consequently the regime "had to make some allowances."[48] On the other side were the NSC liberals, Sandy Berger, Richard Feinberg, and Morton Halperin, who also desired to exploit the opportunities created by Cuba's economic crisis to implement a more sophisticated policy approach than much of the old reflex thinking had allowed. The central problem for these officials was how to prevail over a foreign policy bureaucracy "that was in default mode, that was doing what they'd been doing for forty years."[49] Dennis Hays maintained that Clinton's domestic advisers were "much more in tune with us over here [in the State Department] because we were actually much more sensitive to the domestic political realities [of Cuba policy]," while at the same time implying that the White House itself was "split" over which side to support.[50]

But as Hays was boasting supporters in the west wing of the White House, a disagreement erupted among his Department colleagues over how to operationalize any new approach and the role CANF should play in any proposed policy shift. "We didn't argue about 'Is Cuba's government a bad government and we should be doing what we can peacefully to try to have an impact on moving it toward a different sort of government?' " said Richard Nuccio. "Everybody agreed with that. But how do you do that? Do you tighten the noose more and try to drive them to the wall? Or do you find ways to open up the embargo that might be good for the U.S. but also have an impact on developing a future in Cuba that looks different from now?" There was no wrangling over the idea of easing the embargo. Instead, the disputes centered around two key questions: What measures should be implemented and whether they should test the limits of what the exile community – "in operational terms that meant CANF" – found acceptable. Nuccio and Reagan–Bush political appointee Philip Peters sent memos to Assistant Secretary Watson outlining a package of measures consonant with the provisions of the CDA, which, in turn, produced countermemos from Skol and Hays calculating the likely political backlash if the suggestions were accepted. Ultimately, the far more cautious approach espoused by Skol and Hays won the day. "My biggest achievement during that period," Nuccio recalled with some exasperation, "was to persuade Dennis that we should extend licenses for educational exchanges to undergraduate students instead of just graduate students. It was a ridiculous little change and yet even that had a big fight about it."[51]

In any event, the big picture demands by Washington did not rule out selective cooperation with Havana to solve discrete problems. Yet on those occasions American officials were quick to emphasize that these contacts would not lead to any softening in the basic U.S. policy position. In September, Cuban authorities cooperated with the U.S. Drug Enforcement Agency (DEA) in the arrest of two suspected cocaine smugglers who had fled to the island. Two weeks later, Hays visited Havana and laid the groundwork for a bilateral agreement to repatriate to the island 1,500 Cubans who had fled during the 1980 Mariel boatlift and were subsequently convicted of serious crimes in the United States. Engaging Cuba over this issue, which benefited Washington more than it did Havana, appealed to some midlevel State Department officials frustrated at the failure of the hardline policy to achieve much in the way of desired outcomes.[52]

The section chief of the U.S. Interest Section in Havana was part of this group. In a memo to his superiors, Alan Flanigan wrote that engaging Cuba would place Washington in the best position to influence any future political transition on the island. *The Wall Street Journal* also reported that NSC Adviser Anthony Lake held two meetings with senior administration officials in late 1993 to discuss alternative approaches to dealing with the "problem of Cuba."[53] Nonetheless, the obstacles to any major policy shift remained formidable. Recent conversations with the president had left Robert Torricelli in no doubt that "he is totally committed to maintaining maximum pressure on Cuba."[54] Reaction to the Flanigan memo did little to indicate that the proponents of engagement would have an easy time mobilizing support within the foreign policy bureaucracy. "Taking steps to ease tensions with Cuba sounds good, but what if it backfires?" said one State Department official. "Dealing with Fidel can be tricky." In any event, another administration official stressed, domestic realities always intruded when it came to Cuba: "Politically, you can never be too tough on Castro."[55]

One possible means of changing the domestic realities to facilitate new thinking about Cuba policy was to look for allies in the Cuban-American community who did not espouse the hardline CANF approach. Even before he formally assumed the post of Assistant Secretary of State for Inter-American Affairs in July 1993, Alexander Watson seemed receptive to pursuing this line of action: "I had always thought it would be a good idea to stay very far away from Mr. Mas Canosa. Before I even took the job, before it was announced I was going to have the job, he wanted to come to see me." Initially reluctant, Watson did eventually meet with the exile leader in the company of outgoing Assistant Secretary Bernard Aronson. However, Watson was already trying to construct a different approach to selling the administration's Cuba policy based on maintaining "very good relationships" with CANF while simultaneously cultivating links with other Cuban-American voices – particularly among Democratic Party supporters.[56] The obstacles to success, however, were difficult, not easily overcome, and persisted into the Clinton's second term. As late as May 1999, one involved NSC official accused "the moderate Cuban-Americans [of being] feckless, disorganized and [using] too much left-wing rhetoric. They are also fucked over by the [actions of] the Cuban government."[57]

For the moment, however, CANF and its Capitol Hill supporters remained the locus of Cuba policymaking beyond the administration, and neither was about to let the president forget the message that "politically, you can never be too tough on Castro." The anti-Castro lawmakers, said one Senate foreign policy staff specialist, "were the only people [on the Hill] with intensely strong views on Cuba, and they were prepared to spend every day dealing with Cuba issues."[58] Another remembered that they "didn't care if the change was going to be violent or not, but they did care whether the change came sooner rather than later."[59] Lincoln Díaz-Balart initially stoked expectations within the exile community, claiming that an oil embargo of Cuba was under consideration by the White House. His colleague, Robert Torricelli, complemented personal lobbying of Clinton with proposed new legislative measures to further tighten the embargo. At a Miami conference in early November, he called for legal action targeting the American assets of foreign corporations that bought or leased properties confiscated in Cuba after the 1959 revolution. Meanwhile, demonstrations involving as many as 100,000 Cuban-Americans thronged the streets of Miami to show their continued opposition to the Castro regime.[60]

Not that there was much cause for concern about Clinton backsliding on Castro's Cuba. Eager to allay any doubts about his resoluteness in prosecuting a hardline policy, the president declined to meet with Elizardo Sánchez when the prominent Havana-based dissident visited the United States in late 1993. Clinton even refused to acknowledge or reply to Sánchez's letters.[61] He reminded the anti-Castro constituency of "the support I have given to the Cuban Democracy Act, to Radio Martí and TV Martí – no Democrat in my lifetime, in the White House at least, has come close to taking the strong position I have on [Cuba] with the Cuban-American community."[62] New selective shifts toward the market by the Castro regime, including decisions to open up 100 occupations to self-employment and give more autonomy to the island's cooperative farms, met with the traditional White House rebuff. Clinton saw "no indication that [Cuba], or that the leadership, the Castro government, is willing to make the kind of changes that we would expect before we change our policy."[63] Gestures of this sort more than reassured the exile community. At one fundraising dinner for Clinton in March 1994, Cuban-Americans showed their appreciation by donating more than $500,000 to the Democratic Party coffers. "All of a sudden a segment of the [exile] community is starting to understand that this guy isn't as bad as they were led to believe he would be," declared an effusive Florida Party chairman Simon Ferro. "They see that he is not going to establish relations with Castro and, in fact, that his policy is clearer and firmer than it was under Presidents Reagan and Bush."[64]

Five months earlier, State's Alexander Watson and the Treasury's OFAC Director Richard Newcomb appeared before a House Foreign Affairs subcommittee hearing on Cuba policy. Newcomb reported that the CDA legislation had all but eliminated U.S. subsidiary trade with Cuba; in 1993 it was valued at a miniscule $1.6 million, compared with more than $700 million in 1991. He further testified that the administration had drafted and rigorously implemented policy guidelines to keep dollar payments to Havana resulting from the new telecommunications links to an absolute minimum. Although travel restrictions had been eased and licenses extended to bona fide humanitarian organizations, Treasury officials were again keeping a close watch on other groups, such as Pastors for Peace, who were deemed to be violating the license provisions for purely political purposes.[65]

Under questioning about the new Cuba travel regulations that required a specific license for each trip, Newcomb proved more evasive. California democrat

Howard Berman voiced concern that Treasury's approval authority was couched in such excessively vague language ("in appropriate cases") that he found it impossible to pin down the OFAC director on the criteria used, or the standards applied, in making such decisions. Finally, Newcomb conceded that although the intent of the CDA was to increase educational, religious, and humanitarian people-to-people contact, Treasury's interpretation of the regulations was undercutting this objective.[66]

Watson spoke in more general terms about a country "at a dead end [whose] economic and political systems have failed." The administration would pursue a two-track policy of "maintain[ing] our economic embargo until there is true democratic reform and respect for human rights, while reaching out to the Cuban people." As Treasury's interpretation of the travel regulations had shown, "reaching out" meant different things to different executive branch departments. Some years later, Watson recalled that his "whole approach was to make whatever progress we could in establishing contacts with Cubans inside Cuba who might be able to play a constructive role when things began to change in that police state – but without provoking a domestic political hassle that I nor the State Department couldn't manage."[67]

What State could manage, and what the CDA also permitted, was a carefully calibrated loosening of sanctions in response to positive developments by the Castro regime. Despite "no movement toward democracy or respect for human rights," Watson told legislators that the emphasis on people-to-people contacts would continue, principally through licensing additional donations of food and medicines to individuals and nongovernmental organizations in Cuba, and facilitating more travel to the island. "We are trying to strike a balance," he concluded, "between the U.S. interest in promoting democracy, to enhanced information exchange, including by travel and our pursuit of other U.S. foreign policy and security goals."[68]

This exposition of the administration's guiding principles toward Cuba seemed increasingly at odds with the policy as it evolved in practice. Over the following months, visas were denied to Cuban diplomats, artists, and intellectuals who had been allowed to visit the United States during the Reagan–Bush years and, in February 1994, the State Department announced that it had excluded Cuba from any decision to relax specific license travel restrictions to embargoed countries. According to *The Miami Herald*, Undersecretary Peter Tarnoff, instead of throwing his support behind one side or the other, decided to temporarily halt an intra-agency battle pitting the hardliners in the Bureau of Inter-American Affairs against those officials with more general responsibilities in the areas of human rights and economic sanctions who favored an easing of travel restrictions to Cuba.[69]

Maintaining the travel restrictions in place was not unrelated to a desire to ensure there was no let up in efforts to limit Cuba's access to American dollars needed more than ever by Havana to fund critical imports during this period of severe economic crisis. A bid by four American telephone companies to improve communications links with the island was rejected because the proposed payment to Cuba of a $4.85 fee for its share of collect calls to the mainland was deemed exorbitant. This seeming gap between the administration's rhetoric and action was not all that surprising given the broader context within which policy was being made, perhaps best illustrated by the different interpretations placed on the CDA legislation by the major actors in the drama. Whereas Assistant Secretary Watson testified before Congress that its twin objectives were to increase pressure on the Cuban government to introduce reforms and establish more ties with the Cuban people, only weeks earlier, Robert Torricelli, the bill's author, had told a Georgetown University audience that a key CDA goal was to "wreak havoc" across the island.[70]

The United Nations Special Rapporteur's 1993 report on Cuba seemed to substantiate Torricelli's prediction. Carl Johan Groth concluded his trenchant critique of the human rights situation on the following note: "[A] policy vis à vis Cuba based on economic sanctions and other measures designed to isolate the island constitute[s] . . . the surest way of prolonging an untenable internal situation, as the only remedy that would be left for not capitulating to external pressure would be to continue desperate efforts to stay anchored in the past."[71] Clinton officials dismissed such criticism, whatever its source, and in March 1994, successfully lobbied the United Nations Human Rights Commission (UNHRC) to adopt a resolution condemning Cuba's human rights violations and extending the special rapporteur's mandate.

Tightened embargo provisions were certainly a pretext, if not a cause, for the Castro regime to undercut Washington's objectives in the human rights sphere. The State Department's report on developments in Cuba during 1993 reached conclusions that diverged little from previous studies. Castro's regime "sharply restrict[ed] basic political and civil rights," attempted to "neutralize dissent through a variety of tactics designed to keep activists off balance, divided and discredited," used organized mobs to harass antigovernment activists, and "mete[d] out exceptionally harsh prison sentences to activists whom it considered a threat to its control."[72] Still missing was any acknowledgment of positive developments the Cuban government had pursued or awareness of the larger context within which the abuses persisted. By contrast, *Human Rights Watch* offered a more nuanced assessment. It reported on "several important human rights gestures" by the Castro government, including the early release of some political prisoners and the eased travel restrictions on dissidents, while stressing that such modifications did not address the core problem of "legal and extra-legal reprisals" against dissidents and critics of the regime.[73] Yet this kind of analysis did not resonate with administration hardliners. "Cuba is a country that can and should do well," Director of the Office of Cuban Affairs Dennis Hays observed. "[The problem is] just one goddam megalomaniac who doesn't know when his time has gone."[74]

Havana's dilemma in seeking to engage Washington through political and economic changes constantly ran headlong into the same problem: a lack of clarity on the U.S. side about precisely what constituted openings worthy of a response. Appearances by senior administration officials on Capitol Hill during March 1994 to defend Cuba policy did little to challenge a perception that the changes being demanded could never be met by the current regime. Testifying before a House subcommittee in March 1994, Principal Deputy Assistant Secretary of State Michael Skol equivocated about precisely what steps Havana must take to elicit a positive response from the administration. The best he could do was repeat the by now standard wish list of broad, general demands: "free and fair elections with international supervision, the release of political prisoners, the end to the rules which prohibit outward travel of Cubans to the United States or elsewhere, the dismantling of one of the most repressive States in the world [and] a much more profound freeing up of [the workplace]." Asked to explain why this list of demands applied only to Cuba yet were not preconditions for improved relations with China and Vietnam, Skol feebly replied that "It is because the country situations are different." This refusal to acknowledge the inherent contradiction in singling out Cuba for special treatment produced the following exchange between Skol and an unconvinced Mike Kopetski (D–Oregon):

> SKOL: With regard to China, the jury is still out. But the fact that there was movement, there has been change, there is a trend of change.
> KOPETSKI: That is my point, not because we close them off, but because we opened the door.[75]

Nevertheless, U.S. officials remained convinced that, as Hays put it, "everything we tried we got slapped down on [by the Cubans]. Everything. Everything!"[76] Yet Havana well understood that the only concessions likely to seriously engage Washington were those that prefigured a political transition and the end of the Cuban Revolution. Privately, Clinton officials made no secret of the strategic objectives driving their actions. Confided Michael Skol:

> To me, the point of the various strategies of the embargo was not to change Castro's mind or to change Cuba while Castro was still in power, to gain Castro's acquiescence in democracy in Cuba, or to force him to change.

The point of the embargo was to impoverish the government so it could not be adventurous and to make sure that when Castro's end comes there would be insufficient movement to make possible a continuation of that regime.[77]

Within days of Skol's visit to Capitol Hill, the House Western Hemisphere Affairs Subcommittee began hearings on a Free and Independent Cuba Assistance Act. Proposed by Cuban-American Robert Menéndez (D–New Jersey), the legislation would require the Castro regime to take specific measures pertaining to human rights, democratic elections, and free market–oriented reforms in return for any future U.S. trade and economic assistance. Assistant Secretary of State Watson testified that the White House was reluctant to endorse this bill largely on the grounds that it would further constrain the president's authority over the making of Cuba policy. More specifically, it would eliminate his prerogative to determine the benchmarks against which an easing of the embargo might be judged, or what developments in Cuba would merit a "calibrated response" under the provisions of the CDA. Retaining this authority, Watson said, was necessary to "enable the president to develop and carry out effective policy responses to unpredictable and fast changing situations – just the kind of situation we face in Cuba."[78]

The latter's testimony, however, concealed more than it revealed. During interagency discussions, Watson "had argued in favor of supporting" the Menéndez bill but "we got shot down," largely by AID Administrator Brian Atwood, who "did not want to get into any country-specific special aid legislation and all the precedents it would set," and State's congressional liaison Wendy Sherman, who also maintained it would set a dangerous precedent. "I always thought," Watson said later, "if we had [supported the Free and Independent Cuba Assistance Act], we would have done something with Bob Menéndez and his colleagues on Cuba and might have attenuated, to some extent, the energy that poured into the Helms–Burton Act."[79] Michael Skol had also "argued very strongly" in support of the bill, which he viewed as a positive extension of the CDA in that it "offered a blueprint of what would happen if Cuba became a democracy and opened up." The White House decision to oppose it, he believed, "was not so much because of views about Cuba, but for a more narrow view. No administration or AID wants to be told how to spend its money by the Congress."[80] Irrespective of the reason, all that mattered to leading House advocates of the bill was that "the administration didn't want it and that was a sign to us that Clinton wasn't serious [about Cuba]."[81]

During 1994, Washington continued to ignore conciliatory Cuban gestures, such as Foreign Minister Roberto Robaina's meeting with former anti-Castro activists and exiled representatives of the reform movement *Cambio Cubana*, and downplayed the significance of the economic and other reforms process taking place on the island. Increasingly, official U.S. statements justifying or explaining Cuba policy seemed to do little more than highlight the flawed logic that seemed to lie at the heart of Washington's approach. The announcement in June, for example, of a drastic reduction in the size of Cuba's armed forces and a reported halving of the 1994 military budget made no impression on U.S. policymakers. As in the case of the Cuban agreement to withdraw troops from Angola five years earlier, the "positive developments" Washington demanded as a prerequisite for a calibrated response seemed permanently beyond Havana's capacity to achieve. Later, Richard Nuccio conceded that U.S. policymakers at the time – and for some considerable time thereafter – had no defined calibrated first step in mind with which to entice the Cubans to do anything.[82] Thus the essential thrust of U.S. policy toward Cuba remained consistent from the beginning of 1993 to the summer of 1994, partly due to uncertainty among Clinton policymakers about the outcome of Cuba's economic crisis and how best to capitalize on this opportunity and partly because political calculations entrenched the policy inertia. It would take a crisis in neighboring Haiti to focus a spotlight on the disingenuous nature of this approach and demand some degree of modification.

THE NEW NUMBERS GAME: MIGRATION

The crisis was precipitated by a dramatic increase in the number of Haitians fleeing the brutal military junta that ousted the democratically elected President Jean Bertrand Aristide from office in September 1991. During the election campaign, Clinton had been sharply critical of the Bush decision in April 1992 to forcibly repatriate the refugees, but once in office, he adopted the same general policy approach based on a negotiated settlement with the ruling generals that would return Aristide to the presidency, but with his power more circumscribed than in the past. Despite their professed commitment to a consistent approach on democracy throughout the region, American officials personally assured the junta leaders that the institutional interests of the armed forces would be protected in any arrangement that provided for Aristide's return. This assurance was all the more remarkable given the spiraling migrant outflow as Haitians in their thousands sought to escape the depredations of the thuggish dictatorial regime. During 1993, approximately 2,000 Haitians put to sea in search of asylum in the United States; in June 1994 alone the number suddenly jumped to 5,603, and nearly 6,000 more took their chances crossing the Florida Straits in the first four days of July.[83] Still, Clinton did not begin to publicly demonize Haiti's military leaders until September, and, even as a U.S. invasion force steamed toward Port-au-Prince, the president was prepared to entertain and accept a deal with them, if it could be arranged.[84] The mere possibility of broad talks between Washington and Havana, however, was, for all practical purposes, conditioned on Castro's exit from power.

Cubans were soon engaged in a parallel exodus. By the end of July, fifty Cubans a day were being picked up off the Florida coast by the U.S. Coast Guard. The sharp increase in the numbers wanting to leave was not the only new feature of this latest exodus; more and more were prepared to use force to get their way. On July 26, a Havana harbor ferry was hijacked and set on course for the mainland. Fifteen of the thirty Cubans on board subsequently chose to return to Cuba. A second ferry was hijacked on August 3, and this time seventy-six passengers and crew were taken to the United States against their will. Neither of these boats was apprehended by the Cuban Coast Guard, which was apparently under orders not to risk another July 13 tragedy, when a tugboat stolen by would-be refugees sank after being rammed by a Cuban border guard vessel with the loss of thirty-seven lives. However, although the hijackers were regarded as dangerous criminals by Cuban authorities, in the United States they were granted asylum and hailed as heroes by conservative Cuban-Americans.

Not surprisingly, still more Cubans were encouraged to try their luck. On August 4, an attempted ferry hijacking resulted in the death of one policeman and the presumed death of another who went missing overboard. Thousands of people gathered on the Havana waterfront the next day after hearing rumors that additional ferries were being allowed to leave for Florida. A riot broke out when police attempted to disperse the crowd. In the biggest antigovernment demonstration since 1959, several thousand people threw rocks and bottles at police, smashed the windows of a downtown tourist hotel, wrecked a dollar store, and chanted anti-Castro slogans. When order was finally restored, Castro blamed the sudden surge in people wanting to leave the island on a number of factors: lax U.S. surveillance of its coastline; Washington's failure to honor its part of the 1984 migration agreement to grant 20,000 annual Cuban entry visas and its policy of granting automatic residency after twelve months to Cubans reaching the mainland by whatever means (under the Cuban Adjustment Act), thereby encouraging illegal emigration by rewarding impatience and law breaking. Castro warned that his government might respond by "let[ting] those who want to leave, leave."[85] Refusing to shift from an oft-repeated head-in-the-sand approach to this issue, Clinton officials insisted that Fidel Castro would not be allowed to dictate U.S. immigration policy, or to instigate a replay of the 1980 boatlift, when 125,000 Cubans left the port of Mariel for the United States just as the presidential election campaign was gathering steam.

That uncontrolled influx of Cubans had dealt a severe blow to democratic incumbent Jimmy Carter's reelection prospects. It was simply the latest in a series of foreign policy crises that reinforced the image of a weak and indecisive leader. The episode also left an indelible mark on then Governor of Arkansas Bill Clinton. Some 20,000 Mariel refugees were sent to the state's Fort Chaffee military base for processing. A June riot at the camp that spread into surrounding neighborhoods creating a mixture of fear and anger was a key factor in Clinton's gubernatorial reelection defeat. Suddenly, a second Mariel crisis loomed on the horizon – more than 30,000 Cubans had been intercepted by the U.S. Coast Guard fleeing the island from the start of the rafters crisis through early September 1994[86] – as the White House was preparing for midterm congressional elections in November and laying the groundwork for the president's reelection bid in two years' time.

Prior to the August 5 riot in Havana, Clinton had already decided that the overriding objective of Cuba migration policy would be "No new Mariel." That same afternoon, interagency deliberations over how to deal with another major wave of Cuban rafters settled on a decision "to activate long-standing contingency plans to preempt any repeat of Mariel." The State Department seemed happy to dust off old strategies. As presented by Office of Cuban Affairs Director Dennis Hays, they called for placing the rafters in military bases and camps around the United States. The NSC simply "blew up" at this suggestion, which ignored Fort Chaffee and the political scars Clinton still carried from that episode.[87] For the White House, it was simply not an option. As the president's Chief of Staff, Leon Panetta, explained: "[Clinton] wanted to make sure that we never again fell into another situation where we had a repeat of what happened then."[88] Another policymaker involved in devising a response made much the same point: "There was very little to be gained in replicating the experience of establishing camps in the United States, whether in Arkansas or anywhere else. The resistance would be too great; the potential disturbances were very risky."[89] On August 11, an interagency meeting was called to discuss various options. Amid this flurry of bureaucratic activity, a consensus began to form among middle-level officials around the idea of providing safe havens for fleeing Cuban refugees at Guantánamo Naval Base and elsewhere but denying them entry into the United States – and thereby reversing a thirty-five–year "Special Status" policy.

If Clinton linked his future electoral prospects to a swift solution of the Cuba migration problem, Florida's democratic governor, Lawton Chiles, had even more cause for concern. Locked in a tough reelection contest of his own against republican Jeb Bush, the possibility of new waves of Cuban boatpeople and Haitian refugees risked turning the gubernatorial race into a referendum on immigration. The state's social services were already under strain from the latest batch of new arrivals, and an anti-immigration backlash was gathering momentum among Miami residents. The crisis took a turn for the worse when a Cuban naval officer was killed during a ferry hijacking attempt at the port of Mariel. Castro repeated earlier warnings that authorities would ease restrictions on the migration outflow unless Washington reversed its positive signals on illegal immigration. Other than new orders to the Coast Guard to interdict private vessels going to the assistance of rafters, Secretary of State Christopher merely observed that the United States would maintain its present policy. Angered by Washington's refusal to repatriate the naval officer's accused killer, Castro decided to translate his words into deed. On August 15, efforts to prevent Cubans from fleeing the island by boat were halted. Two days later, the U.S. Coast Guard picked up 547 rafters in twenty-four hours, a figure that exceeded the total for all of 1990.

Fearing a major electoral backlash in response to this new wave of refugees, Governor Chiles called for federal assistance, declared a state of emergency, and prepared to use the National Guard to incarcerate the rafters in state-run camps and other facilities. Yet he hesitated to put such an extreme measure into practice without first informing the administration. Believing that Attorney General Janet Reno, a former Dade County chief prosecutor, was most likely to appreciate the looming political crisis for Florida democrats, Chiles established initial contact with the Justice Department.

Although Reno did not initially share Chiles' state of alarm, even to the point of denying that a crisis existed on the morning of August 18, she was sufficiently concerned about the situation developing into a serious political problem to seek advice from NSC Adviser Anthony Lake. By then, the wheels had already been set in motion to take swift and decisive action. That afternoon, Lake chaired a White House principals meeting attended by Defense Secretary William Perry, Undersecretary of State Peter Tarnoff, the Joint Chiefs of Staff's Admiral William Owen, and the president's senior domestic adviser Leon Panetta. The Pentagon was especially concerned about the problem being dumped on its doorstep. "We knew that if there was a mass migration, the Coast Guard would take some of it," said the head of the Defense Secretary's Cuba Task Force, "but we would ultimately have to use our resources to help clean up the mess. So the Pentagon wanted to make sure, first of all, that there were no problems, no major confrontations with the Cubans."[90]

The principals meeting did not take long to arrive at a consensus in favor of the safe haven approach. "The change was necessary," one of the principals recalled, "to protect a basic fundamental policy of no massive influx that looked like Mariel." Only a week earlier, the White House had received a CIA report forecasting "a slow-motion Mariel" during the remaining months of 1994.[91] On the evening of August 18, blaming the latest exodus on the "failing policies" and "callous disregard for the lives of its citizens" of the Castro regime, the attorney general announced that "effective immediately," all refugees interdicted at sea would be placed in detention "pending a determination of how they should be processed by the [Immigration and Naturalization Service]."[92]

The White House put the onus for this policy change squarely on Castro's shoulders, accusing him of trying to dictate American immigration policy. Precisely what U.S. officials meant by such statements was not immediately obvious, especially when set against the negative impact of the embargo on island living standards and Washington's repeated rejection of offers by Havana to negotiate outstanding differences. Furthermore, Clinton seemed to be demanding that the Cuban leader do exactly what he had long been criticized for doing – restrict the freedom of his people to leave the island.

Because Castro was clearly in a no-win situation, Washington had to take its own steps to end the crisis. In a historic first, Clinton referred to "illegal refugees from Cuba" and announced that they would be taken to the Guantánamo Naval Base. If the base facilities proved unable to cope (14,000 Haitians were currently housed there following the May 1994 decision to end automatic repatriation and substitute case-by-case processing), the possibility of setting up safe havens in third countries would also be explored. Yet whatever option was pursued, warned Attorney General Reno, the "odds of ending up in the United States are going to be very, very small."[93] Cubans picked up at sea would no longer be eligible to enter the United States without first returning to Cuba and applying for either an immigration visa or refugee status at the U.S. Interest Section in Havana. By putting Cubans on the same par as Haitians, Clinton hoped to at least quiet the criticism from human rights groups. However, he could not expect much sympathy from anti-Castro legislators who took the view expressed by Senator Connie Mack that the White House was "punishing the rafters as opposed to punishing Fidel."[94] Nor could he hope to avoid a clash with conservative Cuban-Americans and the Florida democrats vying for their vote.

Nonetheless, the migration decision did constitute an immediate and potentially longer-term setback for CANF and the congressional Cuba lobby. First, the debate had revealed an important alternative constituency, particularly in Florida, that was fed up with a policy that allowed the unregulated flow of refugees into the United States. Second, the safe haven announcement signaled a more subtle but no less consequential development: a shift in the locus of Cuba policymaking from the State Department, where it had been since the Bush presidency, to the NSC. The latter was dramatically confirmed on the evening of August 19, when Clinton interrupted his own birthday party at the White House to meet with Governor Chiles, CANF Chairman Jorge Mas Canosa, and four other Miami Cuban-American "influentials" to discuss the refugee crisis. The attendees, who also included Vice President Al Gore, Deputy NSC Adviser Sandy Berger, State's Dennis Hays, and Attorney General Reno, thrashed out a compromise of sorts. Everyone agreed "that Castro was the problem," said Chiles. "Mas Canosa wanted a full blockade right away and the President said he would not take it off the table but it was not something he would consider right now."[95] Richard Nuccio was informed of the meeting as it was taking place by Assistant Secretary of State Watson, who showed him a copy of the agenda with its "list of possible punishments including the cutting of remittances, Cuban-American travel and direct flights to Cuba." When Nuccio exclaimed that "these are all stupid things" guaranteed to undermine the president's people-to-people strategy to open up Cuba, Watson reassured him: "Dennis [Hays] is there to make sure nothing bad happens" to counterbalance the migration decision.[96] In the political heat of the moment, however, such concerns were brushed aside. Clinton convinced the delegation to support the new policy in return for a commitment to get tougher on Castro by strengthening the very embargo that arguably bore the greatest responsibility for the crisis itself. Hays and the State Department had been sidelined.

Soon after, the White House fulfilled its part of this bargain with CANF and Chiles by implementing a new set of measures that ran counter to those bureaucratic advocates of a shift toward engagement with the Castro regime. The core goal of this latest chapter in embargo tightening was what it had always been: to crackdown wherever possible in order to deny the Castro regime access to badly needed hard currency. First, a ban was imposed on the flow of family remittances from the United States to Cuba, estimated at between $400 million and $500 million annually. Second, the general license for travel to the island by family members, scholars, and other researchers was terminated (which cut such travel by approximately ninety percent). Third, new steps were announced to increase anti-Castro broadcasts to Cuba, including the use of American military aircraft to augment Radio and TV Martí. Finally, the administration promised to mobilize international pressure more aggressively on the Castro regime concerning its human rights record.[97]

The new sanctions were neither an incentive to Castro to cooperate in trying to halt the exodus nor a deterrent to Cubans determined to take their chances on the high seas. After all, sectors of the Miami exile community openly ignored Attorney General Reno's instructions not to assist rafters. One exile group, Brothers to the Rescue, had six aircraft searching for boatpeople in the Florida Straits – and few imagined that they would meet a hostile reception in the United States. Almost 12,000 rafters were picked up by the U.S. Coast Guard between August 21 and August 25, more than triple the number for all of 1993.[98] With

Cuba's illegal migrant outflow spiraling upward, the White House faced the very real prospect that the detention policy would not end the crisis.

Convinced Havana had engineered the crisis to pressure Washington to ease the embargo, Leon Panetta raised the possibility of a far more drastic action that revived memories of the U.S. military efforts to topple the revolutionary regime in the early 1960s: a naval blockade of the island. "We have got to continue to put pressure on Castro," he said, "because the problem here is not . . . refugees [or] migrants, it's the problem within the Castro regime."[99] Clinton had earlier told Mas Canosa that such an option would not be totally ruled out; Panetta's statement served to confirm the lengths to which the White House might be prepared to go to prevent the Cuba situation getting out of hand. Pentagon officials were quick to play down talk that the blockade was a live option, denying that it was "at the forefront of our planning."[100] Secretary of State Christopher almost winced at the idea, which he called an "act of war."[101] Nonetheless, this option "was looked at very seriously," according to a department official involved in the crisis management exercise, "and the principal reason it was discarded was that the Navy and Coast Guard said it would take an enormous amount of vessels in the Florida Straits to try to monitor the situation effectively. It was simply not practical to have a naval blockade. There was also the fear that Castro could increase the flow."[102]

Panetta's proposal was only the most extreme manifestation of the divergent views within the Clinton administration about internal developments in Cuba. Assistant Secretary Watson recalled that the August 5 riot did not shake the operating assumption among senior policymakers that Castro would survive the current crisis. He certainly "never thought" the unrest threatened the regime's hold on political power because "no matter how bad the economy got, the regime controlled everything. They weren't going to go down."[103] Office of Cuban Affairs Director Hays took a less sanguine view of developments on the island:

Castro has always, episodically, used the outflow of people to relieve pressure on the regime, and there's always a point up to which that is healthy for him because the malcontents, the discontents pack up and go. But there is a point beyond which he always cuts off, when it hits regime-threatening proportions, and then things just stop or the country would eventually implode.

This time, Hays believed, Castro had let the situation deteriorate to a point at which it did pose a threat to the government itself: "The country basically stopped, everybody was either becoming a rafter, thinking about becoming a rafter, selling things to the rafters, or watching the rafters. The paralysis was striking the rest of the island as everybody just watched to see what was going to happen."[104] For administration hardliners like Hays, now was the time to escalate the pressure on the Castro regime.

In the meantime, strenuous efforts were being made to bed down the new detention policy. On August 22, the first group of 800 Cuban rafters arrived at Guantánamo Naval Base. Asked whether they had any chance of being admitted to the United States on political grounds, INS Chief Doris Meissner replied bluntly: "No, they do not." Attorney General Reno was adamant that she would "not parole them" to the mainland.[105]

The next day the flow of rafters reached 3,253, the highest daily total in almost a quarter century. If Clinton and his senior policy advisers had privately reached a consensus that the changes already implemented were not working, they refused to accept Castro's proposal for broad, high-level talks. "This is not a problem to be resolved between the United States and Cuba," said Undersecretary of State Peter Tarnoff, who confidently asserted that the administration could "manage the crisis for as long as necessary."[106] Within forty-eight hours, Tarnoff's boast succumbed to domestic political imperatives. The exodus was seemingly incapable of being halted in the absence of some kind of direct contact with the Cuban government. A scaling back in the estimated number of Cuban refugees that Guantámano could hold from 60,000 to less than 28,000 gave added urgency to finding a solution to the crisis. On August 27, with 13,000 Cubans decamped at the base, both governments announced an agreement to hold mid-level talks on migration at the United Nations in New York. The U.S. delegation was headed by State Department hardliner Deputy Assistant Secretary Skol. His counterpart on the Cuban side was the former foreign minister and now president of the Cuban National Assembly, Ricardo Alarcón.

From the beginning Washington set the parameters, insisting that the talks be confined to addressing the interrelated issues of ending the refugee exodus and increasing legal immigration. Havana's demands that the meeting(s) address the question of the embargo as a contributing factor in the crisis and that the August 20 sanctions be dropped were categorically rejected. The administration also ignored calls from Cuba's Catholic bishops, moderate Cuban-American exile groups, Havana dissidents, democratic and republican congressional leaders, and prominent media outlets to broaden the scope of the negotiations.[107] *The New York Times* editorialized that in diplomacy, "it is often more important for governments to talk to their enemies than to their friends."[108]

Peter Tarnoff continued to insist that "we're not going to negotiate broader questions" or contemplate any easing of the embargo, because to do so would "delay, not hasten, reform." Interviewed on CBS's "Face the Nation," Secretary Christopher was just as emphatic: "We're going to have talks with the Cubans on the one subject where we've got something to talk about, and that is migration."

He simply repeated the standard line that the United States stood ready to respond "in a carefully calibrated way" to democratic openings in Cuba.[109] Michael Skol followed that script to the letter: "I headed the negotiations with Alarcón. We told the Cuban-Americans that we were not talking about anything up there [in New York] but the migration issue." At his first New York press conference prior to the talks, Skol engaged in a little theatrics to drive the point home. "I responded to a question about whether or not more was being considered by holding up my briefing book and pointing to the table of contents," he said, "noting that it showed 'A to M – nothing but migration.' "[110]

As the discussions got underway, the administration moved to erase all concerns within the exile community that they were a harbinger of any larger policy shift. Senior officials, including State's Richard Nuccio and Treasury's Richard Newcomb, were despatched to Miami to reassure Cuban-Americans that the talks would produce no surprises. A meeting attended by thirty leading conservative exiles warned Nuccio that the Miami Cuban community would "explode" if Havana wrested any concessions. CANF President Francisco Hernández demanded assurances that only immigration issues were being discussed, or no one "at this table is going to hold anybody back."[111] Nuccio promised the gathering that relations with Havana would not improve until Cuba undertook fundamental political reform. Newcomb's words to the community were even blunter: Clinton policy still aimed to hasten the end of the Castro regime; any significant policy change was still premised on that outcome. Significantly, the itineraries of both officials did not include meetings with any moderate exile groups despite Nuccio's expressed determination to build a Cuban-American constituency that could offset CANF's influence.[112] Back in Washington, Undersecretary Tarnoff again restated the precise nature of the brief he had given the U.S. negotiating team: "Our people have no authority to deal with what we regard as extraneous matters."[113]

On September 17, after eight days of talks, the two sides finally arrived at a solution to the crisis: In return for Havana's agreement to do all within its power, using "mainly persuasive methods," to prevent illegal migration to the United States, the Clinton administration agreed to accept 20,000 legal immigrants a year and pledged to speed up the admission of another 4,000 to 6,000 who were already on the visa waiting list. This constituted the most substantial diplomatic accord reached between the two countries in a decade. It also amounted to a modest change in U.S. policy. The 1984 accord had set a *maximum* number of Cuban immigrants at 20,000 annually, but individuals still had to meet the normal criteria, and only about 1,000 to 2,000 qualified annually. The 1994 agreement set the *actual* number at 20,000 annually; those who would normally qualify either on grounds of family ties or job skills and any remaining spots filled by lottery from among Cubans who applied at the U.S. Interest Section. A senior State official acknowledged that absent Cuban concessions – specifically, Alarcon's willingness to drop the demands that the United States rescind the August 20 embargo-tightening measures and restrict hostile radio broadcasts beamed to the island – there would have been no successful outcome.[114]

At a Washington news conference announcing the agreement, Tarnoff declared that "the United States continues to believe, as it has over the past three decades, that there should be a peaceful transition to democracy in Cuba. We will continue to work to that end."[115] An unhappy Dennis Hays was far from assuaged by Tarnoff's words. Believing the onus for finding a solution lay solely with Havana, he had wanted Skol to drive a much tougher bargain: "I felt we'd missed some opportunities where, instead of giving Castro things, we might have actually gotten things from him in this area."[116]

Nonetheless, the crisis was averted – at least for the moment. No sooner had Cuban authorities begun reenforcing the ban on illegal migration than the refugee count dropped off dramatically, and virtually ceased by late September. However, with the signatures barely dry on the New York agreement, Cuban-American leaders began to lobby the administration to reverse its policy of requiring the Guantánamo refugees to apply formally for immigrant visas and take their place in the processing. "It's not possible to keep thousands of Cubans in detention camps some 90 miles away from their relatives in Florida," warned Francisco Hernández.[117] Nor, it seemed, was it possible to pursue the debate within the administration about shifting to an engagement policy with the Castro regime in the politically charged atmosphere generated by the situation in the detention camps.

CONGRESS UPS THE ANTE: "A STUPID PIECE OF LEGISLATION"

The White House was convinced that the migration decision had saddled it with a political problem in Florida. Unless quickly diffused, it had the potential to create a major political embarrassment for the president at the December Summit of the Americas in Miami even though Cuba itself had been excluded from the meeting. Officials conjured up visions of the exiles "burning the whole damn town down around the president's ears over migration." Richard Nuccio was appointed White House liaison to the Cuban-American community, and given the job of calming the populace down, which was made easier by the fact that "substantively, what was going on during that period was [an administration] inventing excuses to bring the Gitmo [Guantánamo] people into the United States."[118]

CANF was certainly doing its bit to pressure Clinton to relocate the Guantánamo Cubans to the United States. Initial meetings with State Department officials produced concessions in the way of better food, more autonomy, and access to telephones for the 25,000 now housed at the camps – which reinforced the belief among the refugees and their advocates that the White House would eventually buckle under the pressure. Such optimism was also fueled by the tensions building up among the 7,000 to 8,000 detainees being held in overcrowded facilities in Panama, where riots in December over living conditions resulted in injuries to several dozen American troops.

Mas Canosa and his supporters had other reasons to be hopeful about forcing the administration's hand. Unexpected republican gains in the mid-term November 1994 elections gave the GOP control of both the House of Representatives and the Senate for the first time in decades. In the process, leadership of the two key foreign policy committees shifted from moderate democrats to conservative republicans extremely hostile to the Castro regime. North Carolina's Jesse Helms took over the chairmanship of the Senate Foreign Relations Committee from Claiborne Pell (D–Rhode Island), who, despite his late-blooming support for the CANF line on Cuba, had recently called for the lifting of the embargo and described U.S. policy as "more a product of shortsighted domestic politics than of prudent foreign policy considerations."[119] In a public appearance the day after the election, "Helms ticked off a 10-point agenda for changing the course of U.S. foreign policy. Cuba was at the top of Helms's list."[120] On the House International Relations Committee, outgoing Chair Lee Hamilton, another critic of the embargo, was replaced by a Cuba coalition supporter, Benjamin Gilman from New York. Any setback resulting from one of CANF's staunchest allies, democrat Robert Torricelli, being forced to relinquish the top position on the House Western Hemisphere subcommittee turned out to be more illusory than real. His replacement, Indiana's Dan Burton, was a long-time vocal opponent of the Havana regime. The Cuban-American community, a gushing Mas Canosa declared, "could not have expected a dearer friend or someone more devoted to securing Cuba's freedom to assume the chairmanship of the subcommittee."[121]

Administration officials were under no illusions about what this electoral boost to the anti-Castro forces on Capitol Hill meant for any change for the better in U.S.–Cuba relations. "Things probably will get nastier before they get better," said one Clinton official.[122] Within weeks, Burton began to repay the faith the conservative exile community had placed in him with warnings that he would investigate Mas's complaints against companies doing business with Cuba, and by pressing for the repatriation of the Guantánamo refugees to the United States under the auspices of CANF's Valladares Foundation. Meanwhile, he and Helms were preparing to introduce legislation that would ratchet up the economic sanctions against Cuba to a degree not even sought by the author of the CDA.

Also determined to play an active role, Robert Torricelli ushered in the new year by demanding that any financial bailout package for Mexico, once more on the verge of debt default, be conditioned on that government's agreement to cut all its Cuba aid programs. Florida's Cuban-American House members, Republicans Lincoln Díaz-Balart and Ileana Ros-Lehtinen, on the lookout for any backsliding by the White House, complained to the president about reports that the NSC's Morton Halperin was pushing for sanctions against Cuba to be eased, not tightened. The response from Clinton was quick and concise: His Cuba policy would not change.[123] In ways such as these, according to Chief of Staff Panetta, the new republican-controlled Congress forced the administration to become "much more defensive in terms of trying to hold our ground on Cuba as opposed to trying to advance it."[124]

In February 1995, Helms and Burton launched a major effort to secure passage of legislation that would dramatically increase the political pressure on the White House to get a lot tougher with Cuba. Their Cuban Liberty and Democratic Solidarity [Libertad] Act, named in honor of Poland's anti-communist Solidarity Movement, aimed to more severely punish foreign governments and corporations and global lending institutions pursuing economic relations with Fidel Castro's government.

Although the House and Senate versions of Helms–Burton were not identical, the provisions of each combined a threefold objective: to further Cuba's global economic isolation, to promote a political transition on the island, and to compensate former American property holders in Cuba and protect the rights of U.S. property owners worldwide. The key provisions were quite specific and not subject to interpretation: former U.S. owners of nationalized properties would be granted the right to sue foreigners who invested ("trafficked") in these enterprises in American courts: any foreign business executive who owned or profited from such properties would be denied a visa to enter the United States; countries buying sugar, molasses, or syrups from Cuba or trading in these sweeteners would lose their right to sell such products in the American market; U.S. contributions to the World Bank and the IMF would be reduced by the amount of aid either institution might decide to grant Castro's government in the future; U.S. economic assistance to Russia would be withheld equal to the amount (roughly \$200 million) that Moscow provided Havana in payment for the electronic intelligence facility at Lourdes; and the president was authorized to develop an aid program for a post-Castro Cuba once a number of political and economic reforms specified in the legislation indicated a transitional or democratic government was in place (a measure that was largely taken *in toto* from Robert Menéndez's 1994 Free and Independent Cuba Assistance Act).[125] "Let me be clear," declared Helms as he introduced the bill in the Senate, "whether Castro leaves Cuba in a vertical or horizontal position is up to him and the Cuban people – but he must and will leave Cuba."[126]

Jesse Helms's crusade to champion the rights of expropriated American property holders with outstanding claims against foreign governments was a major inspiration for the bill. Yet, over the years, the Castro regime had made a number of offers to negotiate settlements involving disputed properties similar to those concluded with Canada and other countries. Typically, however, they were accompanied by one condition that Washington always found unacceptable: comprehensive talks on bilateral relations. Ironically, with few exceptions – notably Bacardi, which encouraged Helms to pursue a legal avenue to secure compensation – those U.S. companies with claims against confiscated properties in Cuba seemed less excited about or interested in the issue than their elected representatives. "Most of the claimants had discounted this stuff years ago, written it off their books," Assistant Secretary of State Alexander Watson discovered. Meetings with companies' representatives were always at his instigation, and Watson recalled always leaving with the sense that "many of them might even have just wanted to forget all this and, if they were still interested, go back in some other way."[127] The Office of Cuban Affairs had a similar experience. "The owners of the expropriated properties did not badger us," recalled Dennis Hays.[128] The president of Alamar Associates, a Washington DC–based consultancy firm working with U.S. corporations interested in pursuing trade and investment opportunities in Cuba, more or less confirmed this lack of interest. "Over recent years, I've taken a bunch of companies down to Cuba who have claims, and I've never heard a single one, a single sentence of interest in recouping their claims."[129]

Dan Fisk, however, tells a different story. Soon after he was appointed to the staff of the Senate Foreign Relations Committee in July 1994 and given the task of drafting legislation that reflected Helms's concerns about Cuba, certified claimants did start appearing at the door to his office: "We had businessmen coming to us and saying, 'I'm competing in the international market against my sugar and my nickel in Cuba.' And they were right. In Europe they do have to compete with Cuban nickel, which, in our view, they are the legal owners of. They are also the legal owners of that sugar produced in Cuba from our perspective. That's what Helms–Burton was meant to say, that these people still have rights regarding ownership, and until they're compensated, they'll have a remedy beyond just waiting for the State Department to sit down and negotiate."[130] Yet these old, mainly corporate, claimants were not the only beneficiaries of the proposed legislation. The Helms bill also significantly extended the pool of claimants to include Cuban-Americans whose properties were confiscated before they became U.S. citizens. One effect of this would be to increase the competition for whatever settlement monies the Cuban government might eventually agree to pay.

This waiting game on Cuba became an increasing source of frustration to Helms, Torricelli, their congressional allies, and Miami supporters who were now beginning to criticize Clinton in language reminiscent of their earlier unhappiness with Bush: He was not doing enough to hasten the fall of the Castro regime. As far as Helms was concerned, "no one [in the administration] was giving any thought to Cuba"; the White House was doing little more than indulging in "Monday morning quarterbacking," simply implementing the self-enforcing provisions of the CDA. To some extent, a tactical error by Clinton officials appears to have fueled this perception. Fisk accused Nuccio of only maintaining lines of communication with the democrats on the Hill: "What Ric would do was go talk to the democrats. The republicans felt like we kind of got shut out."[131]

Helms and his aides were determined to keep a tight hold when it came to drafting the new legislation. "From the beginning," recalled Fisk, "this was going to be our legislation. We were going to make the decisions as to what went in it and what didn't go in it and how it was shaped." Suggestions from CANF, property claimants, and other legislators were welcome, but this would not be a rerun of the CDA experience. Indeed, by the time Fisk met personally with Mas Canosa in December 1994, he "already pretty much had the bill drafted." What the authors of the Senate bill wanted CANF to do was "approach legislators" and, in the process, help round up the sixty votes needed if it became necessary to pass a cloture motion to end debate. Although CANF may have chafed at the limitations placed on their role and "got really pissed off" over the subsequent decision to delete the Title III provision in order to get cloture, "they were wedded to us. Once that bill was introduced, they couldn't reject us."[132]

This consultative process was as much about making inroads into Clinton's Florida constituency as it was about finessing Cuba policy; the challenge was to offer incentives to mobilize support for the legislation while keeping the initiative firmly in the hands of Helms and his staff. Although similar legislation was being readied by House Western Hemisphere subcommittee Chairman Burton and his aides, there was no doubt about who was driving, and in charge of, this process. As one Capitol Hill Cuba specialist put it: "Burton and his people were along for the ride."[133]

If the bill landed on the president's desk, it promised to replicate the dilemma Bush confronted over the CDA. The administration response to the bill was cautious. In testimony before a congressional subcommittee in March, Assistant Secretary Watson said the White House was broadly sympathetic to the bill's objectives and "stand[s] ready to work with the Congress to make enforcement of the embargo more effective." However, its support was qualified by inclusion of specific provisions that "might have consequences which could impede our ability to further our shared goals" and the need to guard against any actions that could have "major adverse effects on broader U.S. interests." He identified five provisions as creating the greatest concern: the threat to withhold aid to Russia equal to the amount Moscow offered Cuba in return for use of the Lourdes intelligence facility, which could be interpreted by the Russians as "interfering with their exercise of their right under the START treaty to monitor [U.S.] compliance with the agreement" and so damage broader national security objectives; the proposed ban on the entry of sugar and sugar products from third countries that imported Cuba-origin goods of this kind was inconsistent with U.S. obligations under the World Trade Organization and North American Free Trade Association, and could be seen "as a secondary boycott similar to the Arab boycott of Israel, which the United States has long and vigorously opposed"; a specified program of assistance to a transition or democratic government in Cuba would limit the president's flexibility to determine when a transition of this kind was in place and how to respond; a cluster of provisions that "appear to infringe on the president's constitutional responsibilities for the conduct of foreign relations"; and, finally, the extraterritorial reach of some provisions that "would cause disputes with our allies and could be difficult to defend under international law." These differences, Watson stressed, however, were not insurmountable obstacles to reaching a consensus, and the executive was willing to work with the bill's sponsors to achieve this outcome.[134]

The legislation's potential for creating a major rupture between the United States and its alliance partners was the overriding issue for the State Department's chief liaison official with Congress, Wendy Sherman. In a detailed analysis, she argued that the bill in its current form "would anger allies of the United States and force Washington to violate several international agreements." Some of its provisions were deemed unreasonable or too sweeping; others would "undermine the longstanding U.S. [opposition to] secondary boycotts." Whatever the domestic political costs of opposing Helms–Burton, Sherman concluded, "the potential foreign policy troubles this bill will create outweighs those concerns."[135] Not everyone, however, saw it this way – one reason being the failure of U.S. allies to translate their complaints and threatened retaliation over the CDA into action.

In practice, they did almost nothing. Consequently, when the EU sent a letter to House Speaker Newt Gingrich (R–Georgia) in March describing key provisions of the Helms–Burton bill as "objectionable" and "illegitimate," and warning that its extraterritorial thrust "ha[d] the potential to cause grave damaging effects to bilateral EU–US relations,"[136] it was easy to ascribe an element of "crying 'wolf'" to the message. Moreover, the EU's unease was tempered by the unlikely prospect of Helms–Burton becoming law; the main focus of Europe's anger over Washington's Cuba policy remained the CDA. "The Europeans weren't getting too anxious about Helms–Burton at that point," recalled a State Department official then based at the U.S. Mission in Brussels. "The Europeans were alarmed that the legislation had been proposed, but they were confident that the administration was doing everything it could to oppose it."[137] State Department officials working directly with the EU took the criticisms of Helms–Burton seriously, but generally placed them within the broader European attack on Washington's proclivity for applying unilateral economic sanctions as a blunt instrument in pursuit of foreign policy goals. Director of the Office of Cuban Affairs Hays described one response to Helms–Burton by diplomats and government officials on both sides of the Atlantic: "Oh God, another headache. First it was Iran, now we're going to do more to Cuba, and then its going to be Iraq, and then what about Libya. To these guys it was just one more issue, just one more pariah country, and do we really want to piss off the EU over yet another of these matters?"[138]

Following an interagency review of the proposed legislation, Clinton himself weighed into the debate in late April during an interview on CNN. "I support the Cuban Democracy Act, which was passed in 1992 and which we have implemented faithfully. I think we should continue to operate under it. I know of no reason why we need further action."[139] However, the administration waged no sustained campaign against the legislation that was thought to have little chance of going anywhere – and certainly not in a direction that some Clinton policymakers hoped Cuba policy might take.

At the beginning of March 1995, reports surfaced that leading State Department and NSC officials wanted the president to shift to a policy of limited engagement with the Castro regime to test the latter's interest in pursuing major political and economic changes on the island. A degree of support for engaging Cuba had been percolating for some time among a number of midlevel State Department officials worried about the possibility of internal chaos on the island leading to another large-scale migrant outflow. It was also disclosed that NSC Adviser Anthony Lake had decided in the summer of 1994 to recommend that Clinton lift the embargo only to put the idea in cold storage following republican gains in the November election.[140]

Certainly, Michael Skol was convinced that "somebody in the administration wanted U.S. policy changed." Having chaired the interagency committee examining Helms–Burton, which rejected his proposal that negotiations be held with the bill's authors "to get out a piece of legislation that was more acceptable to the administration," Skol nonetheless prepared testimony that would reflect his sentiments on Cuba policy for a scheduled House International Relations committee hearing. This effort was thwarted by an NSC directive to his State Department superiors "that nobody would be testifying for the administration before the committee." According to Skol, those leading "this effort to change policy" were Undersecretary of State for Political Affairs Peter Tarnoff, NSC staff member Morton Halperin, and State's Head of Policy Planning James Steinberg. Skol also charged that the Bureau of Inter-American Affairs "was deliberately being cut out of it."[141] Whatever the veracity of his assessment, there is no doubt that he and Alexander Watson were in the process of being ejected from, or marginalized within, the Cuba policy-making loop. At the same time, the advocates of change were realistic, and under no illusions about how far they could push the process: "The disposition of the White House was always that we should look for opportunities and we should try to have as much so-called Track II exchanges with Cuba, but that there was not going to be anything major or sweeping. There was not going to be a secret trip to Havana like there had been [by Nixon] to Beijing."[142]

Even so, the anti-Castro hardliners in the new Congress reacted angrily to these indicators of a policy shift in the wind. Helms introduced an amendment to a defense appropriations bill to tighten the sanctions rather than loosen them. In the House, Speaker Gingrich (R–Georgia) demanded that the administration "move in the opposite direction," while Torricelli pledged to "fiercely resist" any change in Cuba policy. A senior Clinton official explained that the proposal to revoke the August sanctions was simply motivated by a desire to be "proactive" at a people-to-people level "and not just sit on the [existing] policy for another few years." Yet no rationale for easing the Cuba embargo could satisfy Helms, Connie Mack, and Robert Dole (R–Kansas), who warned Clinton in writing that they would oppose him "through every means at our disposal" if he made any move in that direction. The White House immediately retreated into denial. Insisted spokesman Mike McCurry: "There is no review or change in our view that the embargo of Cuba is an effective tool."[143]

Attempts to deflect congressional hostility toward any kind of engagement with Cuba, along with the debate over Helms–Burton, were temporarily put on hold by the possibility of a new immigration crisis in mid-1995. Following a trip to Guantánamo, Senator Bob Graham triggered "serious alarm bells" in the White House about the need for a comprehensive solution to the refugee problem. The situation in the camps, he told the president, was a "tinderbox" that "couldn't last through the summer without the strong potential of a riot." General

John Sheehan, Commander in Chief of the United States Atlantic Command, was relaying the same message to the Pentagon: the status quo on Guantánamo was not a long-term solution, but a recipe for "civil disturbance." The senator and the general also agreed on a solution: repatriate the more than 20,000 refugees to the United States. "We were facing a double whammy when all we want is to keep foreign policy problems off the screen," remarked one official. "The word [from the White House] was: Solve it. Make it go away with the least amount of turmoil."[144]

Responsibility for "disappearing" the problem was handed to Deputy NSC Adviser Sandy Berger, Morton Halperin, and Peter Tarnoff, who had been Jimmy Carter's secret envoy to Cuba during the late 1970s, developed a "long-standing close personal relationship with [Ricardo] Alarcón," and been used by the Clinton administration as a "back channel" to Havana since the 1994 migration crisis.[145] Weighing the views of Graham and Sheehan, the prospective multimillion dollar financial costs to the Pentagon of housing the Guantánamo Cubans, the domestic political fallout of antagonizing an important electoral group and their powerful congressional allies, and the growing national anti-immigration sentiment, they quickly reached a consensus: Change the refugee policy, but appease the exile community by meeting their demand that the "Gitmos" be allowed to enter the United States. To make a lasting settlement possible, however, required negotiations with Havana. Tarnoff and Halperin also viewed this domestic crisis as a wedge for moving toward a broader policy shift based on engagement rather than confrontation and hostility.[146] The decision to solve the problem diplomatically was made quickly, not only because the executive branch hardliners were deliberately excluded from the policy review. It was also propelled by the situation at Guantánamo and the failure of other options (including refugee camps in third countries such as Panama) to stem the flow. "Therefore," explained one knowledgeable U.S. official, "the question emerged in the minds of those who were working on the subject of actually having an understanding with the Cuban government."[147]

During the latter half of April, Tarnoff and Alarcón held secret talks in New York and Toronto on a new immigration accord. The negotiations, in Tarnoff's words, were "very tightly held [in order] to avoid the very real possibility that rumors about these talks might trigger a massive exodus of new migrants" in anticipation of a new agreement. Alexander Watson and Attorney General Reno were "aware" of the talks, but took no part in them. By contrast, Principal Deputy Assistant Secretary of State Skol was kept totally in the dark; so too was Director of State's Office of Cuban Affairs Hays, whom Tarnoff did not trust,[148] which was not surprising given Hays's insistence on vetting every proposed Cuba policy shift with CANF before proceeding. Richard Nuccio, who was Watson's senior policy adviser at the time, contended that Hays and Skol "were kept out of it entirely because they were seen as unable or unlikely to implement the decision, or they would immediately leak it to their friends in the Foundation."[149]

On May 2, the secret negotiations reached a successful conclusion. The agreements, Tarnoff reassured Congress, "[stood] alone" and did "not signal any change" in U.S. policy toward Cuba.[150] Under the terms of the new accord, the United States agreed to admit the vast majority of the Cuban detainees being held at Guantánamo Bay, but credit them against the 20,000 annual migration figure negotiated under the September 1994 understanding. In the future, however, all boat people picked up in international waters attempting to reach the mainland would be returned to the island and advised by the U.S. Interest Section of their right to apply for legal migration. The Cuban government in turn pledged that no returnees would suffer reprisals and agreed to allow U.S. officials to verify its compliance with this commitment. The Tarnoff–Halperin engagement signals were further bolstered by a decision to inform the Cubans in advance that the president intended to notify Congress he would oppose Helms–Burton. More surprising, a senior official even referred to "some promising changes" in Cuba, such as the legalization of private farming, which might qualify for a "carefully calibrated" response.[151] Indeed, Tarnoff and Alarcón had secretly agreed that "if the accords went well, perhaps this could lead to other kinds of things" that could be discussed at the biannual meetings to review the progress of the agreement.[152]

Florida's two leading democratic political figures praised the May 2 agreements. Governor Chiles said they "will ensure that Florida should never again confront a massive wave of uncontrolled immigration from Cuba." To Senator Graham, the outcome "makes it clear that the United States is in control of our borders and that we will not allow Fidel Castro to use immigration as a foreign policy weapon."[153] However, if the objective had been to solve this refugee problem "with the least amount of turmoil," the result produced some problems, nonetheless. After news of the secret talks broke, Hays and his deputy, Nancy Mason, protested their failure to be consulted and asked to be reassigned to other positions. The conservative Cuban-American leadership was just as outraged. The decision to admit the Guantánamo detainees met one of their prime objectives, but could not assuage their feelings at being completely excluded from any input into the process. Moreover, if the Clinton White House could implement a policy change that, by applying the existing asylum law to Cubans picked up at sea, indirectly neutralized legislation that had given Cuban refugees special status for almost a decade and a half without consulting the exile community, what were the implications for future Cuba policy decisions? In State's Office of Cuban Affairs, the May 2 agreement was certainly interpreted as something of a turning point in the administration's relations with CANF: "After that, they [CANF] felt that we couldn't be trusted as much as before."[154]

For Senate Foreign Relations Committee Chairman Helms and his aides, the failure to inform Congress about the Tarnoff–Alarcón talks merely heightened their feelings that the executive branch was acting in a duplicitous fashion. They were particularly angered by the decision to assign responsibility for maintaining public contact with the Hill to Dennis Hays, who had been totally excluded from the policy-making loop, rather than Peter Tarnoff, who "was involved in the real negotiation where the deals were cut." To Fisk, this tactic "really raised the question if the administration wasn't really up to something nefarious, why have this bait-and-switch game they were playing, including manipulating their own foreign service officer?"[155]

Maintaining CANF's rage, Mas Canosa led a protest against the migration deal by several thousand Cuban-Americans in Lafayette Park, across from the White House. He was now "on the other side of the fence," he told the gathering, and would no longer support Clinton's Cuba policy.[156] This anger, however, had more to do with a sense of betrayal and CANF's loss of assumed privileges than with any substantive change in U.S. policy. Administration officials, for instance, dismissed an unprecedented June meeting between Castro and *Cambio Cubano*'s Eloy Gutiérrez Menoyo, a proponent of engagement and lifting the embargo, as merely an "individual interaction" of no wider significance,[157] and then revealed they were formulating a new set of initiatives to undermine Castro's leadership and promote democracy in Cuba. The latter turned out to be an extension of the CDA Track II provisions, focusing on expanded academic, religious, educational, and cultural people-to-people exchanges that had been routinely opposed by State's Office of Cuban Affairs when Hays was in charge.

The decision to restore full diplomatic relations with Vietnam in July provided further evidence that the basic policy approach remained in place. The announcement ruled out any similar move with regards to Cuba. Newly appointed Special Adviser to the President and Secretary of State for Cuba Richard Nuccio spoke of "some fundamental [political and economic] differences" between the two countries.[158] But, domestic political considerations were never far from the minds of Clinton policymakers. Justifying the White House refusal to treat Cuba with the same leniency as various other authoritarian Third World regimes in late 1995, one senior foreign policy adviser put the case bluntly: "There are no votes riding on how we deal with Indonesia, and not many on how we deal with China. Castro is still political dynamite."[159]

Nonetheless, the second half of 1995 also brought with it some signs that a shift was taking place in the domestic dynamics of Cuba policymaking.

The State Department began to adopt a relatively more assertive posture in its dealings with the exile hardliners, beginning with a warning against incursions into Cuban territorial waters and airspace after a flotilla sailing from Florida ventured too close to the island's coast. It added that U.S. authorities could offer little practical assistance if the Castro government made good on its statement that "any boat from abroad can be sunk and any airplane downed."[160] When the USIA Inspector General's Office voiced criticism of Mas Canosa's role as head of the Presidential Advisory Board on Cuba Broadcasting, Clinton officials were noticeably slow in rushing to his defense. Meanwhile, Special Adviser Nuccio had resumed his efforts to build an alternative, non-CANF constituency that would support a more sophisticated and nuanced policy approach. Nuccio's strategy rested on exploiting the CDA Track II provisions – which allowed the licensing of church-based agencies, educational groups, foundations, and environmental organizations – to mobilize domestic groups who would work with the U.S. government to strengthen independent organizations in Cuba. Its success demanded that CANF no longer be "treated as the gatekeeper for access to the Clinton administration." Nuccio now proceeded to invite a range of groups both inside and outside the exile community to meetings on Cuba. Predictably, indignant Foundation leaders absented themselves from most of these gatherings. "I wasn't excluding them," Nuccio argued. "They were excluding themselves."[161] In a September visit to Florida, Nuccio confined his discussions to moderate Cuban-American groups. CANF responded to this rebuff by shifting the focus of its anti-Castro efforts to Capitol Hill and that group of legislators most intent on blocking or reversing any policy move in the direction of engagement with the revolutionary regime. Yet if a broader domestic input into the debate over Cuba policy was being encouraged by some officials, not all went along with this effort.

Adding to the practical difficulties of trying to cultivate a more diversified community voice was the immediate challenge of the Helms–Burton legislation. Testifying before a Senate subcommittee in late May, Undersecretary Tarnoff had restated the administration's belief that the current embargo measures were "working" and remained "the best leverage the U.S. had to promote change in Cuba." Apart from its potential to "infringe" on the president's ability to make foreign policy and limit his "flexibility" in dealing with "evolving situations," key provisions of the proposed legislation would almost inevitably create a whole new set of problems for American global policy.[162] But few executive branch officials were under any illusion that devising an effective strategy to combat Helms–Burton would be plain sailing. One of Nuccio's first tasks was to organize interagency meetings attended by officials from State, Defense, Justice, the NSC, the CIA, and the IRS to "try to get everybody going in the same direction on Cuba policy." He worked closely with three State Department officials – Peter Tarnoff, Deputy Assistant Secretary Ann Patterson, and Deputy Director of Policy Planning Roberta Jacobson – all of whom "hated Helms–Burton, thought it was a stupid piece of legislation, and that we should do everything we could to defeat it." High on their list of targets was Title II, the refurbished Menéndez bill provision, intended to "basically establish this incredible new protectorate over Cuba by the United States by defining [the nature of] the transition."[163] Perhaps the biggest obstacle to Nuccio's efforts was that few senior administration officials, much less the White House, shared his own sense of urgency about Helms–Burton. "We didn't think it would take off," said one.[164]

Revised versions of both the House and Senate bills, including a presidential waiver on aid to Russia if the president deemed it to be in the national interest, did little to ease the concerns of Tarnoff, Nuccio, and other officials. On the eve of the House vote on its amended bill, at Tarnoff's suggestion, Secretary of State Christopher wrote to Speaker Gingrich that he would recommend a presidential veto if the legislation ever reached the Oval Office because it still contained a number of unacceptable provisions. Tactically, Nuccio recalled, the White House "was perfectly happy to get a letter from Warren Christopher which it could choose to ignore."[165] In the event, the secretary's warning went begging. On September 21, the House voted by more than two to one (294–130) in favor of the legislation.

In the Senate, a democratic filibuster supported by a few moderate republicans produced two failed efforts by Majority Leader Robert Dole and Jesse Helms to close off debate on its revised softer version of the House bill. Nuccio and two colleagues actively lobbied to prevent the bill getting to the floor of the Senate. Yet the dilemma for Nuccio was that he could never actually say that the president would oppose the legislation and exercise a veto if it arrived on his desk for signature: "Until the day the [February 1996] shootdown occurred, I was still trying to get an answer from the White House as to whether President Clinton opposed Helms–Burton, supported it, supported it under certain conditions, or what." The White House domestic advisers were still trying to discern which way the political winds were blowing. Nuccio felt as though he "was in this 'no man's land' in which I am the president's Special Adviser on Cuba working against Helms–Burton, but I don't really know if the president is against Helms–Burton or not."[166] To gain the required sixty votes for cloture, Helms was ultimately forced to delete the contentious Title III provision allowing U.S. citizens to sue "traffickers in confiscated properties" for damages in American courts. On October 19, the Senate passed its version by an overwhelming seventy-four to twenty-four vote.

SLOW RESPONSE: U.S. BUSINESS AND HELMS–BURTON

During the interim between the House and Senate votes, forty-seven CEOs representing some of America's biggest corporations met with senior White House, NSC, and State Department officials before departing on a trip to Cuba organized by Time Inc. For Special Adviser Nuccio, who was responsible for issuing travel licenses to the CEOs (over which an angry Treasury filed an ethics complaint against him), this meeting was another step toward establishing a non-CANF domestic constituency. However, this initiative did not produce exactly the result Nuccio had intended. He not only earned the predictable ire of the Foundation; one of the charges leveled by Cuban-American supporters of Helms–Burton was that the administration was attempting to exploit growing U.S. business community opposition to Cuba sanctions to defeat the legislation. Even if true, the perceptible shift in corporate sentiment regarding Cuba was not so much country-specific as part of a larger unhappiness over the increasing tendency of the Clinton White House to use the blunt instrument of unilateral economic sanctions to solve foreign policy problems. On those few occasions when corporate executives lobbied against the Cuba embargo, Michael Skol remembered, it was "mainly as part of the debate about sanctions in general. They rarely talked about Cuba because it was not a big market."[167]

In fact, the business community was extremely slow to rally against Helms–Burton, despite its manifest lack of enthusiasm for the legislation. "They didn't understand the implications of it," said one Senate foreign policy staffer.[168] According to Nuccio, this reluctance was "partly because they felt it was too complicated, too dangerous, and too politically difficult."[169] Fear of reprisals by the exile community was one factor; another was past cases of being "hammered" by the government and the media on the grounds that their opposition to sanctions was largely self-serving. But there were also reasons specific to Helms–Burton, including a widespread perception among U.S. overseas investors and traders that this legislation was not only unnecessary, but also had no hope of congressional passage. "To be blunt," explained Willard Workman, vice president, international, of the United States Chamber of Commerce, "the initial reaction was, 'Why beat up on a bunny rabbit? We already have an embargo against Cuba. Why do we need this?' " In the unlikely event that Congress passed the bill, the business community assumed it would be subject to a presidential veto.[170]

Andrew Semmel, foreign policy adviser to Senator Richard Lugar (R–Indiana), believed that the absence of any tangible U.S. business stake in Cuba, and thus no interests that required protection, was a key factor in the corporate world's failure to "fully understand the implications of Helms–Burton."

By and large, this was true, with a few exceptions. At least one law firm was contracted by business interests to "walk through the legislation" with Semmel, pointing out "why this was bad legislation."[171] Nonetheless, there were few, if any, public declarations of hostility. Most companies were simply content to leave it to peak organizations such as the Chamber of Commerce and the National Association of Manufacturers to issue statements of in-principle opposition to unilateral economic sanctions. The weakness in this approach, as Workman conceded, was that it could be easily dismissed when the issue was a country-specific piece of legislation that no one corporation was prepared to challenge in public.[172]

Some outward-looking business sectors did, however, take a slightly more forceful approach. Appearing before a House subcommittee examining the implications of renewed trade with Cuba for American agriculture in May 1994, industry representatives repeatedly stressed the potential gains that would flow from such a development. The rice industry's David Graves was confident a major pre-1959 market could be reestablished, even though there would be "a considerable transition period." Archer Daniels Midland Vice President and leading spokesman for the National Oilseed Processors Association John Reed Jr. went further, placing the future role of the Cuba market within a global context. Because of the "increasingly unfavorable competitive situation" for American vegetable oil exporters resulting from the General Agreement on Tariffs and Trade (GATT) Uruguay Round on world agricultural trade, he told the subcommittee, "the potential importance of the nearby Cuban market becomes even greater than it would be under other circumstances."[173]

A growing number of corporations also wanted some of the existing trade and investment sanctions lifted, not new ones added, as proposed by the bills now winding their way through the Congress. In discussions with administration officials, business executives repeatedly complained that they were being forced to watch "as foreign competitors lock up an attractive emergent market."[174] Such pleas typically elicited little more than a restatement of existing policy. Parrying questions about the contradictory nature of a policy that is willing to engage China, Vietnam, and North Korea but not Cuba, Assistant Secretary of State Watson could only give the stock "special case" answer. Nuccio would not even concede that the embargo seriously disadvantaged American businesses: Foreign competitors were "mostly people who put money in short-term or high-risk investment" and could be displaced by U.S. companies whenever the embargo was lifted.[175]

Following the House vote on Helms–Burton in September, the *Journal of Commerce* accused the legislators of "pass[ing] an ill-considered bill that aims to dry up foreign investment in Cuba."[176] The business response to the Senate vote was only slightly less muted. During Fidel Castro's brief visit to New York in October, some 200 business executives indicated their preference for easing the embargo by meeting with the Cuban president. Others simply headed straight to Havana. Between January and December 1995, Cuban economic officials hosted meetings with approximately 1,300 members of the American corporate community and signed about forty nonbinding letters of intent to do business on the island.[177] In pressing the case for relocating policy to a different track, those business sectors most eager to participate in the Cuba market pointed out that the exile community was no longer united behind a hands-off approach. "There are other voices out there," observed Peter Blyth, president of Radisson Hotels, which had already marked out three hotel sites on the island, "who are asking us to move things forward because there is a generation change, and the grandparents of the exile community are all elderly."[178]

Neither the greater willingness of the business community to entertain dealings with the Castro government nor the fracturing of the Cuban-American community represented the kind of alternative domestic constituency that might encourage, let alone reward, a fundamental change in Cuba policy. However, it probably bolstered what confidence there was in the administration about opposing Helms–Burton or other efforts to tighten the economic screws on Cuba, and was not unrelated to the outcome of an interagency review completed in early October. Clinton announced a limited easing of restrictions on travel to, and other contacts, with the island: U.S. news organizations could open bureaus in Cuba, nongovernmental organizations could apply for Treasury Department special licenses to provide assistance to their counterparts in Cuba, the categories of groups and individuals eligible to apply for similar licenses to visit Cuba were broadened, and Cuban-Americans would be allowed to visit the island once a year. Although the measures taken were consistent with the CDA and left in place the August 1994 sanctions they did, nonetheless, reverse some of the gains Mas Canosa had won at the height of the migration crisis and seemed to suggest that Clinton was now prepared to frame his approach to Cuba by reference to a wider cross section of domestic groups and interests than in the past – if not to a new set of (post–Cold War) ideological assumptions and strategic political outlooks.

The State Department's Office of Cuban Affairs coordinator, Michael Ranneberger, was at pains to dispel the "completely wrong misperception that somehow the October '95 measures were intended to move us in the direction of gradual normalization or even *sub rosa* normalization with Cuba. It was completely off the mark." Having played a key role in formulating the measures, Ranneberger stressed that normalization "was never discussed"; the focus of the interagency meetings "was always how can we penetrate the society, how can we encourage independent activity, and that kind of thing."[179] The reference point for Clinton policymakers was not the collapse of the Soviet Union, but what happened in Eastern Europe during the 1970s and 1980s, "where after the liberation of these countries many of these people came out from former dissidents' positions to high government posts and really did say that the very controlled and always modest exchanges and opportunities for openings had made a significant difference."[180]

Other actions also testified to the persistence of Cold War assumptions and outlooks in the prosecution of Cuba policy. Treasury's Office of Foreign Assets Control continued to assiduously track down and prosecute American firms doing business with Cuba. Fines were levied on Merck and Co. pharmaceuticals, NationsBank, AT&T, and Citibank, among others, during final months of 1995. Clinton made a point of snubbing Castro during celebrations to mark the 50th anniversary of the United Nations in New York in October. Asked why they were determined to avoid so much as a handshake between the two heads-of-state, one senior executive branch official replied: "It is a real power politics approach, but why would you want to give him [Castro] the status and respectability that would come from a meeting with the president *until he has given way.*"[181]

By now, the pressure from the United States on Castro to give way was formidable. The CDA's foreclosure of subsidiary trade with Cuba had significantly ratcheted up the embargo. American officials were openly talking about how the legislation's Track II provisions could be used to encourage the sort of activity on the island that might eventually challenge the regime's grip on power. Clearly, Washington paid no mind to conciliatory Cuban gestures. Cooperation in the migration talks had produced only a limited easing of already tightened restrictions on contacts with the island. When Eloy Gutiérrez Menoyo and other moderate exiles were invited to Cuba in November for the second Nation and Emigration conference, Washington not only refused to sanction the trip, but also warned that it would investigate any attendees' misuse of the humanitarian travel permit. An exasperated Cuban Foreign Minister Roberto Robaina explained Havana's refusal to budge on core U.S. demands: "How can we abandon the one party system today when the Americans still want us to disappear?"[182]

If "disappearing" the Castro regime was Washington's solution to its Cuba problem, the same could not be said for the Europeans, whose reaching out to Cuba was making Clinton officials increasingly suspicious of precisely what plans the allies had for engaging the Castro regime. It also produced serious concerns about the extent to which this approach might weaken the impact of Washington's more confrontational strategy. "The big issue for us with the Europeans at the time," said a Brussels-based U.S. diplomat, "was our concern that the Europeans were moving forward rather quickly to implement an agreement with the Cubans, an economic agreement on development assistance."[183] The result was a decision to shift away from automatically opposing any initiative of this kind in favor of applying diplomatic pressure on EU governments to attach "some conditionality" to any cooperation accord they signed with Havana.[184]

American officials were particularly concerned about a scheduled visit to Cuba in February 1996 by EC Vice President Manuel Marin to negotiate an aid agreement that would commit the Castro government to respect human rights and permit a gradual opening up of Cuba's political and economic systems. In return, Marin offered EU development and economic cooperation, and support for Cuba's membership of the Rio Group, which would bring a new degree of international respect and recognition.

When Washington first became aware of the impending economic cooperation agreement in the latter half of 1995, Richard Nuccio visited six European capitals to lobby for the inclusion of a "democracy clause" that was part of similar agreements the EU had reached with Mexico and Indonesia. "This time we weren't trying to block any agreement, we were just trying to better it," Nuccio explained. U.S. pressure on Marin to wrest concessions did not end with Nuccio's trip. On February 7, the day Marin was scheduled to leave for Havana, he met with then U.S. Ambassador to the EU Stuart Eizenstat, who delivered a blunt message. The White House desired to attach its own conditions to any EU–Cuba development aid agreement in order to avoid giving the Cubans something for nothing: "Look Manuel, you're Spanish, you speak the language, you understand the culture, your going is a big thing and it shouldn't be cost free to the Cubans. You ought to be more vocal in terms of human rights violations and democracy. Don't just go down there and talk about increased trade. You were giving Castro a feather in his cap and you ought to get something for it."[185]

While most of what Eizenstat said was consistent with EU demands for reform of the civil code in respect to property, the rule of law, free speech, and the like, his "final demand," according to Nuccio, was that Castro agree to a meeting between Marin and the human rights group Concilio Cubano "and understand that the EU would officially recognize Concilio and extend its protection, and acknowledge that these [dissidents] were legitimate figures who were now under the protection of the EU." In return for meeting these conditions, Cuba could expect Washington to make the first of its much vaunted "calibrated responses."[186] Marin agreed to deliver the offer to Fidel Castro.

To Marin, accommodating these U.S. demands was not tantamount to a newfound consensus between the White House and the EU over how to approach the problem of Cuba. He still regarded the aid agreement as a fundamentally European initiative that was part and parcel of "a very commonsensical approach that was quite different from U.S. policy."[187] The Cuban president, however, failed to appreciate any difference. After eleven hours of talks with Marín, he rejected every item on the latter's agenda. Although the EC Vice President was permitted to meet with Concilio Cubano members, no sooner had he boarded his plane for the flight back to Europe than those he had spoken to, and other leaders of the group, were arrested. Seeking to explain this harsh action, some U.S. observers contended it was deliberately planned to kill off a joint EU–U.S. initiative that would have significantly bolstered local support for domestic opponents of the Castro regime. This view may also have been shared by senior administration officials.[188] However, if Castro had qualms about the possible impact of the conditions on an offer for better relations with the EU or the United States, he could have simply rejected them outright. This had been the approach taken when Caribbean Community initially requested specific human rights commitments in return for closer ties. To have embarrassed the vice president of the EC in this way was completely unnecessary, and would have been tantamount to using a sledgehammer to crack a nut.

More likely, Washington's reflex hostility to any engagement with Cuba, and the suspicions it roused in Havana (which island dissidents had been warning about for years), formed the backdrop to this crackdown and the dramatic events of early 1996. In mid-January, the Miami-based exile group Brothers to the Rescue made an illegal leaflet drop over Havana urging Cubans to engage in peaceful acts of civil resistance against the regime. Warnings from Cuban authorities that actions of this kind would not be tolerated, and by the State Department that the Cubans likely meant business, continued to go unheeded. Four weeks later, authorities again cracked down on Concilio Cubano. On February 24, the day the group's request to hold a national meeting was canceled, Brothers to the Rescue attempted to mount another leaflet drop over Havana. Cuban MiG-29 fighter jets shot down both planes, killing the four crew members and plunging U.S.–Cuba relations into their worst crisis in thirty years.

Helms–Burton and the Triumph of Politics over Policy

I have one message for Mr Castro today: Adios, Fidel.

Senator Jesse Helms, following the announcement of an agreement between the Clinton White House and Congress on passage of the Helms–Burton legislation

T H E shootdown by Cuban jet fighters of two unarmed civilian planes piloted by members of the Miami exile group Brothers to the Rescue (BTTR) occurred two weeks before the Florida presidential primary. The timing was bound to figure in Clinton's calculation of a response, but the fact that it weighed so heavily shocked even the most seasoned Cuba hands in the State Department. When news of the incident broke, the president took the dramatic action of immediately ordering U.S. Air Force jets to the crash site area to protect Coast Guard rescue teams searching for survivors. Secretary of State Warren Christopher, who was in Central America at the time, condemned the attack as a flagrant violation of international law amid contradictory evidence as to whether the planes had been shot down inside or outside Cuban territorial waters. The United Nations Security Council passed a resolution "strongly deploring" Havana's action, but set aside much harsher language proposed by Washington and rejected its request for the imposition of worldwide mandatory sanctions on the island. On February 26, Clinton announced a set of retaliatory measures: the suspension of all charter flights between the United States and Cuba, an expansion of Radio Martí's broadcasting range, new restrictions on visits to and travel within the United States by Cuban officials, and prompt action to reach agreement with Congress on the Helms–Burton legislation "so that it will enhance the effectiveness of the embargo in a way that advances the cause of democracy in Cuba."[1] Subsequently it was learned that the president had also directed the Pentagon to draw up a list of possible targets inside Cuba should a military strike either by U.S. Air Force planes or cruise missiles be deemed necessary.[2]

THE SHOOTDOWN AND THE POLITICS OF REELECTION

In the crisis atmosphere that pervaded the days following the shootdown, a prime objective was to avoid any serious escalation of the bilateral conflict. "Our goal at that point," said White House Chief of Staff Leon Panetta, "was to do everything possible to make sure those relations don't deteriorate."[3] Clinton was sensitive to the possibility that Cuban-American extremists might themselves seek to exploit the crisis, while a nervous Defense Department did not want to be placed in a situation where it was forced to act as "military protectors of these groups."[4] The task of managing the U.S. response fell to Richard Nuccio, who, by his own account, found himself suddenly an isolated figure within the foreign policy bureaucracy, partly due to "a perception that there may be a fundamental change in policy provoked by the crisis, and the bureaucrats didn't know which side to be on, so they stepped back so they would not be caught on the wrong side of the swinging door."[5]

The anti-Castro hardliners in Washington and Miami were disappointed and angry at the initial sanctions, which they characterized as "weak and ineffective," and demanded a more forceful response. Senator Bob Graham (D–Florida) even refused to categorically "rul[e] out military action."[6] Helms–Burton was the one weapon Clinton had at hand with the best chance of mollifying these forces while keeping the risk of escalating the crisis to a minimum.

Throughout 1995 the administration supported the intent of the bill but took exception to specific provisions, arguing that they restricted the president's prerogative to make foreign policy, contravened international law, were likely to clog the federal court system with lawsuits and would almost certainly damage relations with important trading partners. The shootdown transformed the dynamics of the whole debate: limiting its domestic political fallout became the overriding concern. Panetta put it simply and bluntly: "It was clear that the politics of the issue had turned around. The shootdown was an act nobody could sanction. Regardless of the politics of Florida, you're now talking about the politics of the country."[7] National Security Council (NSC) Latin American specialist Richard Feinberg remembered that the shootdown did not automatically produce a new consensus in support of Helms–Burton: "the [foreign policy] bureaucracy as a whole [still] opposed important parts of Helms–Burton, but those concerns had to be swept aside in the emotions of the moment over the shootdown."[8]

From a strictly political point of view, the legislation had two features to recommend it. "It wasn't military action," said a State Department official, "and the Cubans didn't like it."[9] For most administration officials debating a response, these were compelling, if simplistic, reasons. At a meeting of the

99

president's senior foreign and domestic policy advisers the day after the shoot-down to formulate a recommendation to the White House on Helms–Burton, Nuccio was surprised to discover widespread ignorance about key provisions: "Until the day of this meeting, none of the cabinet members there were aware that the embargo had been codified." Lincoln Díaz-Balart (R–Florida) had per-suaded Helms to add this amendment immediately after the shootdown in view of the distrust among congressional hardliners about Clinton's willingness to stay the course of a harsh new turn in Cuba policy. After Nuccio made his open-ing presentation, the first response came from Attorney General Janet Reno, who exclaimed with a certain incredulity that " 'what Ric has just described must be unconstitutional. The president can't possibly sign this bill.' " This was the consensus view until the two White House domestic policy advisers among the group, George Stephanopoulus and Chief of Staff Panetta, spoke up. "When they got to George Stephanopoulos, he said, 'I disagree. The president has to sign this legislation.' And right next to him was Leon Panetta who said, 'I agree with George. The president has to sign this.' And [NSC Adviser] Tony Lake said, 'Well, that's it. I agree with George and Leon.' End of meeting." When the meeting broke up, Nuccio complained to Panetta that signing Helms–Burton would be the worst move the president could make. "I know, Ric," the latter replied, "but we'll just have to fix that after Clinton's [re]election."[10]

The shootdown, Panetta argued, created a new political reality that the White House could ignore at its peril: "With the country reacting as it did to what took place, demanding we take a strong position, and with it being strongly supported on Capitol Hill, there was no question that, if the president had vetoed Helms–Burton, Congress would have overridden the veto in big numbers. It wasn't that we were enthusiastic about it. It was just that this was life as we saw it in dealing with Capitol Hill." Clinton's still-reluctant foreign policy officials eventually went along because "one way or another it was going to happen. So the real question was, 'Can we try at least to negotiate so that some of it [Helms–Burton] would be more acceptable?' "[11]

Clinton hoped he could reach a compromise on the final version of the bill, but when a Nuccio-led State Department delegation arrived on Capitol Hill, it soon discovered that the congressional sponsors and supporters of Helms–Burton were in no mood to make any substantive concessions. "The time for compro-mise is over," one Senate republican staff member commented. "If they want to propose some minor modifications, we're willing to listen, but at the eleventh hour, we're not going to rewrite the legislation."[12] Given Clinton's now public commitment to embrace Helms–Burton, Nuccio had little bargaining leverage: "I go up and say, 'Here I am, let's compromise,' and they say, 'OK, you sign what we tell you and that will be a good compromise.' "[13] Other members of the delegation conceded they "got no traction" in their negotiations with GOP foreign affairs staffers. Clinton's compromise proposal, said one, had "more loopholes than a cheap suit," not least being the lame effort to preserve the president's authority to determine when punitive measures against Cuba were appropriate.[14] Helms and Burton themselves exuded confidence that Castro was "on the ropes" and they were about to hammer "the last nail in his coffin."[15] These sentiments appear to have had an intoxicating effect on members of the conference committee attempting to reconcile the different House and Senate versions of the bill. Attending one of its meetings, Andrew Semmel, foreign policy adviser to Senator Richard Lugar (R–Indiana), saw "not the kind of deliberative process you would want to remember. It was disorganized, chaotic and not a very coordinated process, even though it was an important policy issue."[16]

In this politically frenzied environment, nobody at either end of Pennsylvania Avenue was paying much attention to the pleas of corporate America that passage of the legislation would make it virtually "impossible to develop a position within the Cuban market while providing more opportunities for companies in other countries."[17] The rush to find a politically acceptable response before the Florida presidential primary and the climate of noncompromise in the Congress meant it was no longer realistic to expect that changes in Cuba policy would be left entirely to the discretion of the White House.

On February 28, Clinton announced that agreement had been reached on a slightly reworked version of the original bill. Undersecretary of State Peter Tarnoff called the final outcome a "reasonable compromise,"[18] and the president indicated that he would work to secure passage of the legislation, which constituted the most punitive set of measures taken against Cuba since the early 1960s. Helms–Burton imposed two major new sanctions designed to obstruct Cuba's access to foreign investment capital. First, Title III, which a senior administration official had described as "the part of the bill that bothers us the most,"[19] allowed American nationals to sue for damages in U.S. federal courts those persons who "traffic" in property nationalized by the Cuban government after 1959. The right extended to Cuban-Americans who became U.S. citizens after their properties were confiscated. The legality of this provision was questionable under international law, and even U.S. property claimants were divided over its merits. Bacardi Rum, which had vast holdings in Cuba before the revolution, lobbied hard for the property claims settlement measures. Other major property claimants, including ITT, Exxon, Goodyear, and Sears Roebuck, opposed Title III as unnecessarily complicating their prospects for eventually reaching negotiated settlements with the Cuban government.[20] Title III would take effect on August 1, 1996, but the president was given the authority to delay its implementation for periods of six months at a time if he determined that such a delay was in the national interest and would expedite a transition to democracy in Cuba. The administration hailed the waiver as a hard won concession. Senate Foreign Relations Committee staffer Dan Fisk termed this something of an exaggeration. He and his colleagues, said Fisk, first began "floating the idea" after the failed cloture votes in September 1995, and a firm decision was taken to propose a waiver in an attempt "to seduce the administration" into signing the bill at a meeting in his office during the first week of February 1996.[21] Nor was this concession viewed as an unqualified gain for the White House. The six-month renewal requirement ensured that Congress could regularly monitor the president's efforts to justify delaying implementation of the measure.

Second, Title IV denied foreign citizens (including CEOs and other senior corporate executives, principals, or shareholders) who were a party to the expropriation of U.S. property or deemed to benefit from the trafficking in such property in Cuba entry into the United States. Entry visas could also be denied to the spouses, dependent children, and agents of designated traffickers. This provision was mandatory and could only be waivered on a case-by-case basis for humanitarian medical reasons or for the purposes of mounting a defense in legal actions related to confiscated property.

Helms–Burton also included a basically rewritten version of the rejected 1993 Menéndez bill (Title II), which specified numerous conditions for determining when a "transition" and a "democratic" government had assumed power in Havana, and thus qualified Cuba for various types of U.S. assistance and, ultimately, the suspension of all trade sanctions. A *transition government* was defined as one that excluded Fidel and Raúl Castro; legalized all political activity; released all political prisoners; dissolved the Department of State Security in the Cuban Ministry of the Interior; gave a public commitment to organize free elections for a new government within eighteen months; and made demonstrable progress in establishing an independent judiciary, respected human rights, and allowed the establishment of independent trade unions and other social, economic, and political associations. A *democratic government* was defined as one that achieved power on the basis of free and fair elections; respected basic human rights and civil liberties; supported movement toward a market-oriented economy; and returned confiscated properties to their former U.S. owners in lieu of swift, adequate, and effective compensation.

Other sections of the law prohibited loans, credits, or other funds by any U.S. national, U.S. agency, or permanent resident alien for financial transactions involving any property confiscated by the Cuban government, the claim to which is owned by a U.S. national; and directed Washington to vote against Cuba's admission to any international financial institution of which the United States is a member until a democratic government is in power in Havana. The president was also required (subject to a waiver) to withhold U.S. assistance from Russia by an amount equal to the sum of assistance and credits its provided to Cuba in return for use of the intelligence gathering facility at Lourdes. That the White House received some latitude in implementing this provision was less a substantive concession than a recognition by Congress that much larger foreign policy issues were at stake. After all, even the Pentagon insisted that Moscow must be allowed continued access to its electronic listening post in order to be able to verify arms control agreements. The consensus view remained that to deny or complicate that access could only damage vital U.S. strategic interests.

In return for such minor modifications to the legislation, Clinton agreed to the inclusion of the Title III lawsuit provision that he had previously opposed, accepted various restrictions on the conduct of U.S. policy toward the former Soviet states depending on the nature of their economic relations with Cuba, and above all, agreed to codify all existing embargo Executive Orders and regulations into law (revised Title I) with no presidential waiver loophole – in effect, ceding a great deal of authority to Congress to dictate future shifts in Cuba policy. Initially, Helms himself had been skeptical that the White House would accept this restriction, only to be pleasantly surprised when it did so in exchange for the Title III waiver. Once the bill was signed into law, the embargo could only be lifted when a democratic government (as defined by the bill) came to power in Cuba or when the Congress, of its own accord, agreed to pass another act rendering Helms–Burton null and void. Instead of a U.S. Cuba policy, there was now a U.S. Cuba law, and the president had little choice but to respect it.

Genuine and pressing U.S. interests with respect to Cuba were forced to take a back seat to domestic political considerations in reaching this agreement with the Congress. Only four days before the shootdown, CIA Director John Deutch told the Senate Select Committee on Intelligence that although no Caribbean nation "threaten[ed] U.S. military or economic security [or regional peace and security]," drug trafficking and especially uncontrolled migration from Cuba did constitute potential risks to U.S. interests and required careful monitoring.[22] The White House turnabout on Helms–Burton rendered moot any possibility of a formal bilateral agreement to cooperate in the area of drug interdiction. It also provided Havana with every justification for revoking earlier undertakings to prevent another mass exodus of rafters. At the time of the 1994 migration agreement, Washington had agreed to resist precisely the kind of legislative tightening of economic sanctions that it had now approved; the May 1995 agreement coincided with Clinton's announcement that he would likely oppose Helms–Burton. If Congress was untroubled by the thought that its actions might contribute to worsening living standards in Cuba and that this might provoke Castro to reopen the emigration safety valve, in signing Helms–Burton the

White House signaled this was a risk it was prepared to take to achieve a short-term domestic political advantage.

Other initiatives of potential benefit to the United States were allowed to lapse. In early 1996, for instance, the Defense Department had concluded there was little to be risked and much to gain from pursuing increased military-to-military cooperation with the Cuban armed forces that went beyond simple confidence-building measures to ease tensions on both sides. Taking the longer view, General John Sheehan and other high-ranking Pentagon officials expressed a desire to build bridges "to the most important functioning institution" on the island that was now "playing a much greater and important role in the country's economy." The shootdown ensured that any moves in this direction were stopped in their tracks. "Everything we did in '96, from domestic to foreign policy, was geared to getting Clinton reelected," recalled Raimundo Ruga, who worked at Defense's Cuba desk, "and that was the case with Cuba policy. That was the reason there was no movement on the military-to-military contacts."[23]

Although the core CDA notion of expanding people-to-people contacts (the so-called Track II approach) remained operative, Helms–Burton attached a more clearly antigovernment agenda to such measures along the lines of exploiting new political openings in Cuba to foment subversion. To this extent, it cast a shadow over the status of independent groups such as Caritas, the Catholic charitable organization that in recent months had gained approval from the Cuban government for a significant expansion of its welfare and other activities. This kind of clumsy ideological politics also contributed to the marginalization of alternative voices and harsher treatment of political dissidents on the island. In addition to the February crackdown on *Concilio Cubano*, only weeks later, during a speech to the Central Committee of the Communist Party Politburo, Raúl Castro announced a campaign against scholars who had been involved in a dialog with their U.S. counterparts. Subsequently, Cuban authorities launched an investigation into dozens of academic think tanks and stepped up repression of dissidents and opposition political groups calling for change.[24]

Helms–Burton stripped the administration of its ability to respond in "carefully calibrated ways" to political or economic reform inside Cuba. Although largely confined to rhetorical statements, so long as the White House retained the initiative on Cuba policy, this idea in theory remained a live option. Helms–Burton at the very least severely limited its ability to ease or tighten the embargo as the situation warranted and the president saw fit; it also removed any incentive for Fidel Castro's government to attempt to satisfy U.S. demands for substantive reform given that the demise of the revolutionary regime and its institutions had been written into law as the prerequisite for major concessions by Washington. At the same time, Clinton was running out of options, short of some kind of military pressure, to retaliate against Havana for any further actions or provocations of which the United States disapproved.

On March 1, the White House acted to curtail any repeat of the BTTR shootdown. Clinton directed the secretary of transportation to issue the appropriate rules and regulations prohibiting the unauthorized entry by aircraft or vessels from the United States into Cuban territory and indicating that firm legal action would be taken against violators. The following day he ordered the U.S. Coast Guard to escort a flotilla of Cuban-Americans attempting to sail to the shootdown site for a memorial ceremony, as much to guarantee compliance with the new regulations as to protect them from the being attacked. However, seeking to minimize exile provocations that might create unwanted problems for the White House was not tantamount to any softening in the basic policy approach.

On the evening that the flotilla set sail, U.N. Ambassador Madeleine Albright arrived in Miami to represent the White House at a memorial service for the victims of the shootdown. She was accompanied not by Richard Nuccio, who was preoccupied, as he put it, with "things like deciding whether or not we were going to bomb Cuba,"[25] but by a former chief of staff in Senator Bob Graham's Florida office, Lula Rodríguez. Then a U.S. Information Agency (USIA) official, Rodríguez regularly attended White House meetings on Cuba because of her professed expertise in dealing with the Cuban-American community. Albright gave an impassioned speech before a crowd of 50,000 Cuban-Americans gathered at the Orange Bowl in which she called the dead pilots "the martyrs of February 24."[26] In the course of the trip, she also forged a close relationship with her Miami guide, who was subsequently appointed to a high-level State Department position after Albright became the secretary. According to a Washington-based Cuba specialist privy to the executive branch debate, Rodríguez wielded considerable influence with the new department head and was able "to convince her that that any step taken on Cuba has to be pushed through the sieve of the Cuban-American community, that any change must be OK'd by them."[27]

Ten days after the memorial service, Clinton visited Florida, where he signed Helms–Burton into law to coincide with the opening of the 1996 presidential primary contest in that state. The symbolism of the signing ceremony could hardly be mistaken: Clinton was flanked on one side by CANF Chief Jorge Mas Canosa and on the other by families of the BTTR shootdown victims. Soon after, Nuccio resigned his position as Special Adviser on Cuba, explaining to his superiors that having been given the job of opposing Helms–Burton before February 24, he could hardly be placed in the invidious position of now having to defend and implement the legislation: "Last week I said [Helms–Burton] is black. This week it's my job to say it's white. That presents a problem to me." According to the departing envoy, one White House political adviser replied:

"Ric, that's what we do here. We say it's white, then we say it's black. What's your problem?"[28]

In the weeks and months that followed the shootdown, the White House assiduously courted Florida's Cuban-Americans while ignoring the appeals from political dissidents and other nongovernment groups inside Cuba who opposed Helms–Burton and argued that a "climate of non-hostility between Cuba and the United States would benefit democratic forces in Cuba."[29] The Treasury Department set up a Miami office to encourage whistleblowers to report embargo violators while the federal budget approved by Congress included funds to relocate Radio and TV Martí to Florida. The latter promised to further entrench the influence of Mas Canosa, still chairman of the Presidential Advisory Board for Cuba Broadcasting, and other hardline Cuban-Americans in the policies and programming of the two stations. Meanwhile, a USIA Inspector General's report highly critical of Radio Martí and its senior management was withheld from public release and eventually shelved altogether.[30] During an April fundraising visit to Florida that raised $3 milllion for Clinton's election war chest, his schedule included another high-profile meeting with the families of the shootdown victims.[31] Weeks later the State Department sent the first advisory letters warning three foreign companies – the Canadian mining giant Sherritt International and two telecommunications companies, Mexico's Grupo Domos and Italy's STET – of the risks of trafficking in confiscated U.S. properties, and finalized guidelines to enforce the visa denial provision (Title IV) of Helms–Burton. The State Department's Michael Ranneberger bragged to the House Committee on International Relations that the embargo "is tougher and more comprehensive today than it has ever been," a statement backed up by Treasury's director of the Office of Foreign Assets Control, who singled out corporate America's "high level of compliance with its core prohibitions."[32]

The administration was determined to minimize any friction with Congress over its Cuba policy. Cuban overtures to discuss the issue of compensation for nationalized U.S. properties, for instance, were treated with a mixture of disdain and sarcasm. In June, State Department spokesman Nicholas Burns was questioned about Havana's stated willingness to negotiate a settlement: "Let's check my watch here. My watch says 1996. I believe the revolution took place in 1959. . . . You know, it's just a little late in the game. We're 36 years after the revolution."[33] This attitude of total noninterest could not be explained with reference to Helms–Burton satisfying property claimants now or in the future, given State Department calculations that this new law could generate another 75,000 to 200,000 claims by naturalized Cuban-Americans in addition to the original 5,911 registered claims against the Cuban government.[34] Indeed, U.S. officials had consistently argued during 1995 that settling claims on the basis of this legislation would be a nightmare, the number of lawsuits likely to create gridlock in the courts and drag on for years before actual settlements were reached.

For all its efforts, however, the White House seemed unable to accommodate the demands of the anti-Castro lawmakers. Dan Burton and Lincoln Díaz-Balart needled away at Clinton officials for not doing enough to stop alleged drug trafficking through Cuban territory, waters, or airspace into the United States. It made little difference that the Drug Enforcement Agency (DEA) could find no hard evidence of Cuban government complicity in the drug trade; these two legislators seized every opportunity to criticize Clinton for not moving to indict Fidel and Raúl Castro and other senior Cuban government figures on narco-trafficking charges. As the August 1 deadline approached for activating Title III of Helms–Burton, pressure on the White House not to use its waiver authority intensified. Díaz-Balart urged Clinton to show some "backbone" and not resort to this "blatant example of appeasement." Ileana Ros-Lehtinen (R–Florida), incensed over a meeting between senior U.S. military officials and a Cuban general at Guantánamo, reduced the administration's approach to two simple propositions: "Either Fidel Castro is our enemy or he is not. Either we are involved in a policy of isolating this dictator, or we are not."[35] Dan Burton questioned the State Department's effectiveness in getting the message across to other countries that they should be bringing pressure to bear on Havana to speed up the process of political change. Robert Menéndez (R–New Jersey) dismissed as fanciful the belief that delaying implementation of Title III would "expedite a transition to democracy" in Cuba.[36]

When Clinton decided to activate Title III in July but postpone (waiver) its implementation for six months "after a sharp and prolonged internal debate," pitting economic officials worried about the international reaction against re-election advisers with an eye on Florida and New Jersey,[37] the cacophony of outraged voices among the anti-Castro legislators was loud and vituperative. The president's explanation that the delay would provide an opportunity "to build support from the international community on a series of steps to promote democracy in Cuba" convinced none of them.[38] Burton "was more than disap-pointed . . . I am angry"; Díaz-Balart described Clinton as having the "backbone of Jell-O," while Helms interpreted Clinton's action as that of someone who was "all talk and no substance."[39] In Miami, however, the reaction was noticeably more restrained. CANF was "not completely satisfied" with Clinton's deci-sion, said President Francisco Hernández, but it was nonetheless a "positive" beginning.[40] This was the first sign of a crack in the until now rock-solid public position struck by the exile lobby and its most ardent fellow-travelers on Capitol Hill.

In other quarters there was a sigh of relief. The international outcry against Helms–Burton had been growing louder since March. At meetings throughout Canada in early June 1996, Prime Minister Jean Chretien repeatedly attacked the U.S. efforts to impose its Cuba policy on sovereign states. What Canada primarily objected to was "the notion of extraterritorial application of American law."[41] Having already passed legislation blocking local companies from complying with the reporting provisions of the American law and forbidding Canadian businesses from paying any fines that might be levied by an American court, Chretien indicated that even tougher retaliatory measures were under consideration, including direct penalties on U.S. corporations that sue Canadian companies. On the day the government's measures to counter Helms–Burton came into force (June 17), Foreign Minister Lloyd Axworthy termed Canada's response "the beginning of a chain reaction among other countries in developing a collective response."[42] Ottawa also foreshadowed new antidote legislation to allow domestic companies to countersue U.S. companies in Canadian courts and the filing of a complaint with the North American Free Trade Agreement (NAFTA) against this punitive legislation. International Trade Minister Art Eggleton put Canada's position bluntly: "[Helms–Burton] takes aim at [America's] foe, and then shoots its friends. It undermines the international investment climate and does nothing to encourage trade liberalization."[43] Although the Title III waiver represented "some movement," for Eggleton it did not go far enough: "It's unacceptable to have a sledgehammer over our heads."[44]

The hemispheric clamor against Helms–Burton was just as loud and hostile. State's Michael Ranneberger described the regional reaction as "horrible [and] vehement."[45] The fourteen member Rio Group, meeting soon after Clinton signed the bill into law, minced no words in denouncing the legislation, which, it said, "violates principles and norms established by international laws and the U.N. and the Organization of American States [OAS] charters [and] ignores the basic principle of respect for sovereignty of other states."[46] On June 6, the annual meeting of the OAS in Panama City delivered the U.S. what *The New York Times* called "a stunning defeat" when thirty-two members cosponsored a resolution condemning Helms–Burton.[47] A second resolution, introduced by Canada and Mexico and opposed only by the United States and Domínica, directed the Inter-American Juridical Committee to determine the legality of Helms–Burton under international law. Chile's foreign minister alluded to the contradiction inherent in Washington's vote against a resolution that was, first and foremost, "about freedom of trade, about economic freedom and about international law."[48] Nonetheless, a fuming U.S. Ambassador Harriet Babbitt denounced her colleague for engaging in an act of "diplomatic cowardice."[49]

Yet it was the European reaction to Helms–Burton that held the most potential to damage U.S. interests, particularly those of its overseas corporate sector. Initially, at least, the severity of individual countries' protests varied according to their economic exposure in Cuba (compounded in some cases by investments in countries such as Iran and Libya that were also subject to U.S. sanction laws) and the importance of the Washington relationship. On one point, however, there was a firm consensus: This latest effort by the Clinton White House to subordinate allies' interests to its foreign policy goals was unacceptable. "We heard from all of the EU [European Union] countries very loudly who were saying they didn't like this bill," said a high-ranking official in State's Office of Cuban Affairs. "Whenever senior level officials from the White House, State, or any other agency traveled overseas they were hit with this. And I'm sure a lot of them were surprised by the level of opposition."[50] Another department official said the barrage of criticism was presented in "the most undiplomatic language I've ever seen."[51]

On July 15, the foreign ministers meeting in Brussels indicated that retaliatory measures, ranging from blacklisting American companies and requiring U.S. business executives to obtain visas for travel to EU countries to taking the dispute to the World Trade Organization (WTO), would be activated if President Clinton failed to renew the waivers on key Helms–Burton provisions which were due to expire the following day. "The best way to get change in Cuba," said an exasperated Sir Leon Brittan, the EU's vice president and Trade Commissioner, "is not to clobber your allies."[52] At the same time, there was also a disposition in Brussels to prevent the conflict from escalating further, if at all possible. British Foreign Secretary Malcolm Rifkind sought to dampen down the rhetoric by suggesting that what was occurring was "a rift, not a crisis."[53]

Irrespective of Rifkind's choice of words, the U.S. business community knew enough to fear the worst. At a minimum, individual companies would be subject to European and Canadian laws designed to counter Helms–Burton; in the worst case scenario, they could be dragged into a major confrontation between America and its trade allies. "The business community cared about Helms–Burton because it complicated relations with other countries," an involved Department of Commerce official recalled. "We tended to make that point in the administration rather more actively than anybody else."[54] Clinton's decision in July to postpone the Title III trafficking provision for at least another six months averted any major escalation of the dispute. The EU "welcome[d] the decision as far as it goes" while continuing to remonstrate with Washington over the fact that the extraterritorial nature of the law had not been addressed and that it still hovered over European companies and individuals like a "sword of Damocles." EU Trade Commissioner Brittan was visibly underwhelmed by the White House action, terming it "a very limited response" to European concerns. Not only was Title IV, barring executives of targeted multinationals from entry into the United States, still in effect, but Clinton could reinstate Title III at any time if he so desired. Once more, Europe emphasized its support for the "American objective" of political democratization in Cuba while disassociating itself from the means the United States seemed bent on employing to reach the goal. It cannot be achieved, British Trade Secretary Ian Lange remarked, by "attack[ing] trading partners in other parts of the world who are carrying out legitimate business in Cuba."[55]

This half-hearted European support for Clinton's latest concession paralleled continuing moves to establish the machinery, including a list of specific measures, that would allow for a rapid counterresponse to Helms–Burton if the occasion should arise. Among some EU officials there was even sentiment for implementing reprisals without delay. Beyond that, French Trade Minister Yves Gallard declared that his government "would not leave the answer solely to the European Union. If French firms were hit," he warned, "there would also be a French response taking the form of legislative and legal sanctions."[56]

After testifying before a House subcommittee in mid-July, State's Cuba Office Coordinator Michael Ranneberger was questioned about what the administration was doing to convince the Europeans to "play ball" on Cuba. He responded with a sober, and somewhat pessimistic, appraisal of the "state of play" over Helms–Burton on the continent: "I will say that my view, and I would say the U.S. government's assessment, of the Europeans' reaction is that they are profoundly disturbed by the legislation, despite all the efforts we have made, and I think they are serious about retaliatory legislation." Of course, the U.S. government would continue to work with its allies to send a message to Havana about the need for economic reform and a democratic transition. And notwithstanding the current mood of the Europeans, Ranneberger emphasized that "we have given no ground on this and we have been very, very strong in defense of it."[57] This latter statement to some extent contradicted administration rhetoric about a cooperative effort between the United States and Europe to promote change in Cuba.

In late August, Clinton appointed Stuart Eizenstat as his Special Representative for the Promotion of Democracy in Cuba. On approaching the former Carter official about the job, Clinton is said to have remarked that he "felt bad giving a good guy like Eizenstat the worst possible assignment in the administration."[58] For his part, Eizenstat was astute enough to understand the politics involved: To explain Washington's approach, his first port of call en route to Mexico City, Ottawa, and a number of European capitals, was to Cuban-American leaders in Florida and New Jersey. "I was determined that I was not going to embark on this mission unless I touched base with the Cuban community and they had confidence that I was genuine in my efforts to do this," he recalled. "I knew at the end of the road if I was successful in getting the EU to elevate their human rights concerns that there would be a Title III waiver come along. And so, to have any credibility in recommending that to the president, I had to have credibility from the community."[59]

In his meetings with European officials, Eizenstat pursued a two-track approach: "The public diplomacy part was to defend Helms–Burton as a reasonable act because it didn't sanction mere investment in Cuba or trading with Cuba but only if there was investment in illegally confiscated property." Privately, he held out the carrot of a Title II waiver if governments became "more vocal in defending human rights and democracy in Cuba, and in adopting that as part of their policy." This was an implicit understanding in return for taking these kinds of concrete steps to intensify pressures on the Cuban government.[60] Other U.S. officials described the trip as having the less ambitious objective of "eliciting a sufficient response from other countries to, minimally at least, meet the terms of the [Helms–Burton] Act and avoid imposing sanctions if at all possible, which could have then resulted in countersanctions."[61] All the indications were it was going to be an uphill battle.

To Eizenstat's dismay, he met a veritable avalanche of criticism wherever he went during his fourteen-day trip to the continent. In Brussels, Sir Leon Brittan frankly told him that Helms–Burton was "not the right way to achieve [desired reforms in Cuba]," that it was a "repugnant" law that "offends and attacks America's trusted allies." German Economic Minister Guenther Rexrodt voiced his government's strong opposition and reiterated Brittan's comment that it was "the wrong way" to pursue political and economic changes on the Caribbean island.[62] Even the newly elected conservative government in Spain, despite its public calls for an opening up of the Cuban political system, provided an unsympathetic audience for Eizenstat's pleas. "We succeeded in doing what it is almost impossible to do," lamented an almost disbelieving State Department official working on Cuba. "Every single European Union member state, even the ones who completely agreed with us on human rights, rejected Helms–Burton."[63] Only Whitehall offered a modicum of support for the White House envoy's pitch: "Not one member state liked Helms–Burton, but in terms of getting the kind of trade-off that we were talking about, the British were the most useful, the most helpful."[64]

Eizenstat received similar rebuffs in Mexico City and Ottawa. The Zedillo government publicly and pointedly declared its satisfaction with the ruling of the Inter-American Juridical Committee that key provisions of Helms–Burton were contrary to international law. Both the executive and the legislature left the American envoy in no doubt that they wanted Helms–Burton repealed and the U.S. embargo of Cuba lifted. In Canada, he made no headway whatsoever in discussions with senior foreign policy and trade officials. "We reiterated our position of strong oppositon to Helms–Burton," said Foreign Minister Eggleton, "and we're not backing off that one iota." As far as Ottawa was concerned, engagement and not isolation remained the best approach for solving the Cuba problem.[65]

By now, with the presidential election in full swing and a democratic victory in Florida a realistic possibility for the first time since 1976, the challenge of securing the Cuban-American vote ranked high on the White House campaign agenda. In one sense, this demanded a more nuanced approach than in the past. Generational shifts and the emergence of a more complex exile community attitude about U.S. policy toward Cuba meant that it was no longer safe to assume a more or less perfect community fit with the views of CANF and/or congressional hardliners such as Jesse Helms, Dan Burton, or Benjamin Gilman. Helms–Burton, for instance, had not produced a rush of interest among the 200,000 Cuban-Americans whom the State department estimated might be eligible to take legal action over property claims in Cuba. A department office established in September to handle such claims was underwhelmed by the response. "The phones were not ringing," remarked one official.[66] Even the business community had begun to appreciate that the Cuban-Americans were no longer monolithic in determinedly favoring the toughest possible approach toward the Castro regime. Where previously many companies were reluctant to take a position against the embargo or critical of U.S. Cuba policy in general for fear of inviting retaliatory actions by members of the exile community, threats of boycotts and other actions had noticeably diminished.

Hurricane Lilli, which struck Cuba in mid-October, brought into sharper public focus the growing political and Cuba-specific divisions within the exile community. The hurricane's impact on the island was devastating: thousands of homes were destroyed or left in need of repair; 250,000 Cubans had to be evacuated; many hospitals and factories were severely damaged; and key economic sectors, especially the sugar, tobacco, and banana crops, suffered major losses. This natural disaster sparked an emotional debate within the Cuban-American community over the appropriate response. The State Department was swamped with calls urging a resumption of flights to the island to facilitate donations of food, clothing, blankets, medicine, and other urgently needed supplies. A National Security Council (NSC) official described the response as "a spontaneous happening in Florida."[67] Whether for electoral or humanitarian reasons, the administration waived the ban to allow one relief flight and granted a license to Catholic Relief Services to handle the thirty-two tons of supplies to be distributed inside Cuba by Caritas. However, the question of whether to provide assistance to Cuba, and if so to what extent, clearly divided the Florida exiles. Although many were eager to, and did, help, local participating Catholic charities and the relief flight itself were the targets of anonymous bomb threats.[68]

Clinton's limited response to Hurricane Lilli may well have strengthened his electoral support among ordinary Cuban-Americans. In November, with solid community support, Clinton won Florida by forty-eight percent to Republican Party presidential candidate Robert Dole's forty-two percent. Whatever role Cuba policy played in this result, the president's political advisers could claim vindication for their intervention to override foreign policy experts at critical junctures such as the February 1996 shootdown. Yet if his Florida victory and his reelection to a second term as president was perceived in some quarters as the prelude to a more rational Cuba policy, Clinton would again prove a disappointment. The Cold War approach that had permeated Cuba decision making was not jettisoned, and the second administration, like the first, squandered opportunities to alter the policy direction. Incoming Secretary of State Madeleine Albright set the tone in January 1997, describing the Castro government as "an unacceptable regime and . . . an embarrassment to the international community."[69] What was proving a more obvious embarrassment, however, was a proclivity in the White House to contort policy to conform with short-term domestic political imperatives. Nowhere was this conclusion held with more conviction than among leading members of the U.S. business commmunity.

DELAYED RESPONSE: THE CORPORATE BACKLASH

On January 3, 1997, Clinton again waivered implementation of Title III of Helms–Burton for a further six months. Still, the White House was committed to maintaining diplomatic pressure on America's allies trading with Cuba to increase their efforts to promote economic and political reform on the island, and there would be no compromise on enforcement of the Title IV visa denial provision. "No one is under an illusion that democracy is going to break out immediately under Fidel Castro," explained Stuart Eizenstat, "but what we do believe is the convergence of governments, of business and labor and of nongovernmental interests increasingly focused on the promotion of democracy and human rights will lead over time to more free space and more breathing space for the Cuban people."[70]

Senate Foreign Relations Committee chairman Jesse Helms did not concur with these sentiments or the waiver decision: "I can't understand why [the waiver was granted]. Just as we are beginning to make progress, the president has decided to give up the very leverage that brought such progress about."[71]

At her confirmation hearings, Madeleine Albright, pressed by Helms and other committee members about the waiver, offered a rather fawning response: "I believe the Libertad Act has had a very important effect [in bringing pressure to bear on Cuba]. The president has said that he wants to study how to use the waiver authority and I want to work with you on this subject."[72] United Nations Ambassador–designate Bill Richardson, who had opposed Helms–Burton before the shootdown, told the same committee that he now supported the legislation, not least because those prerogatives the president still retained would be used "to harangue" European and Latin American governments to press for human rights improvements in Cuba.[73] At this stage, only corporate America seemed willing to publicly challenge the hostile signals coming from Congress and the White House about the future direction of Cuba policy. U.S. Chamber of Commerce's Director of International Policy John Howard termed the waiver a prudent and intelligent decision that did not go far enough. "An even more useful step," he exhorted, "would be to seek repeal of the law that established this process in the first place."[74] Radisson Hotel's CEO Peter Blyth worried that Helms–Burton and its treatment of European companies in Cuba could lead to retaliatory measures being taken against U.S. subsidiaries based in Europe. Mariono Marchich of the National Association of Manufacturers contended that the Clinton administration's growing use of unilateral economic sanctions simply heightened global perceptions of U.S. multinationals as "political risks."[75]

The shift by the U.S. business community toward more open and assertive criticism of Washington's Cuba policy represented a significant new development. U.S. Chamber of Commerce Vice President Willard Workman summarized the emerging consensus: "By and large, most American companies look at the Cuba embargo and say basically it doesn't make sense, it hasn't worked, it is inconsistent with our approach to other communist countries and the stated foreign policy objective, which is to have a change in political regime – clearly, it's been a dismal failure." Active public lobbying against additions to the embargo such as the CDA was a low priority for most companies, not only because the measures were hard to combat politically, but also because there were no perceived benefits given that the embargo still remained in place. The passage of Helms–Burton changed all that. The message it sent to the business community was: "It's time for some adult supervision in Washington."[76]

Helms–Burton locked U.S. capital and commerce out of the Cuba market more firmly than ever, which was cause enough for some companies to oppose it. However, it raised far more serious potential problems for American corporations on a global scale. "It put American interests in the position of sanctioning their competitors [round the world]," said a senior Department

114

of Commerce official, "and extended this territoriality beyond what had ever been done before."[77] There were few more dramatic indicators of an executive and legislature perfectly willing to subordinate expanding profits for U.S. capital abroad to short-term domestic political gain and foreign policy exigencies. Moreover, it illustrated in a particularly dramatic way the phenomenon of sanctions creep that had become a defining characteristic of Clinton's international relations. Between 1993 and 1996, some thirty-five countries were targets of new U.S. laws and executive actions authorizing unilateral economic sanctions.[78]

This newfound business enthusiasm for more organized and active lobbying still confronted two formidable obstacles: a White House more attentive to the Cuban-American proponents of a hardline Cuba policy, and a predominantly like-minded Congress, without whose support no fundamental policy shift was possible.

In April, more than 400 American companies (including AT&T, Boeing, Citibank, Dow Chemical, Pepsico, Texaco, and Exxon) formed USA Engage to lobby for a rollback in the entire sanctions regime. Growing concern about the overall drift in U.S. trade policy was the general trigger; Cuba was seen as a test case. "The feeling was that we had gone from a period in the early '90s where most of the focus of the trade community was on getting other countries to lower or eliminate trade barriers – NAFTA, which may have been oversold, and GATT [General Agreement on Tariffs and Trade], that we grossly undersold – to a period where there was a marked increase in the use of unilateral sanctions," expained USA Engage Chairman William Lane. "The CDA and Helms–Burton were two prime examples of that."[79]

Anti-Castro legislators viewed the problem quite differently. They were becoming fed up with Clinton's failure to implement the Cuba laws as vigorously as they desired. By May 1997, "discussion drafts" of new bills to revoke or further restrict the president's ability to waive Title III of Helms–Burton were circulating among senators. So also was another draft of a bill that proposed allowing the Internal Revenue Service to recover tax revenue lost because of U.S. property nationalizations after 1959 by targeting foreign companies currently trafficking in those properties.[80] In the House, Foreign Affairs Committee members approved amendments to the Foreign Policy Reform Act reaffirming a direct link between levels of U.S. assistance to Russia and Moscow's aid to Cuba, the termination of U.S. aid to any country providing economic assistance to Castro's government, and the State Department's obligation to provide quarterly reports on how it was implementing Title IV of Helms–Burton.

However, Jesse Helms, Robert Torricelli (D–New Jersey), and Florida's Cuban-American legislators were not the only ones impatient over the failure of administration policy to produce the desired results. On July 12, bomb blasts rocked two landmark tourist hotels in Havana, the Capri and the Nacional, injuring several people. Cuban officials claimed that materials originating in the United States were used to make the incendiary devices and blamed the explosions on mainland exile groups. Three weeks later, an explosion went off in another downtown Havana hotel. While denying that the bombings were the work of American citizens, U.S. officials deplored these acts of terrorism, which was more than could be said for CANF, which "unconditionally" endorsed the bombings as legitimate tools in the struggle against the Castro dictatorship.[81] Statements by Cuban investigators that a Salvadoran arrested in connection with the bombings had implicated individuals associated with the Foundation were described as "ridiculous and absurd" by CANF officials.[82] The issue, nonetheless, refused to go away. It resurfaced during the latter half of 1998, when a *New York Times* investigation linked CANF to the anti-Castro terrorists responsible for the hotel bombings[83] and the Justice Department indicted seven Cuban-Americans, including CANF officials, over a plot to assassinate Fidel Castro in the Dominican Republic.

Clinton, meanwhile, was busy juggling the contradictions in his Cuba policy. The resumption of migration talks in December 1996 had been preceded by months of wrangling over the administration's reluctance to repatriate, as it was required to do under the terms of the agreement, several Cubans who had used force to enter the United States.[84] In February 1997, a number of U.S. media organizations received licenses to open news bureaus in Havana only to have the White House put their chances of being allowed to do so immediately in doubt when Mike McCurry told a press conference that the White House had "very much appreciated" Helms's advice in the process of its deliberations. The senator had written to the president that he supported issuing licenses to as many media organizations as possible: "If Castro wants to open Cuba to the roving eye of the American news media, we should by all means given him the rope with which to hang himself."[85] Even news organizations were viewed as part of the process of fomenting unrest in Cuba. As for the people-to-people strategy, the White House seemed to have adopted a concertina approach: opening up one area only to close or rigorously enforce another. In August, for instance, the State Department announced travel restrictions would be eased for Americans to go to Cuba for the pope's January 1998 visit. Existing laws relating to travel and certain kinds of humanitarian donations "permits some discretion," was how one official justified the decision.[86] At the same time, Treasury insisted on punishing five Florida port officials and a Jackson city councilman for going on a fact-finding mission to Havana without permission, and investigated a group of students who attended a two-week international conference there for the same reason. Policy was essentially on hold and going nowhere, as one of State's senior Cuba officials plainly admitted: "Helms–Burton and the shootdown, in the short term, snuffed out any possibility of doing anything. It was politically impossible."[87]

Elsewhere, Washington kept up its criticism of Cuba's human rights record but refused to acknowledge any possible connection between the level of political repression in Cuba and the tightening of the U.S. economic embargo. Hence, although the annual unflattering reports of the U.N. Special Rapporteur for Human Rights in Cuba were greeted approvingly by Clinton officials, when Carl Johan Groth told an October 1997 conference in Miami "that [U.S.] hostility directed towards the Cuban government entrenches the present unacceptable practices and also offers an easy excuse for totalitarian and repressive policies," the White House–State Department response was deafening in its silence.[88]

Throughout the latter months of 1997, Clinton showed no signs of grasping the intellectual muddle that lay at the center of his thinking on Cuba. During his first visit to Latin America in October, he told a town hall meeting in Buenos Aires he "still believe[d] that in the end the ball is in Cuba's court, and if there could be some signal that they want to open up and change direction, then I think the hardest-line people in Congress, even the hardest line people in Miami – who are basically responsible for [Cuba] policy – would be open to a different approach."[89] What he neglected to mention was that Helms–Burton had essentially severed the link between a policy shift in Havana and reciprocal concessions by Washington in the absence of a political transition on the island that excluded any role for Fidel or Raúl Castro. Furthermore, if indeed the Miami hardliners "were basically responsible for [Cuba] policy" and Clinton had been "hostage" to their demands over the previous five years – an embarrassing confession of the primacy of politics over policy – the time to reverse this state of affairs could not have been more politically opportune. Instead of attempting to exploit the hardliners' association with recent violent actions in Miami and Havana and the death of Jorge Mas Canosa in late November to justify a major policy review, Clinton stuck to his guns: "I still want [an improved] relationship with Cuba but we have to have some kind of indication that there will be an opening up, a movement toward democracy and openness and freedom if we're going to do that."[90] Just how eager he was for better ties with Havana remained a debatable issue when placed against his still public courting of CANF: only weeks after Mas Canosa's passing, Clinton traveled to Florida and met with the late CANF leader's son and political heir apparent, Jorge Mas Jr.

Meanwhile, pressure had started to build up in Congress for limited changes in Cuba policy and a reevaluation of the use of economic sanctions as an instrument of foreign policy, driven in large part by the concerns of the U.S. business community. In July, a bipartisan group of House members, led by California democrat Esteban Torres, and with the backing of various church groups and sectors of the Cuban-American community, sponsored a bill to remove restrictions on the sale of food and medicines (humanitarian aid) to the island. Lincoln Díaz-Balart and other stridently anti-Castro lawmakers predictably denounced the bill's sponsors for wanting "aid to reach the dictatorship and medicines to be used for torture."[91] In the Senate, a liberal democrat, Chris Dodd (Connecticut) joined with moderate and conservative republicans John Warner (Virginia), Robert Bennett (Utah), and James Jeffords (Vermont) in cosponsoring similar legislation to eliminate restrictions on humanitarian trade.

Paralleling these initiatives was an equally strong desire among some House and Senate members to address not just the specific corporate sector worries about the impact of Helms–Burton. What also disturbed them was a more general problem: the Clinton administration's propensity to employ global unilateral sanctions as a mainstay of its foreign policy. In late October, the ranking democrat on the House International Relations Committee, Lee Hamilton (D–Indiana), and Representative Phil Crane (R–Illinois) introduced legislation requiring the administration to explain the goal of any proposed new sanction, its likelihood of success against the target regime, and the probable costs to U.S. industry and agriculture. "Many [business] executives I have spoken with over the past couple of years have told me that foreign firms and governments are increasingly steering clear of U.S. companies when making procurement decisions," Hamilton told a House Ways and Means subcommittee hearing. "They are concerned that deals with U.S. firms could be jeopardized by subsequent sanctions."[92] Richard Lugar sponsored a matching bill in the Senate, contending that sanctions rarely alter the behavior of target countries and do not always serve broader U.S. interests. Echoing the statements of American CEOs critical of being shut out of the Cuban market, he observed that "sanctions often give a competitive edge to foreign companies by taking U.S. firms out of the game." Just as concerning were the potential longer-term consequences: the consolidation of expanded trade ties between non-American companies and the Cuban government "may be difficult to reverse in the future and may make it difficult for U.S. firms to re-enter that market."[93]

If this renewed congressional debate over the severity and impact of the embargo raised hopes of moving U.S.–Cuba policy off dead center, developments in the executive branch offered little encouragement. The 1998 U.S. AID budget allocation for "democracy-building projects" in Cuba doubled the figure for the previous two-year period, and the bulk of it was slated for groups headed by hardline anti-Castro exiles.[94] Meanwhile, with Defense Department support, plans were proceeding to switch TV Martí broadcasting from VHF to the higher UHF frequency. USIA Director of the Office of Cuba Broadcasting Herminio San Román believed this change would facilitate the expansion of the propaganda war against Cuba to the rest of the hemisphere: "We're letting our allies know what our policy is."[95] John Merrill, the Pentagon's Director for Central America and Caribbean Affairs, described the agency's part in the exercise: "We provide support for TV Martí. It's not a Defense Department mission. It's a mission of the U.S. Information Agency but we provide, on a reimbursal basis, the platform [off the Florida coast] from which TV Martí broadcasting is done."[96] This subtle difference between agency missions may have been lost on the Cuban authorities.

At the beginning of 1998, the policy status quo seemed as entrenched as ever. Yet proponents of a selective easing of the embargo were in the process of transforming themselves from a disparate collection of groups pursuing their own specific agendas into a more structured and organized coalition. A bipartisan mix of legislators, business officials, and religious and humanitarian groups formed Americans for Humanitarian Trade with Cuba (AHTC) and began a "grass-roots [lobbying] campaign" to gain passage of the Torres bill lifting restrictions on the sale of food and medicines to Cuba.[97] The AHTC membership incorporated a range of objectives and motivations. For some, the Torres bill was an end in itself, a means of helping to ameliorate the social and economic circumstances of the ordinary Cuban; others wanted part or all of Helms–Burton and the sanctions regime abandoned. To many of the nearly 100 legislative cosponsors of the Torres bill, the embargo had revealed itself an ineffective and counterproductive means of achieving goals they shared with the White House. Business opposition, however, was fueled by the accumulation of restrictions that had placed Cuba off limits to American capital and commerce. "It does little harm to Cuba because other countries take our place," lamented Archer Daniels Midland Chairman Dwayne Andreas. "They are on the inside. They have influence. We are on the outside looking in."[98] The head of the U.S. Chamber of Commerce's International Policy Committee, Dennis Sheehan, saw the Torres bill as an important step toward eliminating the Cuba embargo.[99]

Not to be bested or outflanked over its support for the suffering of the Cuban people, CANF responded with its own aid plan that would confine food and medicine exports to private donations and channel such aid to particular groups on the island, "especially political prisoners and their families."[100] Shipping costs would be paid for out of frozen Cuban assets in the United States. This represented a shift from the traditional CANF posture of opposing all humanitarian aid to Cuba on the grounds that it simply reinforced Castro's hold on political power. At the same time, its proposal did not constitute support for any genuine easing of the embargo; private medical and food donations to Cuba were already allowed under Treasury regulations. This probably explained Jesse Helms's enthusiasm for turning the CANF option into a legislative proposal. Although Deputy Assistant Secretary of State for Public Affairs Lula Rodríguez, a key administration liaison with the Cuban-American community, gave Helms's initiative a cautious endorsement, White House spokesman Mike McCurry appeared nonplussed by the whole debate on humanitarian assistance. All he could say was that current policy "is designed to bring about change in Cuba [that will] address the suffering that the people of Cuba have faced as a result [of Castro's rule]."[101] Yet the remedies on offer were in the nature of palliative care. Washington was trying to kill off the revolution, and its energies were directed to achieving that result no matter what the danger posed to broader U.S. interests.

COLLATERAL ENEMIES: HELMS–BURTON AND THE CHALLENGE TO FREE TRADE

In every global and regional forum, the Clinton White House made its support for free trade synonymous with its global leadership in the post–Cold War era. To this end, Clinton wheeled and dealed passage of NAFTA through an initially skeptical Congress and talked of extending it to the whole of Latin America within a decade. He also lent America's weight to the push to dismantle trade barriers in the Asia–Pacific region by supporting the fledging Asia Pacific Economic Cooperation (APEC) initiative. Yet overarching these regional free trade organizations was Washington's key role in successfully concluding the prolonged negotiations of the Uruguay Round of the GATT, out of which emerged an agreement to set up a WTO in January 1995. U.S. officials hailed the WTO as the cornerstone of the new global free trade regime. More than a year after it began functioning, with its procedures and practices clearly established, the White House remained as enthusiastic as ever. U.S. Trade Representative Mickey Kantor declared triumphantly that the "creation of the WTO and completion of the Uruguay Round Agreements ensured U.S. leadership in the global economy."[102]

These successes in multilateral diplomacy, however, could not long disguise a swelling restlessness among America's allies over the sincerity of Clinton's commitment to free trade in view of administration efforts to obstruct and limit world trade with Cuba and other Third World nations embroiled in conflicts with the dominant global power. This policy inconsistency encouraged a perception in London, Brussels, Ottawa, Mexico City, and elsewhere that

Washington's embrace of the free trade doctrine was essentially a self-serving policy, to be invoked only in the cause of promoting U.S. interests. At the time of the WTO's creation, the U.S. was already under heavy fire from allies around the globe over the Cuban Democracy Act, which was denounced as an affront to the sovereignty of independent states. Alliance relations came under further strain over Helms–Burton; to virtually every major ally, its extraterritorial provisions demonstrated that the United States was prepared to subordinate its international trade commitments and obligations to domestic politics and discrete foreign policy goals. Clinton's subsequent uncompromising defense of the new law seemed to confirm his preparedness to risk seeing the core free trade instrumentalities undermined, and American corporate interests damaged in the process, rather than his own increasingly eccentric approach on Cuba compromised.

When Clinton signed Helms–Burton into law, the EU trade spokesman angrily reminded the White House that one of the WTO's key principles "is that you don't export your laws and your principles to other countries."[103] In June 1996, when the EU asked the global body to institute consultations on Helms–Burton, the U.S. government began to qualify its enthusiasm for the WTO's procedures. "After hundreds if not thousands of discussions with the Latin countries, the European countries, Canada and Mexico, we understand their concerns," explained State Department spokesman Nicholas Burns in totally rejecting the EU course of action. "They ought to understand a few things. [Helms–Burton is] the law of the land. We implement U.S. law. We're going forward with it."[104] At the G-7 meeting in Lyon, France, later that same month, EU officials told Clinton that "go-it-alone" tactics such as the extraterritorial provisions of Helms–Burton were contrary to the spirit of inter-Alliance relations.

The Europeans were particularly upset by Washington's attempt to legitimate and impose "secondary boycotts" on nations trading with countries on the U.S. embargo list, and they threatened to retaliate. "There will be a price to be paid," vowed a senior official in Britain's Department of Trade and Industry.[105] Foreign Minister Malcolm Rifkind accused the Clinton administration of weakening Alliance unity and posing a threat to global free trade as a result of its "short-sighted, unilateral actions." Nor could he resist pointing out the fundamental contradiction in U.S. policy of opposing the Arab attempt to boycott companies dealing with Israel only to turn around and support equivalent measures to prevent countries from trading with Cuba, Iran, and Libya. "The cases are precisely comparable," he insisted.[106] According to a senior State Department Inter-American Affairs official, no Helms–Burton provision triggered more hostility than Title IV: "It was hugely controversial in our relations with the Europeans, who were saying, 'That sounds like extortion to us.'"[107] This was no empty rhetoric. To underscore just how objectionable it considered

Helms–Burton, the EU initiated procedures to bring the United States before the WTO disputes settlement panel.

Such allied anger was met with a combination of U.S. arrogance, dismissiveness, and threats. "Countries that are teeing off on us now," State's Nicholas Burns retorted, "ought to just sit back and cool it and understand that we're going to implement this law."[108] When Clinton announced in July that he would defer implementation of Title III for six months, Deputy National Security Adviser Sandy Berger indicated that "the meter will be ticking" on Cuba's trading partners nonetheless.[109] "This is bullying," commented Canada's Foreign Minister, Lloyd Axworthy. "But in America you call it global leadership."[110] To another senior White House official, it was the return to the world of a single superpower that best explained Clinton's decision to act unilaterally and ignore worldwide opposition to Washington's Cuba policy. In the post–Cold War era, he said, America is *the* dominant global hegemon, and those of its allies leading the charge against Helms–Burton would ultimately come to terms with that reality: "It breaks the rules, but it works, and the president says, 'We're doing it.' In the end, they'll get over it. We're America, and they'll get over it."[111]

Interestingly, senior State Department officials at the time were not united on the likely outcome of a WTO adjudication of Helms–Burton. According to one participant in the policy-level discussions, some "thought a dispute about Cuba policy was not what the WTO was there to handle, while the minority view in State was that we would win. The third option was to apply the 'national security exemption.' The issue was not purely trade and not purely Cuba policy."[112]

Given the complexity surrounding this issue, it was clearly going to be difficult to find a resolution satisfactory to all sides and consistent with the intentions of Helms–Burton. Advising the Europeans to simply accommodate themselves to a *fait accompli* was hardly likely to mollify those governments whose multinational corporations were under threat. The dilemma for the White House was of a different kind: If it allowed the EU to proceed with its challenge to Helms–Burton in the WTO, where only a minority of knowledgeable State Department officials were confident enough to predict a verdict in Washington's favor, it might have dealt the U.S. law a powerful setback, even restoring much of the president's prerogative to make Cuba policy, but such an outcome would inevitably produce a virulent congressional backlash over an issue that Clinton had little stomach to contest. "Politically, you couldn't let the EU proceed with the WTO challenge," said one State Department official. "The WTO was already under fire, the WTO was being questioned by members of Congress. And our attempt to get others to join the WTO, and our efforts to build the WTO up as a credible organization, would have been completely undermined."[113]

For these reasons, a compromise solution had to be found. "I don't think anyone wanted the Europeans to just sort of go ahead and try to carry through the process," recalled a senior official in State's Cuba Office.[114] Temporary waivers on the implementation of Titles III and IV might satisfy Congress because they left the legislation on the statute books and could be enforced retroactively. However, the Europeans were likely to balk for precisely those reasons. Still, the White House wanted to ensure that it remained "in a strong position to defend the waiver."[115] This suggested that any decision on waivers was always going to be based on pragmatic, rather than principled, considerations.

In mid-October 1996, responding to Washington's lack of substantive flexibility, the EU requested the WTO to organize a disputes panel to examine whether Helms–Burton contravened WTO rules. This was not the message the White House was waiting to hear from the EU; it immediately vetoed the request, contending that the issue in dispute was one of diplomacy, not trade. U.S. officials began applying intense pressure to permanently terminate this EU challenge. The effort was couched in terms of "further discussions," but the U.S. representative to the WTO, Ambassador Booth Gardner, left America's allies in no doubt what this meant: "What we hope happens between now and November 20 [when the EU would have a second opportunity to request a disputes panel which would then be automatically set up under WTO rules] is that we will work with the EU and that *they will reconsider* whether or not this is the appropriate forum of discussion."[116] In other words, the aim of "further discussions" was to convince the allies to give ground and accept the American position. One frustrated European official complained that the Americans "[are] trying to frighten us away from pressing a panel, and just letting sleeping dogs lie."[117]

The EU's refusal to capitulate to these demands induced Washington to adopt an even more ominous posture. Ambassador Gardner warned that "proceeding further with this matter would pose serious risks" to the WTO, which was still "a very fragile institution." Special Representative on Cuba Stuart Eizenstat cautioned the Europeans that if they insisted on dragging the United States before the WTO over Helms–Burton, it would likely "invite an incitement of [domestic] protectionist pressure."[118] The EU's trade commissioner, Sir Leon Brittan, dryly commented that "my American friends seem to have a hard time understanding that if they had not enacted this law, we wouldn't be discussing it."[119]

An exasperated U.S. government now shifted tack to its third option, arguing that Helms–Burton was permissable under the WTO agreement's national security exemption, which allows a member state to take "any action it considers necessary for the protection of its essential security interests" in circumstances involving fissionable materials or arms trafficking, or in respect to action "taken in time of war or other emergency in international relations."[120] Eizenstat, in full hyperbolic mode, told a Washington conference on Helms–Burton that Cuba still posed a national security threat to the United States as well as Latin America: "[The U.S.] has had a bipartisan policy since the early 1960s under President Kennedy based on the notion that we have a hostile and unfriendly regime 90 miles from our border, and that anything done to strengthen that regime will only encourage the regime to not only continue its hostility but, through much of its tenure, to try to destabilize large parts of Latin America."[121] In making such a claim, he seemed unaware of the contrary views of senior military officials as well as a 1995 Pentagon report entitled "U.S. Security Strategy for the Americas" that concluded that Cuba posed no military threat to the United States. Equally significant, he appeared willing to discount the island's reestablishment of political and/or economic ties with almost all countries in the region over the previous decade.[122]

Constructing a national security defense of Helms–Burton also sat oddly with a rationale constantly invoked by Washington to justify its tightening of the Cuba embargo: the absence of political democracy on the island. Explaining why he supported the Helms–Burton provisions against Cuba but opposed secondary boycotts of Israel, President Clinton argued that the latter targeted a country "simply because [it] exists" and were therefore unacceptable, whereas the former "is directed against the only country in our hemisphere which is not a democracy."[123] This skated over the fact that Helms–Burton also dictated the internal policies of a future democratic Cuba – in particular, its embrace of free-market economic reforms – and required the Europeans and other allies to drop their opposition to, and participate in, what White House spokesman Mike McCurry described as "the effort to confine Cuban communism to the trashbin of history."[124]

Not only was this the first time since the establishment of the global free-trade body that a government had invoked a national security argument to defend its position; this precedent-setting American stance also raised the possibility of other countries acting in a similar fashion to quarantine their restrictive trade practices from scrutiny by the WTO. One European trade diplomat observed that any such refusal to play by the WTO rules "would be like pressing a nuclear button" in terms of the multilateral trade system.[125]

As the crisis in trans-Atlantic relations deepened, and the November deadline produced no resolution of the problem, the WTO Disputes Settlement Body agreed to a second EU request for a panel to investigate whether Helms–Burton violated WTO rules. However, in their continual search for a compromise solution, the Europeans adopted the "Common Position on Cuba," which identified the promotion of democratic reform and respect for human rights in Cuba as core policy goals. It declared that henceforth, future economic aid would be tied to the nature and pace of political changes on the island. Although "the Europeans didn't particularly like being shoe-horned into this 'Common Position,'" observed a State Department official,[126] they were realistic about the price that had to be paid to secure another Title III presidential waiver. The pressure from Washington on its allies to take some action that would be "enough to keep the measure on ice"[127] had been relentless. Although Eizenstat called the EU document "a major advance,"[128] it paradoxically highlighted the different approaches favored by each side for dealing with Cuba. The Common Position encouraged a peaceful transition to democracy as a result of Cuban government initiatives, not external coercion. It also linked future aid and other support to evidence of visible progress toward democracy that would be the subject of periodic EC reports to the Council of Ministers of Economy and Finance. The reports would include assessments of the status of respect for human rights in general, the release of political prisoners, reform of the criminal code, and government policy toward dissidents. At the same time, the EU committed to maintaining a dialog with Havana, acknowledged the economic reforms that had been implemented, and pledged to continue humanitarian aid disbursements through appropriate nongovernmental organizations.[129] A Dutch Foreign Ministry official emphatically denied U.S. assertions of a direct relationship between the Common Position and Helms–Burton: "This is absolutely not the case."[130] Engagement, not coercion, he explained, was the driving force behind European actions.

The Common Position produced another six-month presidential waiver of Title III but failed to extract a more permanent American response. Thus, on February 12, 1997, in a last-ditch effort to avoid litigation, the EU requested a one week postponement to the formal start of the disputes panel hearing in the hope that this might elicit a reciprocal response from the White House. At the same time, the latter's national security defense continued to evoke scorn and ridicule from those governments it was intended to impress. EU Trade Commissioner Brittan termed the U.S. position "not credible" and a threat to the viability of the organization. "For the WTO to be effective," he said, "it must not be possible for one country to evade its operation simply by proclaiming that national security is involved, however far-fetched such a claim may be."[131] The State Department would not budge, insisting that Helms–Burton was "a foreign policy issue," and as such, the WTO could not adjudicate on it.[132]

The conciliatory EU stance produced no substantive concessions from Washington. On February 20, after further meetings failed to produce any proposals that would meet European concerns, the WTO named three international experts to judge the legality of Helms–Burton within global trade rules and set an April 14 deadline for the EU to present its brief. In Washington, enraged Clinton officials announced that the United States would boycott proceedings on the grounds that the WTO lacked the authority to pass judgment on an issue of American national security. "We will not show up [when the panel convenes]," a senior administration official declared. "We do not believe anything the WTO says or does can force the U.S. to change its laws." Eizenstat put it even more succinctly: the WTO has "no competence" to rule on matters of foreign policy.[133] State's Michael Ranneberger, who attended the high-level interagency meetings that framed this response, stressed that "we were deadly serious about that; we would have walked away from it."[134] A steadfast Sir Leon Brittan dismissed the U.S. argument as fanciful: "It is not credible to suggest that protection of U.S. national security requires interference in the legitimate trade of European companies with Cuba."[135] As far as the Europeans were concerned, the United States had placed itself above the very international trade law it had been the driving force in promoting.

Still, a U.S. boycott of WTO proceedings could well have proved fatal for the fledging global organization, and Washington's refusal to recognize the authority of any umpire in this dispute would have set trans-Atlantic relations on a runaway collision course. The stakes were high, and the pressure for some sort of circuit breaker enormous. "It was a real cliffhanger," said Michael Ranneberger. "In the end, the Europeans realized we were prepared to walk and risk the whole WTO in the process."[136] On April 11, three days before what U.S. officials described as a "drop-dead date" for ending the challenge, Eizenstat and Brittan announced they had successfully negotiated a deal.

Under the terms of the agreement, the EU offered to defer its challenge to Helms–Burton until October 15; in return, the White House agreed to continue waiving Title III and "open a dialog" with Congress to amend or eliminate other contentious aspects of the law.[137] In the meantime, both sides would collaborate on devising investment rules to govern property confiscated by the Cuban government after 1959. Yet for all practical purposes, the arrangement asked more of the Europeans than it did of the Americans. Eizenstat made it quite clear where the onus for a successful outcome lay: "As this process unfolds, the administration will open a dialogue with the Congress with a view toward obtaining an amendment providing the president with waiver authority for Title IV of the Libertad Act *once these bilateral consultations are completed and the EU has adhered to these agreed disciplines.*"[138] In effect, the EU was being saddled with the responsibility for making prior concessions to the White House on a promise, not a guarantee, that the legislature would respond by giving Clinton the waiver authority.

The April 11 agreement postponed the crisis but remained far from solving it. Indeed, the proposed understanding had triggered a vigorous debate among the EU countries themselves, during which Belgium, France, Italy, and Spain "expressed reservations, some of them quite vehemently."[139] Dutch European Affairs Minister Michiel Patijn described this U.S.–EU deal as a "precarious armistice."[140] German Foreign Minister Guenter Rexrodt called it "a step in the right direction," but declared that "it is still unacceptable, that a country aims to carry out its foreign policy goals by imposing sanctions against companies in third-party countries."[141] Washington remained on notice that the Helms–Burton extraterritorial provisions were unacceptable, and that any new American measures against European companies would trigger an immediate reopening of the WTO disputes panel. Canadian Trade Minister Art Eggleton put the allies' viewpoint bluntly and concisely: "I want to get rid of [Helms–Burton]. I want to either amend it or end it."[142]

Although the conflict had been temporarily defused, two potential obstacles seemed certain to complicate any successful longer-term resolution: the proposed new investment disciplines the Europeans were being asked to adopt were clearly intended to deter further EU (and other Western) investment in Cuba; and White House policy was now hostage to the demands of Congress. "There [was] no guarantee," Eizenstat acknowledged, that the legislators would give their seal of approval to any negotiated settlement.[143]

If U.S. negotiators imagined that the April 11 agreement would freeze European investment in Cuba, they were quickly disabused. On April 25, less than a week after the EU formally suspended its WTO challenge, France signed a major new trade deal with Cuba and warned the Clinton administration not to interfere with its companies doing business in the island nation. Washington's predictable criticism of the French initiative was dismissed by the other EU countries who insisted that it did not breach the April 11 agreement or complicate efforts to resolve the larger dispute between the United States and its allies over economic relations with Castro's Cuba. Nevertheless, the timing of the agreement between Havana and Paris was important. It very clearly signaled that the EU objection to the extraterritorial application of U.S. trade laws was as strong as ever, and that the temporary suspension of the WTO option did not mean that the Europeans had any intention of lamely falling into line behind Clinton's policy. When the State Department's Nicholas Burns told reporters, apropos of the French decision, that "we do not favor any other countries normalizing their economic relations with Cuba," France's Industry Minister Borotra riposted that his country was "an independent republic" and "master of its own decisions."[144]

Over the next six months, ongoing discussions between EU and U.S. officials remained inconclusive. Disagreements persisted over a number of key issues: whether disciplines on expropriated property to "inhibit and deter" such investment should apply only to new investments or imply a blanket prohibition on all investment in confiscated enterprises; whether European companies with investments in expropriated properties who decide to resell those properties should be subject to the disciplines; whether the disciplines should apply to improvements in existing investments; and whether to include guidelines relating to the extraterritorial application of national law or confine the disciplines to situations in which companies are receiving contradictory directives from two trading partners.

Any possibility that the EU's October 15 deadline for an accord would be reached seemed remote. For good measure, the White House was now fighting the war on two fronts. Not only had it failed to persuade Congress to reconsider the impact of Helms–Burton on America's trade allies; on the contrary, the mood among Capitol Hill lawmakers for even harsher action against Cuba seemed to intensify. In the House, Florida republican Bill McCollum introduced legislation to strip the president of his authority to keep postponing Title III, while Senator Helms wrote to Secretary of State Albright demanding that Clinton implement Title IV against senior executives of all foreign companies trafficking in confiscated Cuban properties.[145] The EU decision to suspend its WTO challenge was interpreted by anti-Castro legislators as proving that the hardline, uncompromising stance works, and that Clinton's attempt to avoid a nasty imbroglio with America's leading allies by diluting the more contentious parts of Helms–Burton was an unnecessary concession to blustering governments.

During a three-day visit to Washington in late September, EU Trade Commissioner Brittan was subdued about the possibility of "convert[ing] the armistice into a lasting peace." Following meetings with U.S. Trade Representative Charlene Barshefsky and members of Congress, he told a press conference that "we're working hard [but] it takes two to tango."[146] The core sticking point was reaching an accord on the confiscated property issue, whether it should be applied retroactively or only to future investments. As the October deadline fast approached, Washington also kept pressing the Europeans to support tough disciplines on investment in Cuba, including a ban on government commercial assistance to any business deal involving expropriated property formerly owned by American citizens.[147]

As Brussels and Washington dueled over property issues, a new potential obstacle to resolving the Helms–Burton conflict arose when the French oil multinational Total signed a $2 billion natural gas development contract with Iran in late 1997 in contravention of the Iran–Libya Sanctions Act (ILSA), another piece of extraterritorial legislation passed by Congress and signed into law by Clinton during 1996. Its key provision authorized the president to impose sanctions on any company investing more than $40 million in either country on the grounds that both were sponsors of international "terrorism." Secretary of State Albright denounced the contract as "beyond her understanding," and accused France of refusing to support American efforts to isolate Iran.[148] White House threats to impose sanctions under ILSA unless Total rescinded the agreement provoked widespread scorn in Europe. Newly elected French Prime Minister Lionel Jospin bluntly rejected this latest effort by Washington to "impose [its] laws onto the rest of the world," while EU officials warned that any U.S. retaliation against Total would be "illegal and unacceptable," and lead to automatic renewal of the WTO panel on Helms–Burton.[149] The British government offered a more subtle but equally pointed warning: The White House should "reflect long and hard about the wisdom of taking any action against Total."[150]

To defuse the possibility of a new transatlantic clash over unilateral U.S. trade sanctions and put an end to constant European reminders that failure to waive sanctions on Cuba and Iran by mid-October would lead straight back to the WTO, the State Department indicated it might be willing to exempt foreign firms, including Total, from compliance with the law if their governments worked to "ratchet up the pressure" on Tehran and Tripoli to end their sponsorship of global terrorism.[151] Sir Leon Brittan, however, still held out for a comprehensive diplomatic solution. Failure to waive the Act, he said, could trigger a much more profound rupture in inter-Alliance relations over this issue than had hitherto been the case: It "risks setting in motion a chain of events which could seriously damage the wider relationship."[152]

For all this displeasure, the EU member governments were clearly reluctant to get involved in a trade war with a superpower ally that had dug in its heels under intense congressional pressure. Although European officials continued to denounce Helms–Burton and ILSA as intolerable forms of "American imperialism,"[153] the EU decided to indefinitely extend its October 15 deadline and not resume its complaint to the WTO over Helms–Burton. Yet Washington's perceived lack of a sufficiently flexible bargaining posture continued to irritate European diplomats. "We're not closing the door," said one, "but in order to negotiate effectively, the other side has to show genuine commitment."[154]

In the House of Representatives, Lee Hamilton and Phil Crane prepared to introduce legislation limiting the use of trade sanctions. They were motivated partly by the concerns of American business sectors opposed to the Cuba embargo policy, but perhaps even more so by the threat Helms–Burton posed to the future of the WTO. "If ongoing U.S.–EU talks on an 'out of court settlement' failed," observed Hamilton, "just about every scenario points to a weakening of the rules-based international trade system."[155] However, they were in a clear minority. For the powerful anti-Castro lobby in the House and the Senate, any move to weaken or terminate key provisions of Helms–Burton was an unacceptable dilution of the administration's commitment to bring about the collapse of the Castro government. Although increasingly reluctant to go back to the WTO in the absence of a solution, the Europeans were still committed to expunging the bill's extraterritorial reach features. No amount of presidential waivers was likely to meet their in-principle objection to Helms–Burton. In both public and private, they had taken too strong a stance to back off without some major concession.

American and European diplomats persisted in efforts to resolve these now intertwined disputes, but a significant breakthrough remained elusive. Washington's continued insistence that the onus was on its allies to move the discussions forward virtually guaranteed that any final agreement would be a drawn-out affair. At the same time, Europe's clear signal that it was prepared to do all within its power to avoid a return to the WTO probably emboldened American officials in the belief that this hardline approach would eventually produce a result acceptable to the White House. "What we have been trying to achieve in the negotiations . . . is effective disciplines, one that would fully achieve the objective of inhibiting and deterring investments in illegally ex-propriated property," Assistant Secretary of State for Economic and Business Affairs Alan Larson told a congressional hearing on the WTO disputes panel in March 1998. "We have made clear that while we are talking about a global set of disciplines [they must] cover American property in Cuba that was expropriated illegally without consultation."[156]

Some weeks earlier, the White House extended its waiver on Title III of Helms–Burton and agreed to review its sanctions policy. EU officials cautiously welcomed the latter while reserving final judgment until "we . . . see what it means in reality."[157] The EU's ambassador to the United States, Hugo Paeman, warned that any punitive measure against Total, which remained a "live option," according to Eizenstat, would bring transatlantic negotiations to an abrupt halt with all the consequences that implied.[158] As for the Title III waiver, the European response was the same it had always been: positive but unenthusiastic in the absence of any U.S. decision to simply annul this and other extraterritorial laws.

In a decidedly provocative move that served to highlight the sharply differing approaches to Cuba adopted by European capitals and Washington, the EU published details in late January of a plan to further European investment in the island. It called for the establishment of a committee to put together a business opportunities guide and to organize seminars in Havana "to discuss ways of attracting investment in Cuba."[159] Ambassador Paeman termed this initiative "in line with" Europe's belief that engagement was "the most likely catalyst for bringing about economic change to the island."[160] Much to the chagrin of Clinton policymakers, this approach was about to receive an endorsement of a hugely significant kind.

130

4

Stirring the Waters:
Clinton's Missed Opportunities

We have a policy that is not predicated on Cuban actions now.
National Security Council Inter-American Affairs Official,
May 1999

ONE year into his second term, the gap between Clinton's stated objectives with respect to Cuba and his actual accomplishments seemed as wide as ever. Within the international community, the policy had isolated Washington far more than Havana. Domestically, it had not only failed to make much headway in satisfying the demands of the anti-Castro forces in Miami or on Capitol Hill, but had also generated new sources of opposition critical of the president's failure to show leadership on one of the few remaining unresolved problems from the Cold War era.

In all corners of the globe, America's punitive extraterritorial legislation targeting Cuba provoked dismay and hostility. In regional and global forums, America's allies maintained their anger over the CDA and Helms–Burton, and refused to be diverted from a belief that constructive engagement with the Castro regime was the best way to promote the changes Washington desired in Cuba. The Clinton administration and European governments remained locked in a simmering dispute over Helms–Burton, whose outcome could yet have serious implications for trans-Atlantic relations, the operation of the World Trade Organization (WTO), and the future of global free-trade agreements. In the United Nations, the United States was forced to suffer the annual humiliation of more and more countries voting in favor of a nonbinding resolution calling for a lifting of the Cuba embargo.

At home, corporate America emerged in the forefront of those attacking Clinton's sanctions-driven foreign policy, its failed Cold War approach to Cuba, and its continuing tendency to accommodate the demands of special interest groups at the expense of sensible overseas trade and investment policies. The agricultural sector, in particular, saw no valid reason why it should be locked out of a small but potentially lucrative market, especially when its European, Canadian, and Latin American competitors were under no such constraints. Entering 1998, the right kind of political opportunity might well provide Clinton the basis for taking advantage of this rising tide of internal and external sentiment to rethink his Cuba policy – if he was so inclined. Coincidentally, he was about to be handed the first of several such opportunities. On each occasion, his response indicated no desire to move in new directions or relocate policy along a different track. Refusing to contemplate serious negotiations in the absence of a regime change on the Caribbean island was a policy set in concrete.

COAXING THE POPE AND SIDELINING FIDEL

At first glance, Pope John Paul II's decision to visit Cuba in January 1998 was a major setback to Washington's attempts to isolate Cuba and a major challenge for U.S. policymakers. In public statements, administration officials appeared relaxed and even upbeat about the possibility that the pope might do for Cuba what his 1979 visit did in Poland: help trigger the eventual collapse of communism. President Clinton was "glad" the Pontiff was going to Cuba, and hoped that he might manage "some real progress towards freedom and opening there."[1] These comments masked the fact that there had been what Michael Ranneberger characterized as "a pretty good debate about how we should play the visit." According to State's Cuba Coordinator, "there was one school of thought that said this is going to legitimize and bolster Fidel tremendously. The lines weren't clearly drawn. A lot of it was one eye on the Cuban-American community and one on the Hill." The former were "tremendously against the visit," as were a number of conservative legislators. "So we were kind of scratching our heads. Ultimately, it was State who took the lead in arguing that this could only be a positive development, that it would be constructive and we ought to get behind it and be very proactive." Once a consensus was reached on the ability to limit any negative domestic political fallout resulting from the visit, "it didn't take a whole lot of convincing. Ultimately, you knew they [Cuban-Americans] couldn't be too hard because it's the pope and they're all Catholics."[2]

The White House was resigned to a condemnation of the embargo. "That was a given," recalled Special Representative Stuart Eizenstat. "We knew that would be part of the equation."[3] Although U.S. officials insisted that there had been no attempt to influence what the pope might do or say in Cuba, the private reality suggested otherwise. Eizenstat met with Vatican officials prior to the pope's departure to urge that he admonish Castro: "I said I simply hoped that if he felt the need to express any criticism about the U.S. embargo, that should be accompanied by an even more fervent statement on behalf of democratic principles." Uppermost in the minds of U.S. policymakers was a concern to get the pope to criticize human rights violations in Cuba "more publicly," not least to minimize the possibility of "a great public relations victory for Castro."[4]

Eizenstat had left Rome a matter days before another high-level department policymaker made the trek to the Vatican. "The upcoming pope's visit to Cuba," he recalled, "was the focus of our efforts to shape policy opportunities in what was otherwise a stagnant policy environment and a stagnant internal political situation in Cuba. I met with Vatican Foreign Minister Tauran for 45 minutes to an hour, and the subject was just Cuba." Reinforcing Eizenstat's plea for papal balance, this official said, "We wanted the Vatican to have a bit more nuanced understanding of everything that was going on in the relationship."[5] Nonetheless, the White House steeled itself for some kind of papal rebuke.

During a press conference at the U.S. Interest Section, Ranneberger gave short shrift to to any notion that the pope's presence would lead Castro to undertake any major domestic reforms: "We view the pope's visit as very positive [but] we do not have expectations that it would produce fundamental change."[6] Senior House Democrat Lee Hamilton (Indiana) put a very different interpretation on the significance of the pope's visit. For him, it represented a subtle but powerful critique of the broader Clinton policy approach: "This is a landmark event," he said. "It's got an awful lot of people thinking. The pope's approach is the exact opposite of the American government's. The pope is trying to engage the Cuban people. The U.S. policy is to isolate the Cuban people."[7]

Even before his plane touched down at Havana's Jose Martí airport, the pope directly criticized the U.S. embargo of Cuba and urged Washington to change its approach, a message repeated throughout his five-day visit. It was no surprise that he also used his mobile pulpit to criticize Castro's government for restricting basic liberties and imprisoning political opponents; less anticipated was the degree of support the pope lent to Cuba's campaign to be accepted as a full member of the international community on its own terms. Although subtlely admonishing Cuba to "open itself to the world" on his arrival in Havana, John Paul II simultaneously called on "the world to open itself up to Cuba."[8]

To what extent the mere fact of the pope's presence in Cuba – and his criticism of the U.S. embargo as "unjust and unethical" – may have convinced more Americans that it was time Washington changed tack on Cuba is difficult to gauge. The papal trip certainly provided the kind of circuit breaker that could have been used to justify a policy shift. Apart from all else, it drew world attention to Cuba and, by extension, to U.S. policy in a noncrisis context. However, the Monica Lewinsky scandal, which broke on the same day that the pope's plane landed in Havana – resulting in the U.S. television networks pulling their high-profile news anchors back from Cuba – significantly reduced the coverage given to the visit. That the historic encounter between John Paul II and Fidel Castro did not produce any major policy reassessment in Washington simply testified to the persistence of politics over policy whenever Cuba required Clinton's attention. The will to confront or pose even a modest challenge to the hardline anti-Castro interest groups and their legislative backers remained absent. The latter showed no such reluctance to use their muscle to at least maintain the policy status quo. In February, some forty groups, including those who had forced the Archbishop of Miami to cancel plans to charter a cruise ship to take pilgrims to the island for the pope's visit, signed a declaration opposing the relatively innocuous CANF humanitarian aid proposal. Predictably, the three Cuban-American House members aligned themselves with these most strident "no-change" voices in the exile community. In a joint statement, Lincoln Díaz-Balart (R–Florida), Ileana Ros-Lehtinen (R–Florida), and Robert Menéndez (D–New Jersey) claimed that any attempt to soften the embargo would only "legitimize erroneous arguments used by those members of Congress . . . who call for an end to the embargo based on the allegation that our current Cuba policy and law insufficiently address humanitarian concerns."[9]

One goal of administration pronouncements at the time of the pope's visit to Cuba was to downplay perceptions that engagement was more likely to wrest changes from the Castro government than Washington's isolation policy seemed capable of producing. Responding to a papal plea, Cuban authorities released 299 prisoners, including more than seventy political detainees. Although the European Union (EU) judged the release a "positive step" and the Vatican "welcomed the decision,"[10] Clinton officials, true to form, offered not so much as a grudging commendation. "Until we have all the information we need," the State Department's James Rubin commented, "it's hard to make a characterization of what the significance of this step is."[11] Testifying before the House International Relations Committee on the impact of the papal trip, the policy adviser to the U.S. Catholic Conference on Latin America and the Caribbean, Thomas Quigley, rebuked the White House over its reluctance to appreciate the significance of recent regime initiatives, including prisoner releases and new religious freedoms. The U.S. Catholic church, he said, viewed them as "more than cosmetic and a good beginning which need to be built upon rather than treated cynically."[12]

The real significance of the pope's visit for U.S. policy, however, as one senior administration official observed, lay elsewhere: it created a "different dynamic" that could be exploited to "sideline Castro as much as possible"[13] by drawing attention to Cubans themselves and encouraging nonstate organizations to take a more active role in their affairs. In early March, Secretary of State

Albright had met with John Paul II in the Vatican, where Cuba, the "Poland analogy," and bolstering the church as a counterweight to the Castro regime were major topics of discussion. Summarizing her discussion for the president, she wrote that the pope's visit could indeed be a "point of departure" for unleashing regime-challenging forces as had occurred after his 1979 Poland trip.[14] Before visiting Rome, Albright had touched base with exile leaders in Miami, and returned to Washington satisfied that there would be no substantial community opposition to the kind of initiatives the White House had in mind to begin the process of sidelining Castro.

From the beginning, this was a dubious tactical calculation. First, in contrast to its Polish counterpart, the Catholic church was a weak and marginal institution in prerevolutionary Cuba, had no historic identification with the forces of Cuban nationalism, and had lost its core constituency in the early 1960s when the white upper and middle classes fled the island for the United States. Second, the local Catholic hierarchy had its own agenda – regaining access to the media and schools, the provision of welfare services, and visas for priests and nuns to work in Cuba – and there was no necessary convergence between its priorities and the broader anti-Castro agenda being pursued by the White House. Indeed, indications of divergent aims and priorities had surfaced back in November 1996, when Eizenstat held talks with the Vatican's Deputy Foreign Minister in Rome prior to an official visit by Fidel Castro. During the meeting, Eizenstat lauded the work of the Cuban church's Caritas relief agency, describing it as "the most effective independent organization in Cuba," and expressed the hope that the Vatican would convey a "balanced message" in its dealings with the Castro regime.[15] The reference to Caritas immediately jeopardized an understanding the Cuban church thought it had with the administration. Fearful that the pope's visit would become too closely associated with the U.S. government, church officials had asked the State Department "not to single them out as a mode of change in Cuba."[16] Praising Caritas had precisely the opposite effect.

Nevertheless, on March 20, two weeks after Albright left Rome, Clinton announced a set of measures "to build further on the impact of the pope's visit to Cuba, [to] support the role of the church and other elements of civil society in Cuba, [and to] help prepare the Cuban people for a democratic transition."[17] First, direct humanitarian charter flights to Cuba were resumed, but other passengers on these aircraft were still restricted to journalists, government officials, educators, church people, and representatives of human rights organizations. Second, the president announced that the 1994 ban on cash remittances to family members in Cuba was being lifted, but limited to a maximum of $300 every three months. Third, licensing procedures for medical exports were simplified and industry executives permitted to visit Cuba to negotiate sales, but all sales and donations were subject to on-site verification and monitoring, and could only be channeled through third country diplomats or nongovernmental organizations. Fourth, the White House would work closely with Congress to determine the levels and timing of food donations to the island population.

The changes amounted to a tampering at the margins of the embargo, and one of them – cash remittances that were already being regularly channeled through third countries in violation of the existing ban – represented no concession at all. Yet, once again, Clinton's objective here was to stretch the net as wide as possible to accommodate those groups impressed by the pope's initiative, those keen to see an increase in humanitarian assistance to ordinary Cubans, those still hopeful that small modifications might soon lead to bigger ones, and those determined to subvert the revolutionary regime. The State Department went to considerable lengths to make clear that these measures and implementing procedures were "fully consistent" with the CDA and Helms–Burton, both of which encouraged people-to-people programs.[18] Secretary Albright stressed that these steps were not a response to "anything the Castro regime has done" or part of a scheme to improve bilateral relations. "On the contrary, we are acting because of the new possibilities that exist outside the government."[19] Her top Cuba official, Michael Ranneberger, sought to assuage any congressional concerns that the measures signaled a weakened resolve to prosecute the economic war. These steps, he told legislators, "[did] not represent a change in U.S. policy."[20] Nor were the measures inconsistent with CANF's recently proposed humanitarian assistance plan for Cuba.

Alfredo Durán, vice president of the Cuban Committee for Democracy, welcomed the March 20 measures as "a positive sign," and Florida's Cuban-American community as a whole seemed reasonably pleased.[21] Not so their lawmakers on Capitol Hill, for whom even the slightest changes conjured images of an embargo in the process of unraveling. "All this does is send a political victory to Castro," said an angry Lincoln Díaz-Balart. "It makes you wonder about President Clinton's insatiable urge to do favors for Castro."[22] On this occasion, such railings failed to produce anything resembling a backlash among their constituents. The U.S. business community's favorable response came as no surprise. The more than 600 members of USA Engage had only recently run a full-page advertisement in *The Wall Street Journal* attacking U.S. policy as "outdated" and serving only to "isolate the Cuban people from American influence."[23] What particularly buoyed Caterpillar director and USA Engage chairman William Lane was the lack of negative reaction to this lobbying initiative: "We received a couple of nasty letters, and that's about it."[24] To the extent that there was any criticism from mainstream America about Clinton's measures it was the U.S. Chamber of Commerce's restatement of its position

136

that measures such as these did not go far enough and that the entire embargo should be lifted.

With the debate continuing over whether the March 20 measures went far enough or too far, the administration was soon grappling with another Cuba problem that had the potential for creating a far more divisive conflict with Congress. The Department of Defense was required by legislation authorizing its 1998 budget to issue a report on what, if any, military threat Cuba posed to the United States. Clinton was in office only a matter of months when senior Pentagon officials had reached a firm answer to this question: "The Cubans were no longer involved in foreign campaigns, so we didn't view them as a threat in the sense of destabilizing the region or anywhere else. They just didn't have the resources to do that any more; they were broke. They probably would be able to put on a very strong defense of their island, but beyond that, the feeling was that this country was no longer a threat."[25]

Since mid-1994, what had emerged as the key Pentagon concern was the threat of unrestricted emigration, not imagined Cuban military forays against its neighbors. As to Fidel Castro, U.S. military planners increasingly perceived him as "a rational player who does not want to provoke the United States."[26] Returning from a visit to Cuba in late March 1998, Major General John Sheehan again voiced the longstanding sentiments of a number of his colleagues in urging the White House to "regularize contacts" between Cuban and American military leaders as one way to defuse tensions between the two countries.[27] Prior to the Defense Intelligence Agency's (DIA) release of its report on Cuba's military threat in early May 1998, the Head of U.S. Southern Command, Marine General Charles Wilhelm, stated that Cuba's armed forces had approximately halved in size since 1991, and "has no capability whatsoever to project itself beyond the borders of Cuba, so it's no threat to anyone around it."[28] News leaks revealed that the DIA report concurred with Wilhelm's assessment.

The three Cuban-American lawmakers and a small group of House colleagues, however, reacted as if the Defense Department had adopted a radically new posture that placed U.S. security interests in the region at risk. In a letter to Secretary of State Albright, they wrote how "appalled" they were by this "current attempt to downplay the Cuban threat."[29] The administration felt sufficiently intimidated to challenge the report's basic conclusion that Cuba "does not pose a significant military threat to the U.S. or to other countries in the region."[30] Secretary of Defense William Cohen returned the report to the DIA with a request that it reassess the basis of its conclusions. In a letter to Senate Armed Forces Committee Chairman Strom Thurmond (R–South Carolina), Cohen wrote that he "remain[ed] concerned about the use of Cuba as a base for intelligence activities directed against the United States, the potential threat that Cuba may pose to neighboring islands."[31] The DIA dutifully reviewed its original findings, saw no reason to fundamentally change any of them but, presumably to satisfy the Secretary's implied demand for some change, inserted a few minor qualifying words: Cuba now posed a "negligible" conventional threat to the United States, and it retained a "limited capability to engage in some military and intelligence activities which would be detrimental to U.S. interests."[32] If this did not pacify the angry legislators, the last and perhaps more calming words came from the State Department's Ranneberger: "Whether or not Cuba is a security threat to the United States, the issue remains that Cuba is not a democratic country, and that we simply are not prepared to have normal relations with a nondemocratic Cuba. And this report will have no bearing on that."[33]

Amid the debates over the March 20 measures and Cuba's military threat, the United Nations Human Rights Commission (UNHRC) voted for the first time since 1991 to discontinue the special rapporteur's monitoring of human rights abuses on the island, largely as a result of a number of Latin American governments abstaining instead of registering their traditional "yes" vote. A high-ranking State Department regional specialist attributed what he called this "surprising" setback to an insufficiently aggressive U.S. lobbying effort: "We had got a little complacent about beefing up cosponsoring and didn't pay enough attention to the vote camp."[34] This explanation did not impress the anti-Castro lobby on Capitol Hill. The UNHRC vote produced a terse exchange between Cuban-American legislator Robert Menéndez and State's Principal Deputy Assistant for Secretary for Inter-American Affairs Peter Romero during a House subcommittee hearing in May. "You're telling me," an angry Menéndez finally said, "that eight out of ten countries in Latin America, that you all met with, that you all signed declarations with, that you all had very close opportunities from the president to the secretary of state, and all of the other personnel, that . . . none of those countries could be convinced, and they were actually changing their votes?"[35]

The UNHRC vote served only to further irritate the most vociferous anti-Castro members of the Congress who looked for new ways of renewing pressure on the White House to attack the Castro regime at its source. One possible lever was Title II of Helms–Burton, under which AID disbursed funds to non-governmental bodies (dissident and human rights groups, families of political prisoners, etc.) for democracy building projects in Cuba that would eventually led to a peaceful political transition on the island. The AID administrator for Latin America and the Caribbean, Mark Schneider, interpreted the law's guidelines as confining assistance to noncash items such as food, medicines, and reading materials. The "Three [House] Tenors," with the strong support of Jesse Helms, baulked at this narrow interpretation of the law and began drafting legislation to force the White House to fund Title II recipients by all available means, overt or covert if necessary, including support to third parties inside and outside of Cuba to undermine the Castro government. Their proposal wanted the president "to send everything from printing presses and fax machines to pens and paper to the 'most extreme victims of political repression in Cuba.' "[36]

Not that the administration was resting on its laurels. Exploring with the Vatican ways of bolstering the position of the Catholic church in Cuba remained high on its agenda. During a second visit to Rome in late March, Madeleine Albright told the pontiff that the United States would channel humanitarian aid to Cuba via the Catholic relief organization Caritas. But this was simply giving Washington's imprimatur to arrangements the church had already put in train. In January, the Manhattan-based Catholic Medical Missions Board had collected more than $6 million worth of pharmaceutical and medical supplies from U.S. companies for shipment to Cuba. The supplies were sent within days of Clinton's decision to reinstate direct flights to the island. Following Albright's visit, the Vatican's Secretary of State, Cardinal Angelo Sodano, also met with Cuban Foreign Minister Roberto Robaina, after which the former confirmed that the Church would act as a conduit for private U.S. food and medical donations to Cuba. What Albright seemed to want was to hitch precisely this church initiative to administration policy.[37]

Unhappy with the pace and uncertainty of such efforts, and determined to head off those newly mobilized domestic forces promoting a major revision of Cuba policy, Helms drafted legislation in May to give effect to CANF's proposal to disburse up to $100 million worth of food and medicines directly to the "victims of political repression in Cuba" over a four-year period.[38] This Cuban Assistance and Solidarity Bill would restrict direct flights to the island to humanitarian relief shipments, force the administration to seek to indict Fidel and Raúl Castro before the International Court of Justice over the February 1996 shootdown, and relocate Radio and TV Martí to the Guantánamo Naval Base. Marc Thiessen, a Helms aide on the Senate Foreign Relations Committee, was perfectly candid about the purpose of the bill, which was to refocus the debate on "ways to subvert the Castro regime."[39]

The executive branch response to Helms's bill was complicated by its May 18 accord with the EU on investment guidelines in Cuba signed on the eve of Clinton's meeting with EU leaders in London and WTO members in Geneva. The terms of this "Understanding on Disciplines" committed the White House to waive sanctions against the French oil multinational Total under the Iran–Libya Sanctions Act (ILSA), to continue indefinitely a waiver of Title III of

Helms–Burton (trafficking provision), and immediately seek congressional approval for a Title IV waiver (visa restrictions). In return, the Europeans agreed to deny government loans, subsidies, or political risk insurance to companies that invest in nations with an "established record" of illegal expropriations, and to participate in establishing a global registry of confiscated properties that would be subject to these binding principles, enabling the former owners to pursue redress in Europe and possibly around the world. In his new position as Under Secretary of State, Stuart Eizenstat termed the agreement "the biggest blow ever struck for the protection of property rights of U.S. citizens and against the efforts of Castro to expropriate property." In subsequent congressional testimony, he optimistically declared that as a result of this "historic breakthrough . . . we have chilled investment [in Cuba] in ways that have not happened in 37 years."[40] The EU, however, made it clear that it would not move to fulfill its side of the bargain in the absence of a permanent Title IV waiver.

In sum, the "Understanding on Disciplines" was a highly conditional arrangement with plenty of tripwires that could reignite the dispute. The U.S. concessions had a "Trust Us" aura about them. Although the administration insisted it had the legal authority to waiver ILSA provisions, it could not make the same claim about Helms–Burton. There was no guarantee that Clinton's successor would stand by the Title III commitment or that Congress would give its assent to the Title IV waiver. In contrast to Eizenstat's attempt to put the best possible spin on the agreement, EU Chairman and British Prime Minister Tony Blair spoke in more measured tones about the breakthrough having "avoided a showdown over sanctions."[41] Notwithstanding Brussel's quid pro quo for the "Disciplines" to become operative, senior Clinton officials were still unable to conceal their delight over what they interpreted as a commitment by EU member states "not to upgrade their political or economic relations with Cuba until or unless Cuba improved their human rights and democratic record."[42] From State's Cuba office came a more candid appraisal of the May 18 deal: "We were trying to come up with a political arrangement. We were not trying to change the law – we've moved beyond that."[43]

On Capitol Hill, meanwhile, the signals were not promising that Clinton would be able to deliver on his end of the bargain even if he was genuinely committed to doing so. "Congress certainly didn't buy off on the May 18 agreement," is how one source succinctly put it.[44] "I don't think there were many people, if anybody, up here who thought that there was any chance whatever for fundamental legislative redrafting of Helms–Burton," explained Andrew Semmel, who was monitoring the debate out of Republican Senator Richard Lugar's office. "But everybody thought the jawboning with the Europeans was worthwhile. Everybody wanted the Europeans to be more compliant with whatever the intentions of Helms–Burton were."[45] However, if the congressional debate revealed a widespread skepticism about Clinton's agreement with the EU, some legislators were more dismissive than others as they pursued their own anti-Castro agendas. A senior aide to Senator Helms, for instance, described the EU concessions as "way too small a loaf. What the EU has basically offered us is a dilution of Helms–Burton in exchange for hot air." Helms's comment on the "Disciplines" was even more scathing: "It will be a cold day in you-know-where before the EU convinces me to trade the binding restrictions in the Helms–Burton law for an agreement that legitimizes their theft of American property in Cuba."[46]

To Stuart Eizenstat, who argued the administration case on Capitol Hill, this was Congress once again "bending to the will of the Cuban-American members for whom any change to Helms–Burton, or any waiver, even with something that is arguably better, is seen as threatening." Yet although Lincoln Díaz-Balart and Robert Menéndez "didn't want to do anything" to implement the May 1998 accord, the pivotal vote was that of Helms: "It was clear that everybody was going to defer to Helms on this issue and he didn't want to do anything either." Eizenstat recalled a number of frustrating meetings with Helms and his senior staff aide, Admiral James Nance, "who was passionately anti-European and didn't trust the Europeans. He said even if this [accord] was good on its face, how do we now they're going to fulfill their part. I said, 'Well, look we will agree in the legislation to a "snap back"; that is, that after X number of months if the president makes a certification that the Europeans are not living up to this, then the waiver is ended. We couldn't penetrate with that." Helms and Nance also took issue over the failure to apply the accord retroactively to investments in confiscated properties. Eizenstat was no more successful in attempting to counter this complaint: "I said, 'Look, first, the Europeans admitted for the first time in an agreement that this property is illegally confiscated. That's a huge step forward. And, second, you can't do anything about that. Those investments are there. What you want to stop is future investments.' But they kept coming back to the fact that we weren't forcing current occupants of illegally confiscated properties to leave."[47]

On June 18, Helms and House International Relations Committee Chairman Benjamin Gilman (R–New York) wrote an angry letter to Secretary of State Albright demanding a number of changes to tighten up the agreement before they would consent to any waiver of Helms–Burton provisions. They attacked the agreed-upon disciplines as "weak sanctions" that would be "almost impossible" to enforce. "We are far from convinced," the letter concluded, "that [the Disciplines] will inhibit or deter the unscrupulous companies that are willing to do business with the likes of Fidel Castro."[48] To assuage their concerns, Albright started to backtrack, giving an ironclad "commitment" that it would reinvoke Title IV if the Europeans failed to comply with the understanding. On the other side of the Atlantic, the EU message was just as firm: There would be no further unilateral compromises over Helms–Burton.[49]

Still deeply suspicious of how committed both signatories to the May 18 agreement were about squeezing Cuba, Helms introduced legislation to expand the Helms–Burton funding allocation to nonprofit groups in Cuba to promote a democratic transition. The 'Cuba coalition' was also busy preparing to scuttle democratic Senator Chris Dodd's amendment to the 1999 Agriculture Appropriations Bill that would have genuinely lifted restrictions on the sale of food-stuffs, agricultural products, and medicines and medical equipment to Cuba. An amendment tacked onto Dodd's by Robert Torricelli prohibited food and medicine sales to countries on the State Department's list of terrorist states as well as those who "systematically deny access to food, medicine and medical care to persons on a basis of political beliefs or punishment." After a failed tabling effort, the Torricelli amendment was overwhelmingly approved by a voice vote of the Senate. At least one U.S. official was moved to observe that Torricelli's language had "vastly improved" Dodd's amendment.[50] Ironically, both amendments were later deleted from the bill after a failure to conciliate differences in the House and Senate versions – ensuring there would be no change to the sanctions status quo. The 1997 Torres bill, meanwhile, was destined to suffer a similar fate. After being referred to several different committees, none of which took any action on it, the bill died when Congress adjourned for the 1998 mid-term elections.

If the U.S. business community was disappointed by the fate of the Dodd amendment in particular, it showed no signs of tempering its efforts to challenge Clinton's seemingly indiscriminate use of economic sanctions to gain foreign policy goals. "Today there are many more companies that are publicly participating in this debate," the president of Alamar Associates, Kirby Jones, told a Havana news conference as he awaited a Treasury Office of Foreign Assets Control (OFAC) decision on plans to take a group of U.S. corporate executives to Cuba in September for a one-day business seminar. "None of them is sufficiently powerful to change an entire policy, but collectively their weight is on the rise."[51] The broader focus of the business community, or what USA Engage Chairman William Lane called "the Fortune 500–type companies," was not the reform of "one specific sanctions regime," but getting the administration to concede that "since unilateral sanctions have had such a dismal track record," it should exhibit "greater due diligence" before imposing any new sanctions. Although "mildly supportive" of Cuba-specific initiatives that targeted unilateral sanctions "that didn't work and therefore gave great clarity to the entire sanctions reform effort," it was peripheral to their larger aim. However, loosening Cuba-specific sanctions was the primary objective of those midwestern agricultural producers and pharmaceutical industry companies for whom White House policy denied access to a potentially lucrative island market.[52] Senior executives of the Washington-based Medical Device Manufacturers Association, which represented 120 companies, bemoaned the fact that this market "is now going to Europeans and Canadians" or, as one put it more colorfully, "foreign boys have eaten our lunch."[53] Rice and other agricultural exporters were perhaps even more frustrated over being prevented from competing in a market they dominated before the revolution. The president of the U.S. Grains Council, Kenneth Hobbie, was convinced that U.S. farmers could displace Asian and European companies currently providing Cuba's needs because "our prices and transport costs are lower."[54]

The administration remained impervious to talk of lost profits; foreign policy goals took precedence. On August 12, OFAC Director Richard Newcomb wrote to Kirby Jones denying permission for the proposed September business seminar in Havana on the grounds that U.S. executives meeting with Cuban government officials were "providing a service" to the regime, and therefore contravening Treasury regulations. One State Department official described the ruling as "fully consistent with U.S. policy regarding Cuba." Another exclaimed: "We have an embargo. You simply can't have business deals with Cuba until Cuba changes."[55] However, a follow-up conversation with OFAC officials gave Jones hope that the conference might still go ahead after he agreed to include meetings with nongovernmental organizations on his agenda, specifically the Catholic church, students, and workers groups. Days later, Michael Ranneberger informed Jones "that these groups did not satisfy his definition of the Cuban people" but "guarantee[d]" a license if meetings were organized with "political dissidents."[56] Then, according to a now exasperated Alamar president, Ranneberger raised the bar again: "He said, 'I will give you permission to go if you hold a press conference when you come back and criticize the Cuban government.' He said it in front of [Richard] Newcomb and was rebuked by Newcomb, who said, 'We regulate laws, not speech.' "[57]

Over the next few days, any likelihood of a reversal of the decision ended when Undersecretary Eizenstat personally told Jones that he supported the Cuban coordinator's position. On September 3, Newcomb fell into line, advising Jones that "it would be contrary to current U.S. foreign policy to authorize" the business summit.[58] State officials maintained that "we didn't pressure [Jones] one way or another," but did not fundamentally dispute his account of the negotiations. They conceded that broader policy issues had shaped the ultimate decision and that it might have been otherwise if Alamar's president had offered a summit program "more palatable to our policy."[59]

This apparent new and tougher administration stance extended to its relations with CANF. During an August 20 meeting with Eizenstat, ostensibly requested as a courtesy call to discuss the trade embargo, pending legislation, and other CANF interests, Jorge Mas Canosa Jr. and Foundation President Francisco Hernández attempted to bring up the forthcoming federal indictment of seven Cuban-Americans, including senior Foundation officials, on charges of conspiring to assassinate Fidel Castro. Mas Jr. warned of the "significant political implications," only to be abruptly halted by Eizenstat and told in no uncertain terms that the subject was a judicial matter, and had he known it was going to be raised the meeting would not have been scheduled. "He put down a very firm marker," said Ranneberger, who was also in attendance.[60] In the circumstances, of course, he had little option but to respond in such a brusque fashion. Eizenstat's response may also have been occasioned by the extreme lengths CANF was going to in order to recapture the momentum it had lost with the death of its founder, Mas Canosa Sr. "It was taking CANF a while to get themselves back together again and to identify a leader," recalled another department official with Cuba responsibilities. "At that particular point, they were almost reacting instead of being proactive."[61]

Even so, under pressure from the anti-Castro lawmakers, the administration hesitated over a United Nations food aid appeal in early September for victims of a severe drought in eastern Cuba. In separate letters to the secretary of state, Ros-Lehtinen and Díaz-Balart reaffirmed their categorical opposition to any form of assistance, while Helms, Torricelli, Mack, Graham, and Menéndez demanded that conditions be attached to any aid package: It should be confined to foodstuffs (no monies), distributed through "international private voluntary organizations," and monitored by U.S. officials to ensure it was not used for other purposes.[62] Not surprisingly, the Cubans rejected those conditions. No such reluctance or hostility surrounded Clinton's decision on November 7 to sign into law a congressional initiative that exempted food and agricultural aid from the sanctions imposed on India and Pakistan in response to nuclear tests carried out by both countries in May 1998.[63]

If the hardliners in Congress still exerted a powerful influence over executive branch Cuba policy, they were less successful in controling the wider public debate. At the urging of a group of prominent former government officials and congressional leaders (including Henry Kissinger, William Rogers, Frank Carlucci, and Howard Baker) Senator John Warner (R–Virginia) wrote to the president on October 13, 1998, recommending the establishment of a bipartisan commission "to review our current U.S.–Cuba policy."[64] The letter was cosigned by fourteen other Senators. Outraged by what they called an "attempt to subvert the will of the American people and the intent of Congress," the three Cuban-American lawmakers implored Clinton to reject the proposal.[65] In a meeting with Albright, they launched a vitriolic attack against corporate America, accusing it of instigating the commission idea for pecuniary benefit. "The people pushing this," said Ros-Lehtinen, "have big dollar signs on their foreheads."[66] In a timely reminder of their political clout and singlemindedness when it came to Cuba policy, Ros-Lehtinen played a key role in adding several new provisions to the 1999 Federal Omnibus Spending Bill designed to crack a whip under the administration over its implementation of Helms–Burton. The State Department, for instance, was now obliged to provide the relevant congressional committees with new reports on its pursuit of Title IV violators. Ignoring the fact that Castro had already announced an indefinite suspension of the work at the Juraguá nuclear power plant, two other provisions denied foreign aid to countries providing nuclear fuel to Cuba and "related assistance and credits," and placed new bans on U.S. contributions to the Atomic Energy Agency earmarked for projects in Cuba.

On December 11, still waiting a response to his original request, Senator Warner dispatched a follow-up letter to the White House. Seeking to downplay concerns that the lack of quick response was a negative sign, a National Security Council (NSC) official commented that the council looked favorably on any proposed panel to review Cuba policy that was "inclusive, representative and composed of distinguished members. If we thought it was a bad idea, you would be getting those vibes." His boss, Sandy Berger, praised Warner for the "constructive spirit" that motivated the idea, implying that it may well have achieved the right mix of domestic political backing to gain Clinton's support.[67] Yet even those administration officials sympathetic to the commission were circumspect in pushing it because, as one high-level Cuba policymaker observed: "The politics are just not there."[68]

Nonetheless, in December, Havana gave an indirect boost to the proponents of the commission plan, permitting forty Catholic priests and religious workers to travel to the island. This was a small concession to the Vatican, but one nevertheless that featured on its list of priorities in Cuba. Furthermore, the church had won additional ground in the previous twelve months, including permission for more open-air masses and processions, some access to state-run media, and a further degree of latitude for Caritas's activities. So long as the Castro regime remained in power, of course, these gains were reversable. In the meantime, they constituted advances on which other successes could be built. Above all, it was evident that the policy of engagement that the church had adopted in the early 1990s and consolidated with the pope's visit had produced far more fruitful results than Washington could claim for its policy based on confrontation and hostility.

THE ILLUSION OF POLICY CHANGE: BACK TO THE FUTURE

Clinton's response to the accumulating pressures for a comprehensive review of Cuba policy and a loosening of the embargo restrictions was tentative and underwhelming, reflecting a continuing reluctance to unnecessarily provoke the Cuba coalition in Congress and their Miami supporters. On January 5, 1999, the administration announced it would not establish a bipartisan commission on the dubious grounds that "there is a broad bipartisan consensus already in support of the objectives of our policy."[69] Acknowledging the lack of a consensus over how best to pursue these objectives, in particular over the wisdom of maintaining the embargo, senior officials were unconvinced that the Warner proposal offered the best solution. For starters, said one, alluding to the codification of Cuba policy built into Helms–Burton, "only Congress can change the law."[70] Although the signatories to the commission proposal crossed the political spectrum, said another, "the community that really matters was strongly opposed."[71]

Privately, the anticlimactic nature of the White House effort to defuse the growing domestic clamor for a policy rethink, particularly its rejection of the bipartisan commission proposal, came as a disappointment to some in the foreign policy bureaucracy. One State Department Cuba official viewed it as a missed opportunity: "It was a win–win situation for the administration. The decision to oppose it was made at higher levels, with the State Department and probably other agencies. It was a very divisive issue and there was too much opposition to it."[72] This "opposition" extended to both ends of Pennsylvania Avenue. On Capitol Hill, Bob Graham and Robert Menéndez restated their "thin end of the wedge" argument: A bipartisan commission would lead only to an unraveling of the embargo. In the White House and on State's Seventh Floor, the litmus test for any decision of this magnitude was how would it play domestically: "In Washington, you never know what straw really broke the camel's back," observed a lobbyist who participated in discussions on the commission proposal. "But Graham played a strong role, Albright had her concerns, and [Al] Gore wasn't going to [anger] Cuban-American voters in key states like Florida and New Jersey."[73] Both Graham and Menéndez warned the vice president of a backlash among Cuban-American voters if the commission went ahead, and of the serious blow this would deliver to his 2000 presidential ambitions. "I made it clear to him," said Menéndez, "that he could kiss away Florida and New Jersey in terms of electoral counts."[74] Conservative Republicans and hardline exile groups reinforced the message by indicating the spin they would place on a bipartisan commission, which they christened "The Gore Commission." Once again, political calculations trumped policy evaluations in the Clinton White

House, and yet another opportunity to turn the clock forward on Cuba policy went begging.

The same day the commission proposal failed to pass White House muster, the president hoped to mute criticism of this decision by announcing a package of measures that reinstituted direct mail services to Cuba, expanded the number of charter flights between the two countries, increased the dollar amounts that could be sent as family remittances, and gave permission for the sale of food and medicines to Cuba to private sector organizations such as religious groups, privately owned restaurants, and farmers who were self-employed or worked in cooperatives selling directly to the private market. Whether the targets of this latter measure would benefit, however, was problematic, given that they required Cuban government authorization to buy imported goods directly from the United States. The president emphasized that "these steps" were "consistent" with the CDA and Helms–Burton, and represented no departure from the antiregime strategy.[75]

The January 5 package was small compensation for a substantive policy review. Even State Department officials admitted quietly that the new measures were "pretty noncontroversial."[76] Leading U.S. business community figures damned the measures with faint praise. U.S. Grains Council Executive Director Richard Tolman termed the food and medicine sales decision "a nice gesture but it doesn't satisfy us."[77] U.S. Chamber of Commerce Vice President Willard Workman dismissed the entire package as little more than "tinkering at the margins."[78] Peak agricultural bodies were equally critical, viewing the measures as unlikely to threaten the EU's role as the dominant supplier of Cuba's wheat and wheat flour imports. The American Farm Bureau Federation (AFBF) described the package as merely a good first step.[79] At the same time, several farm groups had reached the conclusion that their lobbying efforts to win access to the Cuba market would be better served by concentrating on the legislature, where Richard Lugar, with strong broad-based business support, had sponsored a general bill to lift restrictions on food sales to countries subject to unilateral sanctions.

The White House announcement produced a mixed response from prominent anti-Castro legislators. Lincoln Díaz-Balart and Ileana Ros-Lehtinen adopted the toughest posture, still wedded to the belief that even tinkering with the embargo undermined it and prolonged Castro's rule. Benjamin Gilman weighed into the debate, charging that Clinton's new measures "breach" the intent of Congress when it codified the embargo regulations under the Helms–Burton legislation.[80]

Their Senate counterparts were relatively more sympathic precisely because the changes were marginal and, just as importantly, lessened the possibility of a more comprehensive policy review. An aide to Helms explained that the senator supported the measures insofar as they amounted to "a strong reaffirmation of current U.S. law and a rejection of those who want to lift the embargo."[81] Torricelli interpreted the measures as positive contributions to the "war" against Castro. "Nothing here morally offends me."[82] That Bob Graham applauded Clinton's minor steps was no surprise, given that they were based on a study that had originated in his office.[83] Especially since the immigration crises of 1994–5, the White House viewed Graham as a kind of lightning rod on what the domestic political sentiment could accept when it came to changes in Cuba policy. However, even minor adjustments had to be sold to congressional diehards and sceptics in the exile community. Secretary of State Albright was at pains to reassure anti-Castroists that "these steps are neither designed, nor expected, to alter our relations with the Cuban government," and that "we're going to keep our pressure up against Castro."[84] Assistant Secretary of Commerce for Export Administration Roger Majak recalled that within days of the announcement that food and medicines could now be sold to private groups in Cuba, Alamar Associate's Kirby Jones was forced to cancel a conference involving pharmaceutical companies because the necessary licenses for travel to Cuba were withheld.[85]

The broader significance of the January 5 package was less the measures themselves than what it indicated about how Clinton was going to pursue his Cuba policy within the straitjacket of Helms–Burton. At a State Department briefing, Special Assistant to the President and Senior Director for Inter-American Affairs at the NSC James Dobbins asserted that Helms–Burton did not just codify the embargo; "At the same time it codified the president's licensing power," thus allowing him to grant exceptions to the embargo "in cases in which it was deemed consistent with U.S. policy." Hundreds, if not thousands, of licenses had been issued since March 1996 without any complaints that they were inconsistent with Helms–Burton. "The concept that the president would be able to license travel, remittances, other things," concluded Dobbins, "is well accepted [and] well within [the Helms–Burton] framework."[86]

If he was prevented by law from lifting the embargo, Clinton, in effect, could circumvent much of it by choosing to license those activities he desired to permit, irrespective of any concessions the Castro regime might or might not make. "The president has said several times he's ready to improve relations with Cuba when Castro is prepared to make significant steps toward democracy and respect for human rights," Dobbins explained. "But we're not waiting for that to occur to take steps that we can to support a democratic transition in ways that don't strengthen the Cuban regime."[87] In the absence of major policy changes, administration rhetoric sought to convey the perception of a more proactive approach based on initiatives that did not bolster the Castro regime. "We don't do calibrated responses now," an NSC Inter-American Affairs official insisted. "We are no longer in a duet with Cuba. Our policy doesn't depend on Havana. We don't do it expecting them to reciprocate. We have a policy that is not predicated on Cuban actions now."[88]

On January 7, the Council on Foreign Relations (CFR) released a Task Force Report on U.S.–Cuban relations. Chaired by two former Assistant Secretaries of State for Inter-American Affairs, Bernard Aronson and William Rogers, the report argued for a more flexible U.S. policy toward Cuba that would enable Washington to play a key role in shaping and influencing the inevitable post-Castro political transition.[89] The proposals, cautious and modest as they were, seemed almost radical when set next to the Clinton package, and the White House response provided added evidence of the latter's unwavering refusal to tamper with the basic hardline thrust of its Cuba policy. Administration observers participated in each of the Task Force meetings and the NSC even helped shape its recommendations, including a lifting of the ban on food and medicine sales to Cuba without preconditions. An earlier draft included an appendage to this recommendation, signed on to by all the Task Force members, stating that the executive branch had the regulatory authority to lift the ban despite Helms–Burton and without congressional approval. It was deleted, according to an involved CFR official, when individuals "with Congress ties" were alerted to the wording and "the shit hit the fan." References to cooperation agreements in the fight against drug traffickers were also toned down.[90] Such recommendations were too difficult to handle politically. Instead, the White House embraced only the "least controversial" proposals in the report.[91]

The "growing perception" that a political transition in Cuba was on the horizon assumed more importance in U.S. thinking at the beginning of 1999. "As that transition approaches," said Dobbins, "people are more eager to find ways to assist it and to assure that it is peaceful and that it is democratic."[92] High on the Clinton agenda of preferred ways turned out to be a refurbished and updated CDA Track II notion – expanding people-to-people contacts. Baseball diplomacy fell into this category.

When Baltimore Orioles owner Peter Angelos first sought permission to play the Cuban national team in Havana in 1995, the State Department refused to license a "high profile" contact of this kind. Over three years passed before Angelos was finally poised to achieve his long-held desire. Clinton's January 5 measures included permission for the Orioles to play one game in Havana and a return matchup at Baltimore's Camden Park. The background to the decision, however, was not smooth sailing. The most influential bureaucratic supporter of the initiative, NSC Adviser Sandy Berger, had to deal with senior State

Department officials, notably Assistant Secretary John Hamilton and Cuba Office Coordinator Michael Ranneberger, who were still, at best, lukewarm about authorizing the games. Interagency discussions produced a department insistence on a set of petty conditions being met before the games could go ahead. In keeping with the hard-currency denial policy, the primary concern was to ensure that the Cuban government did not benefit financially. The NSC eventually prevailed, but was upstaged by Secretary of State Albright's provocative comment that the games were intended to "provide the people of Cuba with hope in their struggle." If Albright was willing to risk the unraveling of what was still a delicate and fragile baseball arrangement, she seemed equally unconcerned about jeopardizing the post–January 1998 gains made by the Catholic church in Cuba. Taking it upon herself, "without consulting the Cubans or the Orioles negotiators," she nominated Caritas as the administration's choice to receive all game funds due the Cubans.[93]

The Latin American adviser to the U.S. Bishops' Conference, Thomas Quigley, termed Albright's linkage "unfortunate." The Cuban church and Caritas, he explained, were apprehensive about administration plans, "inadvertent perhaps at times, to cover them with the mantle of Track II."[94] Like Eizenstat's public praise for Caritas in November 1996, such cavalier statements by U.S. officials about the role of the church agency served only to subject it to new government strictures and constraints. "When the United States says it will only provide assistance through Caritas," the University of Havana's Professor of Religious History, Enrique López Oliva, remarked, "it makes the hardliners say, 'Look, Caritas isn't anything but a Trojan horse for the United States.'"[95]

For a White House desperate to validate the people-to-people approach, concerns about the church's own interests were shunted aside. The church, after all, was the only powerful independent organization in Cuba, and thus a logical if unwitting (and unwilling) accomplice in the designs and actions of Washington policymakers. Nonetheless, Albright's "Caritas option" proved a nonstarter, stalling the baseball negotiations for another six weeks, during which time senior State officials reiterated their "no monies to the Castro regime" position and even continued to argue against going ahead with the project itself, eventually forcing Sandy Berger to read them the riot act in an early morning telephone conversation.[96]

Suspicions about the underlying motives driving the people-to-people approach were again fueled when Secretary Albright told a *Miami Herald* luncheon in early February that the administration was attempting to strengthen what pockets of civil society existed in Cuba. At a ribbon-cutting ceremony for the new Miami headquarters of the Office of Cuban Broadcasting, again under fire from the State's Office of the Inspector General over its "lax internal practices and procedures," she blithely dismissed as "balderdash" the notion that TV Martí was of little practical use to the Cuban people.[97] Later that month, the department approved new grants to bolster and encourage opposition groups in Cuba. Freedom House received $275,000 to "promote the formation of civil and political leadership in Cuba"; Florida University's Media Center benefited to the tune of $292,000 to help improve stories filed by dissidents to Radio Martí and internet sites; and the Cuban Dissidents Task Force was allocated $250,000 to disseminate analyses of the island's political situation by local opponents of the Castro regime and assist their families.[98]

Havana reciprocated in kind, implementing new measures to limit the ability of dissidents to forge links with American public and private organizations. The National Assembly passed a "Law for the Protection of the National Independence and Economy of Cuba," providing twenty-year jail terms for anyone convicted of collaborating with the U.S. government, its agencies, or its representatives; targeting the possession and distribution of "subversive" literature produced by the U.S. government; meetings and demonstrations facilitating U.S. attempts to undermine the political or economic system; and antiregime journalists sending critical reports abroad. The subsequent crackdown on dissidents included the March conviction and jailing of four human rights activists for "inciting sedition" by calling for peaceful democratic change.

Washington's people-to-people strategy was under pressure on other fronts as well. In February, five U.S. telephone companies became embroiled in a legal wrangle that threatened the suspension of their Cuba links. The source of the problem was a decision by the companies to withhold up to $19 million in revenue payments owed to Cuba's ECECSA phone company while the Florida relatives of four Cuban-Americans killed in the 1996 shootdown sought a court order requiring these funds be set aside for compensation payments to the aggrieved plaintiffs. State and Treasury officials expressed concern and irritation at the possibility of bilateral phone links being canceled over an issue of relatively limited importance when viewed next to the risk it posed to the two-track policy. The garnishing of phone payments, they contended, "could have serious implications for U.S. foreign policy and for humanitarian interests with respect to the Cuban people and the Cuban-American community."[99] With no resolution in sight, Cuba canceled most telephone links on its February 25 cutoff date. Five months later, a U.S. Circuit Court of Appeals in Atlanta provided the Justice Department with a victory of sorts when it ruled that the millions of dollars owed to Cuba could not be awarded to the Florida shootdown plaintiffs.

On Capitol Hill, it was the crackdown on dissident activity in Cuba, not the failure by U.S. companies to honor their international agreements, that concentrated most attention. In early March, Senate efforts to condemn Cuba over its human rights abuses gathered momentum. In opening remarks before a Senate Foreign Relations Committee hearing on the subject, Jesse Helms remarked that those advocates of "unilateral concessions from the United States in order to nudge Castro toward change surely must now acknowledge that appeasement has failed, as it always does. We should make no secret of our goal [which is] Fidel must go."[100]

It was not the most propitious moment to announce that a deal had finally been struck that would allow the Baltimore Orioles–Cuban baseball games to proceed – with all profits funding baseball and other sports-related activities in each country. Cuban-American opinion was divided on hearing the news. Raúl de Velasco, president of the moderate Cuban Committee for Democracy, welcomed the decision, in contrast to Lincoln Díaz-Balart, who said the games would amount to little more than a "public relations coup for Fidel Castro."[101] The administration countered that in no sense could any decision to play one game in Havana be construed as a "rewarding" the Castro government because, as one State Department official cuttingly observed, "there is no behavior to reward"; nor was it the precursor to a normalization of relations along the lines of Richard Nixon's "ping pong diplomacy" that preceded the diplomatic opening to China.[102] Lawmakers opposed to the baseball diplomacy were unconvinced and unmoved. Denouncing a process that had occurred "behind closed doors," Florida's Ileana Ros-Lehtinen told House Western Hemisphere subcommittee colleagues that the "only home run will be for the Castro regime, as it alone reaps the immediate public relations benefits and eventual commercial and political benefits from this game." CANF's Jorge Mas Canosa Jr. regaled the subcommittee with similar predictions: The decision constituted "a disastrous step in [U.S.] foreign policy." State's Michael Ranneberger attempted to parry these and other criticisms, insisting that the administration's resolve to keep the pressure on the Castro regime was as strong as ever, and pleading with the legislators that these games would facilitate the "larger process of people-to-people engagement," which had as its ultimate goal the promotion of political democracy in Cuba.[103]

Ranneberger's argument might have been more convincing if Secretary Albright, a few weeks earlier, had not exposed a contradiction by justifying the U.S. decision to engage China in these terms: "We determined some time ago that it was not a good idea to link human rights and trade, and that we actually make better progress in both when they are not linked."[104] The department's just-released annual human rights report for 1998 had noted a sharp deterioration in China's performance as well as a continuing harsh response to political dissent in Cuba,[105] but whereas the former still warranted high-level diplomatic missions and ongoing efforts to improve relations, the latter served to rationalize and justify a hostile, arm's length approach. At a mid-March conference of U.S. business leaders on the potential for trade and investment relations with Cuba, Ranneberger again defended the embargo with reference to the "deplorable human rights situation" in Cuba. When pressed on why there was one rule for China and another for Cuba, he lamely responded that China was further along the economic reform road and, in any event, the administration was constrained in what it could do by the "simple reality" of Congress's resolute opposition to lifting the trade sanctions.[106] Madeleine Albright had a blunter and more dismissive explanation: "We do not have a cookie-cutter approach to policy."[107]

Although Clinton policymakers took refuge in congressional obstructionism to partly explain the refusal to engage Cuba, moves were already under way on Capitol Hill to make it more difficult to pass restrictive trade or foreign aid laws similar to Helms–Burton. On March 26, a bipartisan coalition in the House and Senate introduced bills to make special provisions for American farmers who sold their products in the world market. This group had been particularly hard hit by the antinuclear testing sanctions imposed on India and Pakistan, which included a halt to agricultural export credits. The bills also gave the White House permanent authority to exempt agricultural and humanitarian exports from sanctions required under the Arms Export Control Act. The legislation's sponsors, such as Republican Senator Chuck Hagel, were, however, quite realistic about the prospects of overcoming formidable obstacles that stood in the way of passage on the floors of both Chambers, among them Jesse Helms and Dan Burton. "We have a few mountains to climb," Hagel conceded, "and the two chairmen are mountains."[108]

Liberal Democrat Senator Chris Dodd returned from an early April visit to the island looking to start a "new conversation" about U.S.–Cuba policy based on "reason" rather than emotion. The time had come, Dodd added, to end trade sanctions, which even the antiregime dissident groups found "largely ineffective and unhelpful."[109] To start the ball rolling, he proposed to submit new bills to lift all restrictions of food and medicine sales and end the prohibition on American citizens traveling to the island. The dilemma facing Dodd, however, was that although such initiatives received the wholehearted support of powerful sectors of the U.S. business community, inside the Congress he was still part of a relatively small, shifting constituency whose capacity to challenge the anti-Cuba coalition was limited.

Dodd's policy critique acquired a harsher edge when the administration decided in late April to ease sanctions on food and medicine sales to Iran, Libya, Sudan, and other countries on the list of U.S. terrorist states – with Cuba the sole exception. Stuart Eizenstat justified the shift to a case-by-case determination in language that once again writ large the inherent contradictions in Clinton's Cuba policy: Sales of food and medicine do not "encourage a nation's military capability or its ability to support terrorism," and to withhold such commodities could increase popular hostility toward American foreign policy in the target countries by shutting U.S. exporters out of the market and worsening the living standards of innocent civilians.[110]

On May 13, the White House added to frustrations of American farmers seeking new export markets when it unveiled the regulations for implementing the January 5 decision allowing limited sales of food and agricultural goods to Cuba. An official involved in drafting the regulations compared them with a thermostat: business and other groups were permitted to canvass all opportunities for increasing contacts in Cuba until they reached a "cutoff point," beyond which they could not proceed.[111] Assistant Secretary of Commerce Roger Majak described the changes introduced by the new regulations as "more cosmetic than real."[112] Somewhat contemptuously, an NSC Latin American official at the time remarked that those U.S. business interests lobbying for a change in Cuba policy would constantly acquiesce under pressure because their objectives were always "very vague [and] because they don't have much staying power."[113]

The president of the American Farm Bureau, Dean Kleckner, surmised that the U.S. embargo of Cuba was costing the nation's agricultural community an estimated $500 million in sales annually, with the potential to quadruple in value over the longer term. In the late 1990s, this market looked doubly attractive to a key sector of the U.S. economy that was "in bad shape," exclaimed Kleckner. "Having lost substantial exports to Asia in the last couple of years, we're looking for exports anywhere in the world."[114] At a June meeting of the House Agriculture Committee, industry representatives vented their unhappiness and disappointment over unilateral sanctions locking companies out of markets in Cuba and elsewhere. The ability to maximize profits on a global scale was being subordinated to foreign policy imperatives of dubious value, producing few, if any, substantive benefits. Daniel Amstutz, president of the North American Export Grain Association, testified that unilateral trade sanctions on Cuba, North Korea, and Iraq, which between them account for fourteen percent of global rice and ten percent of global wheat imports, "have not affected their ability to secure supplies, so it is the American farmers who have been the losers." H.D. Cleberg, CEO of the Kansas-based Farmland Industries, complained that these sanctions "have subsidized our competitors [and] remove[d] markets from our producers." The American Soybean Association's Mike Yost argued that "even more damaging than the losses of annual sales to certain countries [including Cuba], unilateral sanctions establish the reputation of the U.S. as an unreliable supplier."[115]

Much the same message was delivered the following week to a Senate Banking Committee hearing on the Export Administration Act by the Arkansas Farm Bureau's Andrew Whisenhunt, recently returned from Cuba, where he was part of an agricultural trade exploratory mission. What he found "strikingly obvious" was that more than three decades of sanctions had produced "no tangible results" beyond denying U.S. agricultural exporters access to a potentially $1 billion a year market. The time had arrived to "lift unilateral sanctions on agricultural exports and stop making our producers pay the price."[116] This kind of political agitation from the farmbelt states was now beginning to spur even conservative legislators to take up the baton on behalf of their constituents in support of lifting restrictions on the sale of agricultural goods to Cuba and countries subject to U.S. trade sanctions.

Meanwhile, Undersecretary Eizenstat, having previously argued that easing restrictions on food and medicine sales to Iran, Libya, and the Sudan was not an encouragement to "rogue behavior," had changed his tune to the extent of opposing the general agricultural exemption bill sponsored by Richard Lugar because it "would weaken the president's ability to influence troublesome nations through the threat of severe economic sanctions."[117] In Congress, Helms also exhibited a degree of intellectual dishonesty in his effort to obstruct the agricultural industry's lobbying offensive against the Cuba embargo. His maneuver took the form of a proposed compromise that would allow food and medicine sales provided they were licensed by Treasury – an arrangement that could prove just as restrictive in practice as maintaining the status quo. Yet even Helm's minimalist option could not pass muster with the three House Cuban-Americans for whom the only solution to the Cuba problem was to bring more, not less, pressure to bear on the Castro government.

There was no disagreement among the anti-Castroists, however, about the administration's continued failure to satisfactorily implement key provisions of Helms–Burton. Back in March, Robert Menéndez had accused the State Department and its Cuba Office Coordinator Michael Ranneberger of "dragging your feet for the purposes of not fully implementing Title IV," which banned entry into the United States of senior executives of foreign companies benefiting from confiscated Cuban properties.[118] Now, four months later, the chair of the Senate Foreign Relations Committee decided that the time had come to hold the administration's proverbial feet to the fire to force it to implement the legislation more rigorously. Helms refused to hold hearings to confirm the nominations of Peter Romero to be the new Assistant Secretary for Inter-American Affairs and Ranneberger to be Ambassador to Mali. "These nominees have known for some time that their failure to vigorously enforce Helms–Burton is a matter of concern to Chairman Helms," explained an aide to the senator. "We have said to them explicitly, 'Bring us a body,' otherwise these nominations aren't going to move forward."[119]

On July 1, the State Department asked the Spanish hotel group Sol Meliá to reply "expeditiously" to a charge that one of its hotels in eastern Cuba was built on land seized from U.S. citizens in 1961.[120] Pressured by Helms, the department formally notified the hotel chain in August that not one, but three, of its twelve hotels in Cuba were on land claimed by a South Florida family.[121] Sol Meliá was not the first foreign company to be targeted under the Helms–Burton legislation. In 1996, the Canadian mining company Sherritt and two Mexican multinationals, cement producer CEMEX and the telecommunications conglomerate Grupo Domos, had been warned off operations in Cuba by the State Department.[122] But this latest notification had come after the European compromise of May 18 over investment "Disciplines." Any application of Helms–Burton against Sol Meliá now not only posed a threat to the "Disciplines" accord but was also likely to put the EU and Washington back on a collision course in the WTO.

In a parallel development, the White House ordered a "top-to-bottom review" of the Castro government's alleged ties to drug trafficking, buckling to pressure applied by the formidable trio of Helms, Burton, and Gilman for Cuba be placed on the State Department's list of major drug-transit countries.[123] The lawmakers refused to accept the assurances of White House Drug Policy Director General Barry McCaffrey and other senior Clinton law enforcement officials that there was no evidence of recent high-level Cuban involvement in narcotics smuggling, that only a very small proportion of drugs entering the United States passed through Cuba, that island authorities had been singularly cooperative in working to improve joint efforts at drug interdiction with the Coast Guard, and that Havana acted positively "on all the [drug-related intelligence] information we pass on to them."[124] Always sensitive to how any direct contact with Havana might impact on Congress, administration officials tripped over themselves to downplay the significance of a June 1999 meeting between American and Cuban narcotics officials. Michael Ranneberger felt obliged to remind one and all that "working-level operational cooperation ... does not reflect any change in our Cuba policy."[125]

Incremental and low-key steps by the White House to expand people-to-people contacts since the January 5 package, such as lifting restrictions on money transfers and travel and the impending revival of direct charter flights between Havana and New York, also fueled policy unraveling fears among the anti-Castro forces on Capitol Hill. Although State's Ranneberger stressed that "the purpose of all these measures from the outset has been specifically aimed at encouraging independent activity in Cuba," not even attributions of a destabilizing and ultimately subversive intent to these decisions could assuage the lawmakers' suspicions.[126] "The serious [White House] people who do policy stuff are supportive of change," said an involved Senate aide. "[But] at the highest political levels, where they count electoral votes, there's a nervousness about doing anything that changes the status quo."[127]

In August, the legislative supporters of the embargo flexed their muscle to blunt a Senate initiative by farm-state Republicans that would have ended restrictions on food and medicine sales to Cuba, North Korea, Libya, Iran, and Sudan. Initially, Helms attempted to table this amendment offered by John Ashcroft (R–Missouri). The ensuing debate, which focused almost exclusively on Cuba, culminated in the overwhelming defeat of this move. The majority of senators were not willing to subordinate economic self interest to ideological concerns. The amendment itself was subsequently carried by a decisive seventy-eight to twenty-eight vote. Refusing to accept defeat, Helms, Torricelli, Graham, and Mack then persuaded Ashcroft to modify his proposal by requiring a Treasury license in the case of terrorist states, effectively maintaining the Cuba policy status quo. The chamber did authorize the sale of agricultural products to Cuba subject to a licensing procedure but this provision failed to survive House–Senate conference committee deliberations in September that paved the way for floor votes on the $69 billion agriculture funding bill.[128] Asked to comment on the farm sector's efforts to end the embargo on food and medicine sales to Cuba, President Clinton said he would support it under the "right circumstances"; meanwhile, "we should continue to try to put pressure on the Castro regime."[129]

It was not immediately apparent what the White House meant by the "right circumstances." For Clinton and his senior foreign policy advisers, any shift on Cuba policy depended on their ability to mobilize congressional support, or at least neutralize opposition by the most prominent anti-Castro legislators. Assuming an inclination to move in this direction, the executive still confronted an ongoing dilemma: the clear Senate majority that voted for the Ashcroft amendment was either unwilling or unable to challenge, on a sustained basis, the demands of the strategically located clique of hardliners who wanted to force Castro from power by whatever means. This was the key message of Cuba's ultimate exclusion as a beneficiary of the amendment.

For their part, Helms and his allies clutched at every possible opportunity to keep the White House focused on the political consequences of shifting away from a get tough anti-Castro policy. Renewing efforts to demonize the regime, for example, Benjamin Gilman dredged up old allegations about Cuban involvement in the torture of American POWs during the Vietnam War. "There is no statute of limitations on the crimes committed by these Cuban torturers," thundered the House International Relations Committee chairman, and hearings would be held on the subject.[130]

Accusations of drug trafficking continued to offer these lawmakers an even more potent weapon to maintain Cuba's pariah status. The White House was reluctant to designate Cuba a major drug-transit country in the absence of solid evidence. "You could make a blanket case," said one official observed, but without hard facts, it "would not be credible."[131] Yet the problem for the White House was that it was dealing with individuals for whom the numbers and evidence were not prerequisites for establishing the reality as they perceived it. When Clinton announced that he had decided to keep Cuba off the list of major drug transit countries because the "evidence showed that the flow of U.S.-bound drugs through Cuban airspace and waters had 'decreased significantly since last year,' " Gilman exploded and announced a hearing in mid-November to consider legislation to force Cuba onto the list: "Clear evidence shows that massive amounts of legal narcotics bound for the United States transit the Cuban land mass ... air space ... and waters."[132]

Burton and Gilman set the tone of the hearing by accusing the administration of being "an accomplice to [and] a cheerleader for Castro's activities," and the president himself of being "complicit with every ounce of cocaine which goes through Cuba and ends up on the streets of Chicago, Indianapolis, Baltimore and New York." Assistant Secretary of State Randy Beers resolutely defended his superiors' decision, saying it was grounded in a series of reports to the department about "smuggling operations in this region" that all reached a similar conclusion: "We are unaware of significant quantities of drugs transiting Cuba's land mass. The drugs that do arrive in Cuba appear to be mostly for a growing indigenous and tourist market." The Drug Enforcement Agency's Chief of International Operations, William Ledwith, confirmed "an exhaustive review" by his agents could not find evidence to corroborate allegations that Cubans officials were involved in drug trafficking. Few subcommittee members seemed to be listening. "Castro," Dan Burton retorted, "is using Cuba as a syringe to inject drugs into our country."[133]

MISSED OPPORTUNITIES: THE TWILIGHT OF CLINTON'S DEAD-END POLICY

The same kind of emotional arguments were to shape the debate surrounding the rescue by American fishermen of a six-year-old Cuban boy found clinging to an inner tube in waters off Florida on Thanksgiving Day. The boy, Elián González, had been aboard a motorboat overcrowded with refugees who reportedly paid $1,000 each to "people smugglers" to transport them to the United

States. The boat sank mid-route and eleven members of the group, including the boy's mother and stepfather, drowned in the crossing. With the permission of his father, Juan Miguel González, Elián was delivered into the care of his great-uncle, Lázaro González, on November 26. Within twenty-four hours, Juan Miguel had forwarded a request for his son's return. But due apparently to the number of U.S. officials vacationing over the holiday period, immigration officials were not informed until December 7.[134] By then, demonstrations had broken out in Havana for the boy's return, and his fate had become a cause célèbre among Cuban-Americans and a rallying cry for the Cuban government.

The State Department response to Castro's demand that the boy be reunited with his father was immediate and firm: The administration, said spokesman James Foley, was "not intimidated by Fidel Castro."[135] However, its attitude toward Elián's relatives and their supporters in Miami was much more circumspect. Under pressure from CANF officials not to be seen "playing into Castro's hands," Clinton merely insisted that politics should play no part in determining the boy's future and left it to the Immigration and Naturalization Service (INS) and Attorney General Janet Reno to determine what that future should be.[136] On December 31, a full three weeks after Lázaro applied for asylum on Elián's behalf, U.S. immigration officials finally interviewed the boy's father in Havana, resulting in an INS determination that the boy's best interests would be served by returning him to Cuba. By this time, however, the possibility of an easy resolution seemed forlorn as the issue had ceased to be a minor custody dispute between Washington and Havana; it was now a major test of wills pitting the White House not only against Castro, but, more importantly against the Cuban exile community and its Capitol Hill champions.

Buoyed by the prospect of scoring political points, a number of legislators rushed to line up behind the exile community's demand that Elián should not be sent back into what they portrayed as the abusive clutches of Fidel Castro. Well before the INS ruling, Senator Connie Mack, supported by Jesse Helms, Bob Graham, Robert Torricelli, and Majority Leader Trent Lott (R–Mississippi), foreshadowed the introduction of a private bill to have Congress declare Elián a naturalized citizen. In the House, republicans Bill McCollum, Ileana Ros-Lehtinen, Lincoln Díaz-Balart, and Majority Whip Tom DeLay (R–Texas) announced they would sponsor companion legislation while their colleague, New Jersey democrat Robert Menéndez, indicated he was preparing a less ambitious bill that would simply grant Elián permanent residency status. In early December, a Gallup poll showed Americans equally divided over whether Elián should be returned to Cuba or remain with his Miami relatives.[137]

During the congressional winter recess, however, public opinion moved sharply in favor of repatriation. While the issue dragged on with no satisfactory resolution in sight, four separate Gallup polls conducted between January and April 2000 revealed a clear majority now favored the INS position.[138] If more and more Americans were apparently persuaded by the argument that the wishes of Elián's father should be respected, the Miami relatives did their cause no favors with heavy-handed attempts to retain custody of the boy – even refusing to cooperate with an INS request that his Cuban grandmothers be allowed to meet with him – and the shrill protests by the exile community against Elián's return to Cuba cast doubts over both its respect for the law and ultimate regard for the boy's well-being.[139] On January 19, Lázaro González, backed by CANF, filed a federal lawsuit against the Justice Department and the INS to overturn the latter's ruling. When Congress resumed the following week, a number of conservative republican legislators decided to await the outcome of this challenge rather than risk accusations of preempting the legal process by declaring Elián a U.S. citizen. This decision was influenced not only by the movement in public opinion, but also by the religious republican "family values" constituency that tended to think reuniting father and son should take precedence over politics.

Reminiscent of the 1994 Cuban rafters crisis, Clinton seemed aware that the domestic dynamics of this issue had now become more complicated, that there was a wider constituency to take into account in determining the fate of Elián, and that its preferences were not identical to those of the Cuban-American community. On the day Lázaro Gonzáles' lawsuit was filed, Clinton made his most expansive comments to date on the custody dispute in an interview with the *Christian Science Monitor*. Criticizing Castro for the "terrible" way in which he had politicized the boy's dilemma, Clinton said Cuba had once again "blown every conceivable opportunity to get closer to the United States." Still, he added, this was fundamentally an issue about family unity and that meant returning children even to countries where "we don't like the government."[140] If these comments amounted to an expression of support for the INS decision, within days White House spokesman Joe Lockhart issued a clarifying statement that suggested the White House was hedging its bets. The president, he said, would "wait and see what [the Congress] had in mind before making any decisions" on whether to sign or veto a citizenship bill.[141]

Equivocation and an instinctive reluctance to confront the Cuban-American community remained a hallmark of administration policy. During the first four months of the crisis, according to a senior INS official, there had "been almost no debate about [the Elián case] at any agency level."[142] This seemed likely to change in late March after a federal judge in Miami dismissed Lázaro's lawsuit. The initial community reaction was muted – but not for long. The mood soon changed when the Justice Department pressured lawyers for Elián's relatives to accept the INS decision and pursue other legal options quickly. Demonstrators in Miami vowed to prevent any attempt to remove Elián from his relatives and a CANF statement even raised the specter of violence by accusing Attorney General Reno of trying to provoke "another Waco" – a reference to the 1993 FBI raid on David Koresh's cult compound in Texas that resulted in eighty deaths.[143] Siding with the Cuban-American hardliners, Miami Dade County Mayor Alex Penelas declared that he would not allow local police to assist federal agents in taking Elián into their custody, and would hold Reno and Clinton responsible for any civil unrest.[144] Sensing an opportunity to shore up support in Florida, where presidential polls showed him trailing republican candidate George W. Bush Jr., Vice President Al Gore now chose to intervene and risk exacerbating tensions by lending his support to calls to keep Elián in the United States at all costs.

In a move that mirrored Clinton's calculated endorsement of the CDA during the 1992 presidential election campaign, Gore broke ranks with the administration's line on the custody dispute, claiming that U.S. immigration laws may not be "broad enough" to protect Elián's best interests and urging Congress to grant the boy permanent residency.[145] His statement caught executive branch officials flat-footed. "Oh my God, it's unbelievable!" said one. Heated exchanges were reported between White House aides, who attacked the vice president for "craven" maneuvering, and Gore advisers.[146] Democratic legislators distanced themselves from Gore's remarks as polls showed a significant majority of Americans continued to support the INS decision to return Elián to Cuba. As criticism of Gore's unproductive comments increased in volume, and began to damage his political stocks, the original supporters of the Mack bill putting Elián's fate in the hands of Congress also began to have second thoughts as to the wisdom of the initiative. On April 3, Trent Lott told Senate colleagues he was no longer "sure this is something Congress should step into." The next day, Mack himself said he might be willing to set aside his proposed legislation in favor of a nonbinding "sense of the Senate" resolution calling for a panel of psychiatrists to examine the boy and determine his future.[147]

The arrival of Juan Miguel González in the United States in early April further weakened support for those opposed to Elián's return to Cuba. Whether or not administration officials perceived the father's presence as bolstering the case for repatriation, publicly Clinton became noticeably more insistent that the rule of law be upheld; in private, he began to pressure Attorney General Reno to break the deadlock by first taking the boy into federal custody. Continuous negotiations between Justice Department officials and Elián's Miami relatives produced a series of agreed-upon deadlines for releasing Elián into government care only to see the relatives equivocate at the last moment, usually accompanied by new demands for any handover. On April 22, her patience finally exhausted, Reno ordered federal agents to enter the home of Lázaro González and seize the boy.[148] Two months later, all legal appeals against the original INS decision having been exhausted, the boy returned to Cuba with his father.

For some prominent domestic political actors, this episode was something of a turning point in their immediate political fortunes. Vice President Gore's sudden and unannounced breaking of ranks was reciprocated by the White House, which kept him in the dark about Reno's decision to raid the González house to take the boy into temporary federal custody. The clear implication was that Gore could not be trusted.[149] Nor was it possible to discern much in the way of potential electoral advantage accruing to the vice president. Many non-Hispanics in Florida interpreted his shift on Elián's future as pandering to the exile community, whereas among Cuban-Americans he appeared not to have made any significant inroads into their support of George W. Bush Jr.[150] In any event, as a prominent member of the administration, Gore was never going to be able to avoid the negative political fall-out associated with what many Cuban-Americans viewed as Clinton's disastrous handling of the Elián case. These included Democratic Party members angered by the failure to consult them about the April 22 raid. "That sen[t] a strong signal that [Clinton] doesn't give a damn about us. We fe[lt] betrayed," said a Cuban-American activist, suggesting that even loyal party members would have second thoughts about their voting intentions in November.[151]

CANF was an even more obvious loser. The fate of Elián galvanized the Cuban-American community as no other issue had since the 1961 Bay of Pigs invasion. Surprisingly, however, CANF maintained a relatively low profile in street protests supporting Elián's Miami relatives and, ultimately, could not exercise enough clout even to broker a peaceful custody transfer. This raised questions both about the Foundation's credibility as the body best able to promote the community's interests and the degree of influence its post–Mas Canosa leadership still exercised in Washington. CANF's image also suffered because the majority of Americans not only regarded the Miami tug-of-war over Elián as uncivil at best and cruel at worst, but also, whether accurate or not, held the Cuban-American hardliners responsible for what occurred.[152] "If I were a leader of the Cuban-American community, it's something I'd be thinking about," commented one U.S. official. "It could all go away in six months, or it could make people question, 'Why do we have this policy [on Cuba]?' "[153]

Even the usually irrepressible group of anti-Castro legislators were singed in their handling of the Elián affair. Not only did they adopt a stance that ran counter to majority public opinion almost from the beginning, but their failure to muster enough votes in Congress to grant Elián permanent residency, let alone U.S. citizenship, was a profound embarrassment as well. Undeterred by this miscalculation, Connie Mack led angry republicans in demanding a Senate hearing on federal agents' use of force to wrest Elián from his Miami relatives. After declaring they would pursue the issue until Americans could once again feel "safe in their homes," however, they were quickly forced to tone down their rhetoric as polls revealed most Americans agreed with Reno's order. Support for a hearing in both chambers quickly slipped away.[154]

The larger and more pivotal question, of course, was the significance of this episode for the future of U.S.–Cuba relations. Publicly, Washington and Havana had been engaged in an acrimonious war of words over custody of the boy. Behind the scenes, however, officials from both countries had labored to quarantine the dispute from other issues affecting bilateral ties. Privately, some Clinton officials even conceded that the custody dispute had led to an unprecedented level of cooperation between the two adversaries, and proferred the hope that it had "helped our relationship mature to a new stage."[155] Others reacted cautiously and sought to downplay speculation of "anything dramatic" taking place in contrast to the possibility of "moving things ahead in small ways."[156] One U.S. official was more pessimistic, noting that the Castro government had "just built a permanent protest area in front of our Interest Section in Havana and we bashed them [on April 18] in Geneva on a U.N. resolution attacking Cuba's human rights abuses. Gee, I don't think this signals major changes."[157] Once the dust settled on the Elián affair, American officials wasted little time in confirming their lack of interest in any policy reassessment. Acting Assistant Secretary of State Peter Romero accused Castro of manipulating the Elián affair for his own domestic purposes and dismissed any notion of a breach in the administration consensus "that our policy is the correct one – economic sanctions and other kinds of instruments to isolate a renegade regime, an undemocratic regime."[158]

The outcome of the Elián González case was another missed opportunity to move U.S. policy to a more rational footing. With a politically diverse mix of lawmakers, business and other societal organizations, and influential members of the foreign policy establishment calling for a change in approach, and the anti-Castro forces on Capitol Hill and in Miami assessing the damage to their reputations from being on the wrong side of the custody debate, the Clinton White House was handed the most propititous circumstances for undertaking a comprehensive review of Cuba policy since the pope's visit to the island in 1998. In May, the administration did accept a Cuban invitation to station a Coast Guard officer in Havana to investigate narco-trafficking, but generally it chose to persevere with the politically less risky option of defending the embargo while making minor changes such as streamlining the procedures for licensing visits to Cuba by students, athletes, artists and scholars, business and political delegations, and extending direct air services between Havana and the U.S. mainland. According to Treasury Department officials, the number of Americans traveling legally to Cuba had grown by ten percent annually since 1995, whereas illegal visitors had more than doubled during the same period. Other sources placed the combined 1999 figure at 157,000.[159] Asked whether this relatively less rigorous enforcement of travel restrictions was a way of easing the embargo with little or no domestic political repercussions, the Director of State's Office of Cuban Affairs Charles Shapiro responded with an emphatic "absolutely not." All the president is doing, he said, "is mak[ing] some changes in the margins."[160]

The administration continued to exhibit some flexibility regarding the issue of medicine sales to Cuba as well. Between mid-1998 and the end of 1999 it had approved the sale of $45 million worth of medical supplies, even though the embargo constraints and regulations – which saddled exporters with high financing and transport costs, and close monitoring to prove they had not been resold by the Cubans for hard currency – meant that few transactions actually occurred. In January 2000, Washington granted permission for a U.S. Health-care Exhibition to be held in Havana – the first American trade show on the island in forty years. Most exhibitors, however, complained that U.S. licensing and monitoring procedures continued to make sales extremely difficult, and some used the occasion to call openly for an end to the embargo.[161]

Pharmaceutical and other medical supply companies were hardly alone in urging that Washington to do more than just tinker at the margins of the embargo. Farm state legislators, democratic and republican, were under increased pressure from their constituents to do something about the depressed prices for American agricultural products, and specifically to lobby their colleagues for access to the Cuban market. In January, Senate Foreign Relations Committee Chairman Jesse Helms agreed to reconsider the amendment introduced by Missouri's John Ashcroft the previous August to allow licensed food and medicine sales to Cuba, which passed by a wide margin but was subsequently blocked from consideration in the House by the republican leadership at the urging of Florida's Lincoln Díaz-Balart and Ileana Ros-Lehtinen. Every dollar spent by "rogue states" on American produce, Helms argued, was "a dollar they cannot spend on terror and repression."[162] On March 23, the amendment was approved by a voice vote of the committee as part of a trade and anticorruption bill. In the House, conservative republican George Nethercutt (Washington), for the third time in as many years, proposed a companion amendment that would terminate unilateral sanctions on food and medicine shipments to the island.[163]

Advocates of a changed approach toward the government in Havana still confronted a White House adhering to a tough and demanding policy anchored in a notion of Cuban exceptionalism. Clinton's reaching out to Beijing and the administration's rationale for engaging the Asian power vividly highlighted the paradoxical nature of U.S. policy. During an April luncheon with editors of *The Washington Post*, NSC Adviser Sandy Berger claimed that individual Chinese citizens enjoyed much greater freedom in their lives these days. This assertion contradicted Secretary of State Albright's active lobbying in the UNHRC the day before the Senate vote on the Ashcroft amendment in support of a resolution condemning Beijing over its human rights record, and was markedly at variance with the State Department's 2000 global human rights report, which concluded that the situation in China was not improving.[164] Yet, the White House saw no inconsistency in encouraging contacts with China while condemning its human rights record; indeed, it was urging the Congress to approve permanent normal trade relations between the two countries. When it came to Cuba, however, an equally scathing assessment of the human rights climate, in particular the crackdown on hundreds of dissidents prior to the November 1999 Ibero-American Summit in Havana and the ongoing harrassment of independent journalists, served as one more reason for not pursuing a policy of engagement.[165]

Treating Cuba differently was not just confined to U.S. relations with what remained of the communist world. Since 1994, the State Department's annual studies of "Patterns of Global Terrorism" had found no evidence of Cuban "sponsorship" of terrorist activities or "active support" for armed struggle in the hemisphere or elsewhere. Yet this was insufficient reason for deleting Cuba from the list of terrorist states. It was still included on the tenuous grounds that it provided "safe haven" for individual foreign terrorists and "continue[d] to maintain close ties to other state sponsors of terrorism and leftist insurgent groups in Latin America."[166] In 1999, Office of Cuban Affairs Coordinator Michael Ranneberger indicated just how far Washington was prepared to stretch the bow to keep Cuba on the list: "There is no evidence that the Cubans have been behind terrorist incidents, but there is still that kind of networking."[167] Senior colleagues were more candid. "Taking Cuba off the State Department's list of designated terrorist states is not remotely on the cards," admitted one.[168] "After the shootdown," another concurred, "it was pretty much guaranteed Cuba would stay on the list."[169]

In its 2000 Report, the department argued that nothing had changed: that Cuba continued to "provide safe haven to several terrorists and U.S. fugitives." They included members of the Basque ETA movement who were living in Cuba with the knowledge and tacit approval of the Spanish government, and Colombian guerillas who did not pose an obstacle to President Andrés Pastrana's very public efforts to seek Fidel Castro's help in brokering an agreement to end his country's civil war. The most striking omission from the list was Pakistan, even though the report charged General Pervez Musharraf's dictatorship with "harboring and aiding known terrorists." Counterterrorism Coordinator Michael Sheehan's feeble justification was that Pakistan is "a friendly state that is trying to tackle the problem."[170]

These rigidities in U.S. policy and the Cold War ideology that still shaped Clinton thinking about Cuba seemed less and less convincing to more and more sectors of the American population, especially those with an interest in doing business on the island. "Traditionally, it's been the liberal left and church groups pushing to relax sanctions on Cuba," a disgruntled Ros-Lehtinen observed. "But now we've got Wall Street and, unfortunately, Main Street, trying to lift sanctions on all dictatorships."[171] Even so, since the 1994 midterm elections when the republicans gained control of both chambers, the three Cuban-American legislators could invariably rely on ideological "fellow travelers" – some of whom occupied leadership positions in the House and Senate (Helms, Burton, Gilman), and others who exercised considerable influence within the Democratic Party and White House (Graham, Torricelli) – to support a hardline position on Cuba. What united them was an overriding determination to get rid of the Castro regime, even if this meant putting at risk or sacrificing migration accords, possible antinarcotics agreements, and potential markets and profits. By the last year of the Clinton presidency, and in spite of the fact that CANF's influence in Washington had ebbed since the death of founder Jorge Mas Canosa in November 1997, the power of the congressional Cuba lobby remained formidable, and now counted among its number Senate Majority Leader Trent Lott and House Majority Whip Tom Delay.

One pressure point these legislators could still target under Helms–Burton was Moscow's annual $100 to $300 million compensation payment to the Cubans for use of the Lourdes communications monitoring facilities. Similar to other provisions of the Act, this one also included a waiver authority if the president determined that aid to Russia was in the national interest. In late March, Ros-Lehtinen turned her attention to closing this and other so-called loopholes, sponsoring the "Russian–American Trust and Cooperation Act," which tied rescheduling of Russia's $2.6 billion Paris Club debt to the United States to closure of the Lourdes base in Cuba. To no avail, the White House argued that passage of such legislation would endanger U.S. signals intelligence facilities that performed much the same function as the Lourdes facility did for the Russians. The House International Relations Committee approved the bill by voice vote, but adopted an amendment retaining the presidential waiver authority; in July, the full House passed it by a resounding 275 to 146 votes.[172] The waiver provision did nothing to reassure Russia's Foreign Minister, Igor Ivanov, who denounced the bill as "a violation of all international norms because it constitutes interference in the internal affairs of foreign countries."[173]

Still, by mid-2000, the anti-Castro forces in Congress were focusing most of their efforts on stalling or diluting the Ashcroft–Nethercutt intiatives to lift sanctions on the sale of food and medicine to Cuba. In the Senate, Helms managed to attach conditions to the amendment requiring that exemptions for food sales to countries on the State Department's list of terrorist states be reviewed on a case-by-case basis and forbidding any U.S. government financing of these commodities. To facilitate quick consideration of the House amendment, Nethercutt agreed to these changes. The modified amendment then survived an aggressive lobbying effort by House Majority Whip DeLay to delete it from the agricultural spending bill. With fifteen republican members opposing DeLay's motion, the full Agriculture Committee passed the bill by a decisive thirty-five to twenty-four votes. Whether it would survive a House leadership opposed to its inclusion in any appropriations bill remained to be seen.[174] At the White House, concern focused less on the question of terminating sanctions on food and medicine sales and more on the measures that might limit the president's ability to conduct foreign policy. "Our concern with the [House and Senate] legislation as drafted," explained one senior official, "is that it unnecessarily restricts presidential prerogatives across the board."[175] Rather than try to influence the trajectory of the debate, the administration once again indicated it would prefer to await the detail of yet another Hill initiative on Cuba.

American corporate and farming representatives, by contrast, were determined that the momentum of their antisanctions campaign would not be allowed to flag. Returning from a U.S.–Cuba Business Summit in Havana in June, several prominent business figures talked up signs of further positive changes in the island economy. The president of the U.S.–Cuba Trade and Economic Council, John Kavulich, called a Cuban government decision to allow local entrepreneurs to visit the United States a "substantial step forward." It was, said U.S. Chamber of Commerce Vice President Craig Johnstone, an objective "we certainly have been striving for almost a year to achieve," and he encouraged a favorable response to Havana's offer to talk to individual American companies about settling their outstanding claims as the first step toward improving overall bilateral relations.[176] Given initial projections of between $300 and $600 million in yearly agricultural and pharmaceutical sales to Cuba if the restrictions were lifted, it came as no surprise that the American Farm Bureau's Director of Government Relations described eliminating the restrictions on food sales as the "top trade issue at the moment."[177] For John Block, president of Food Distributors International and former republican Secretary of Agriculture, the question was a simple one: "If Ronald Reagan could do that [support food sales] with the evil empire, can't we do that with Cuba?"[178]

This pressure for change undoubtedly concerned the leading anti-Castro forces. "The farm lobby and 'big business' coming together have definitely altered the political landscape," admitted the CANF's Washington Office Director, José Cardenas. On Capitol Hill, an aide to one of the Cuban-American lawmakers reported that "it's like living in a castle under siege." At the same time, they need not have feared any dramatic move by the White House. Although administration officials grudgingly acknowledged that domestic opponents of sanctions had a point – "they can be like killing a housefly with a sledgehammer," exclaimed one[179] – any changes being debated with respect to North Korea, Libya, or even Iran were not likely to be extended to Cuba. "The embargo is the law [as a result of Helms–Burton]," Deputy Assistant Secretary of State Lula Rodríguez reminded journalists in late June.[180]

Rodríguez's comment followed Senate rejection, by fifty-nine to forty-one votes, of a proposal sponsored by Christopher Dodd to establish a bipartisan commission that would undertake a comprehensive policy review in order to prepare a "soft landing" for the island once Fidel Castro relinquished power.[181] Opponents of the Cuba embargo seemed more likely to achieve results by chipping away at specific planks of the policy than via this kind of frontal assault, which was always going to meet a stiff wall of resistance. Facing almost certain defeat in any showdown over the proposed amendment to the House Agriculture Appropriations bill to lift restrictions on food and medical sales to Cuba, the House Cuban-Americans worked with the GOP leadership to find an acceptable compromise. In the early hours of June 27, they announced an agreement to support the watered-down version of the amendment first proposed in May. A euphoric George Nethercutt (R–Washington) hailed the compromise as a "huge breakthrough" for American farmers, whereas Ileana Ros-Lehtinen more realistically observed that the language agreed to would, in fact, "make it as difficult as possible" for U.S. exporters looking to get into the Cuban market.[182]

Under the amended bill, restrictions on food and medicine sales would be eased on the condition that no U.S. government loans or credits, or private bank financing, was made available to facilitate sales; U.S. companies would be barred from negotiating barter arrangements to pay for sales; licenses would have to be obtained by farmers, commodity exporters, and other organizations planning to export to Cuba (although not Catholic charities and other groups already exempted from licensing approval); and Cuban exports would continue to be denied entry to the U.S. market.[183] The House compromise also failed to clarify what impact the 1992 restrictions on ships visiting Cuba calling at U.S. ports for six months would have on the conduct of transactions. Finally, it actually tightened the embargo with the requirement that, in return for the relaxation on food and medicine sales, federal restrictions on Cuba travel be codified into law.

Officials representing peak business and agricultural organizations traduced the House amendment as a "bad break" for U.S. exporters. They also warned that "you don't get a second shot" at such measures. The National Farmers Union said the restrictions would make it "virtually impossible for us to compete with other nations."[184] If Congress passed the bill, Clinton indicated he might sign it so long as it did not limit the president's flexibility in the area of foreign policy. But he would not be a party to any major change to Cuba policy "until there is a bipartisan majority which believes that there has been some effort on the part of the Cuban government to reach out to us as well."[185] Although the House vote for the Russian–American Trust and Cooperation Act in July suggested that a bipartisan majority was as far away as ever, other congressional initiatives provided a limited basis for optimism that sentiment on the Hill was coalescing in favor of some kind of new direction on Cuba. Hard on the heels of the Russian debt vote, the House passed by equally resounding majorities two republican-sponsored amendments: one prohibiting the use of Treasury Department funds to enforce U.S. restrictions on the sale of food and medicine to Cuba (301–116), and another doing likewise with regard to travel to the island (241–174). Both were attached to the Treasury Appropriations bill, only to be stripped by a hostile republican leadership in conference, where they successfully argued that Agriculture Appropriations was the proper bill to attach them to and promised to consider them as part of that legislation.[186]

Meanwhile, relations between Washington and Havana showed further signs of deterioration. In June, Havana announced it was postponing participation in the biannual migration talks to protest the "dry" part of the "wet/dry" policy, the 1966 Cuban Adjustment Act (CAA), which allowed only immigrants who made it to U.S. shores to apply for permanent residency after twelve months, and the drawn-out Elián González decision, which was interpreted as a means whereby the United States was subtlely encouraging illegal exits from the island. Not to be outdone, the State Department's Philip Reeker accused Havana of "systematically violating" the 1994 migration agreement almost from the moment it was signed, while Secretary Albright lodged a formal protest with the Cuban Interest Section in Washington that charged the Castro government with refusing to allow 117 of its citizens who had been issued with valid U.S. visas to leave for the mainland.[187] After a three-month impasse, Havana agreed to resume the migration talks, but not before National Assembly President Ricardo Alarcón had been denied a visa to attend an International Parliamentary Union meeting in New York. The decision was subsequently reversed by the State Department, enabling Alarcón to participate in a September United Nations Millennium Summit, but the visa severely circumscribed his freedom of travel, forcing him to cancel a meeting with the Congressional Black Caucus in the nation's capital.[188] Asked later why Cuban officials were accorded such treatment while North Korean officials were invited into the Oval Office, White House press secretary Jake Siewert had a novel explanation based on a rather twisted logic: "North Korea represents a major security threat to the United States and our allies, Cuba does not."[189]

The administration was also prepared to risk Havana's ire by retreating from its opposition to proposed legislation that would compensate victims of countries deemed to sponsor terrorism by unlocking their frozen U.S. assets. In July, the House approved by a voice vote the Justice for Victims of Terrorism Act, which would make it easier for victims of terrorist acts (and their relatives) to collect damages awarded in federal courts from the offending nation's American assets by eliminating the president's existing waiver authority if national interests were deemed to be at stake. The Senate version was placed on that chamber's legislative calender in November 1999. Both bills were primarily intended to gain financial recompense for the relatives of the Brothers to the Rescue (BTTR) pilots shot down by Cuban fighter jets in February 1996. State and Treasury officials had consistently argued that these funds were bargaining chips for future compensation negotiations with countries such as Cuba, and that unfreezing the assets for this particular purpose would complicate government efforts to resolve other longstanding claims. Traditionally opposed to any expansion of the claimants' pool, several former owners of large Cuban properties still holding out for compensation awards also looked askance at this legislation. However, yielding to pressure from both conservative and liberal democratic senators along with the realization that a Senate bill depriving the president of the authority to protect Cuban [and Iranian] assets was also likely to be approved, the White House shifted track in order to minimize its losses and get this irritant off the political agenda as the election neared.

During the August congressional recess, Deputy Treasury Secretary Stuart Eizenstat and White House Budget Director Jack Lew thrashed out a compromise with the bills' sponsors, Senator Connie Mack (D–Florida) and Representative Frank Lautenberg (D–New Jersey), under which legislation would be introduced into the Senate that included a provision for BTTR claims to be paid principally from Cuban telephone revenues held in escrow. Both chambers swiftly approved the revised legislation making the BTTR family members eligible for payments in excess of $90 million.[190] Not for the first time, presidential prerogatives took a back seat to domestic politics.

These, in turn, were dominated by the presidential election campaign, which by now had entered high gear. On the hustings in Florida, Al Gore and George W. Bush Jr. vigorously competed for the Cuban-American vote with promises to stay tough on Cuba. A key figure in the Bush foreign policy advisory team, Condoleezza Rice, had met Díaz-Balart in April, and assured the congressman that the republican candidate was firmly committed to maintaining the embargo. Díaz-Balart repaid this approach by offering to provide Bush with position papers on Cuba policy, and some of the suggestions these contained were used during the campaign.[191]

Florida's Bill McCollum described the Cuba plank of the Republican Party platform as the most "clear and concise" the party ever had.[192] Speaking before a Miami audience in late August, Bush was adamant that the sanctions would remain "in place," coupled with increased support for Radio and TV Martí, until the Castro regime "frees political prisoners and holds free elections and allows free speech."[193] On occasion, he also implied that the Republican Party commitment to the CAA might be reviewed. During a September meeting with journalists at the Palm Beach International Airport, Bush stated that he "wouldn't change" Clinton's decision to end the policy of automatic asylum for Cuban rafters intercepted en route to Florida. Then, three days later, Díaz-Balart released a letter from the republican candidate that included a commitment, as president, to revisit *all* Clinton executive decisions pertaining to Cuba. Regarding immigration policy, Bush wrote, "I would want to hear both sides" of the "wet foot/dry foot" argument.[194] Whether this apparent shift was simply a tactic to maximize support among a key voting constituency, it nonetheless meshed with the general tenor of the policy he intended to adopt as president to deal with Cuba: "We will keep the pressure on Fidel Castro."[195] CANF officials, with whom he had met on a number of occasions throughout the campaign, could not have been more pleased. Chairman Jorge Mas Jr. personally endorsed Bush's candidacy.

Gore was equally blunt about where he stood on Cuba, insisting he was "a hardliner on Castro."[196] In contrast to Bush, however, he delegated major responsibility for campaigning in the heartland of the Cuban-American electorate to running mate Joseph Lieberman. The democrat's vice presidential nominee had the closest ties of all four candidates with the CANF leadership, dating back to its strong support of his initial 1988 campaign to win a Senate seat in Connecticut. On a pilgrimage to Jorge Mas Canosa Sr.'s grave in late October, Lieberman recounted how he "wasn't supposed to win [in 1988]. But I met with Jorge and [current CANF president] Pepe [Hernández]. We bonded on a matter of principle."[197] Thereafter, in the words of a senior CANF official, he maintained "a perfect voting record on Cuba."[198] With two clearly acceptable alternatives, the Foundation confronted a dilemma that it solved by deciding to remain neutral and not officially back either candidate.

Although the presidential campaign reaffirmed CANF's role as a force to be reckoned with in Florida politics, the political environment was changing on Capitol Hill, and the Foundation's influence was waning. In June, former Director of the State Department's Office of Cuban Affairs Dennis Hays was appointed to head the Washington office with a brief to refocus attention on the misdeeds of the Castro regime and bolster CANF's declining influence over the Cuba policy debate. CANF Chairman Jorge Mas Canosa Jr. told a Washington news conference that Hays's background "will be invaluable in an era where American values . . . have often taken a back seat to economic schemes."[199] A second new top-level appointment was the executive director, 35-year-old Joe García, whose brief was to help rebuild the Foundation's image both in Florida and nationally. Defining the most pressing challenge as that posed by the antisanctions business and farm lobby, García told reporters that "we're going to try to reengage America's conscience" by shifting from a more or less exclusively Washington-based strategy to one that also focused on expanding ties with opposition leaders in Cuba, partly through a quadrupling of funds channeled to dissident groups on the island. By focusing on humanitarian and human rights concerns in Cuba, CANF hoped to more effectively counter the mercantilist forces in Congress pushing for an easing of the embargo.[200] These personnel changes, however, could not mask the Foundation's uphill battle to fill the leadership gap left by the death of its charismatic and politically astute founder Jorge Mas Canosa Sr. Indicative of the Foundation's declining ability to raise funds, the Free Cuba PAC campaign contributions had dwindled from $102,500 in 1997–8 to a mere $35,500 in the 1999–2000 election cycle.[201] "It was Jorge Mas, his personal relationships and fundraising," reflected a congressional aide working with CANF. "That got things done. Now that he's died, his son really hasn't taken up the case."[202]

However, others had, principally the Cuban-American legislators who, assisted by strategically located allies, were still able to exercise influence wholly disproportionate to their numbers. And with Bush and Gore promising to stay tough on Cuba, there was now only a small window of opportunity to moderate Cuba policy in a way that served the wider interest of corporate America, especially its agricultural sector. On October 5, Majority Whip DeLay and other anti-Castro legislators struck a deal to force a vote on the compromise Nethercutt amendment with its financing ban, and on the statutory prohibition on expanding travel to the island. Ileana Ros-Lehtinen boasted that passage of the food and medicine sales measures would amount to "nothing but smoke and mirrors because it won't result in one dollar more in Castro's pockets."[203] When the Agriculture Appropriations bill reached the floor of the House, democrats (who had voted against it in conference) and republicans voted for it; neither party was going to oppose a bill packed with $3.5 billion of emergency assistance to farmers in an election year over Cuba. On October 18, the Senate approved similar legislation that included new travel restrictions and barred U.S. government credit or private financing for any Cuba sales. The American farm lobby was understandably frustrated and disappointed. It was precisely the availability of export credit guarantees totaling $180 million annually that explained Cuba's purchase of seventy to seventy-eight percent of its wheat and flour imports from France.[204]

Unlike the farm lobby and its congressional supporters, Clinton's reaction was more perplexing. "This is one of those things," he told reporters following the House vote, "where somebody can go home and say, 'I made a good deal for farmers,' and it's so close to the election nobody will know whether it's real or not." His other complaint was that the House bill "definitely restricts the ability of the executive branch to increase people-to-people contacts between Americans and Cubans."[205] By implication, a codification of existing travel restrictions also undermined what remained of the original people-to-people strategy for bringing about change in Cuba. This strategy was severely weakened by passage of the Helms–Burton Act, Clinton belatedly told a Spanish-language television audience in November, which was "a great mistake" because it prevented the president from "us[ing] the full panoply of pressures" to support those in Cuba opposed to the Castro leadership.[206] That Clinton should be ruminating about lost opportunities for reaching out to dissidents on the island at the end of his presidency was ironic, given that this was precisely the approach he had rejected during the early years of his administration, preferring to deal instead with the Cuban-American hardliners in Miami. Still, when the Senate passed its version, Clinton grudgingly indicated he would sign the bill, being just as loathe as congressional democrats to put at risk almost $80 billion in agricultural spending during an election year.[207] In Havana, the Castro government dismissed the outcome as a publicity stunt, and rejected any trade under such restrictive conditions.

The amount of effort that went into producing this minor concession (how small would await a determination of the regulations governing any actual sales) only served to underline the extent of Washington's global isolation where Cuba was concerned. A matter of days after Clinton signed the legislation, the annual nonbinding resolution before the United Nations General Assembly calling for an end to the Cuba embargo passed by a record 167 in favor with 4 absentions. Only Israel and the Marshall Islands voted with the United States against the resolution. In late November, an influential sector of the foreign policy establishment added its voice in support of easing the embargo as a way of assisting the transition to a post-Castro era and reducing the risk of U.S. military intervention. This second Council on Foreign Relations (CFR) bipartisan task force report recommended the elimination of travel restrictions to Cuba, regular commercial flights between the United States and the island, permission for American companies whose Cuban enterprises were nationalized to resolve their claims by entering into joint venture arrangements with the government in Havana, and granting Cuba observer status in the World Bank and Inter-American Development Bank.[208]

By comparison with any gains resulting from Clinton's decision to allow food and medicine sales to Cuba, these CFR proposals seemed bold and innovative. Meanwhile, the official, public justification for maintaining a tough Cuba policy looked increasingly idiosyncratic, even irrational. In an address at Hanoi's National University in November, for instance, Clinton told his audience that the United States was not in the business of attempting to impose respect for human rights, democratic politics, and economic reform on Vietnam. "Let me say emphatically, *we do not seek to impose these ideals*, nor could we," he said. "*Only you can decide* if you will continue to open your markets, open your society, and strengthen the rule of law."[209] When it came to Cuba, however, the reverse held true.

Whatever the outcome of the presidential election, there was no likelihood that this "Cuba exception" approach would abandoned by a new democratic or republican administration. Although the disputed Florida ballot count delayed the eventual result, what was never in doubt was that the state's Cuban-American voters had overwhelmingly deserted the democrats in favor of George W. Bush. Election day polling revealed a halving in the percentage of the exile community vote for Gore compared with their support of Clinton in 1996 (from approximately forty percent to less than twenty percent).[210] When Gore finally conceded defeat, he did so in circumstances that could only strengthen the notion that support among Cuban-Americans was crucial for any White House aspirant. His loss in Florida denied him the electoral college votes that would have provided the margin of victory, and his inauguration as the nation's forty-third president. Bush, however, may well have felt he owed a debt of gratitude to the community, which, on the basis of campaign promises, would most likely be repaid at the expense of Castro's Cuba.

In January 2001, as one of his last presidential decisions, Clinton suspended implementation of Title III of Helms–Burton for another six months, removing any immediate pressure on the incoming president to demonstrate his anti-Castro credentials by allowing Americans to sue foreign investors for trafficking in confiscated Cuban properties. As Clinton's second term drew to a close, his

1992 campaign promise to "bring the hammer down on Fidel Castro" remained unfinished business. To his outgoing secretary of state, the disappointment was palpable. In a farewell news conference at the State Department, Madeleine Albright said her major regret on leaving office was that Fidel Castro still governed the Caribbean island, and left no one in doubt that his death could not come soon enough. Her gift to the incoming Bush administration were "the actuarial tables on Cuba,"[211] testifying to the essential bankruptcy of a nonpolicy of "waiting for Fidel to die" that the United States had pursued toward Cuba over the preceding eight years.

Conclusion

THE post–Cold War international environment had a contradictory effect on Washington and Havana: Whereas the former deepened its adversarial posture, the latter systematically reversed what U.S. policymakers previously described as "obstacles" to improved bilateral ties; whereas the White House perceived the end of the Cold War as an invitation to intensify its pressure on the Cuban Revolution, new harsh global realities had pushed Cuba in the opposite direction as it moderated its policies toward the capitalist world, including overtures to the dominant hegemon to its north. Both the Bush and Clinton administrations, however, interpreted Cuban concessions as a vindication of their approach – as weakness gained through U.S. pressure rather than as pragmatic adjustments to a new and changing international order. Reciprocating Cuba's opening to the world market and engagement in regional diplomacy consisted of tightening economic sanctions measures, heightening the ideological war, condemning Cuba's human rights performance by standards inconsistently applied in other parts of the world, and placing conditions on normalized relations that amounted to a demand for an end to the revolutionary regime and its institutional structures.

The collapse of the Soviet Union and Eastern Europe profoundly influenced George Bush's approach toward Cuba, triggering a belief that the devastating impact of the Bloc's demise on the island economy might make Fidel Castro's regime the next communist domino to fall. The possibility of finally achieving this historic strategic goal was more tempting than any thought of rethinking a policy toward Cuba that had singularly failed even to come close to achieving its objectives over the course of the previous three decades. To justify maintaining this Cold War destabilizing approach in the so-called New World Order, the White House decided that major changes in Cuba's political economy were now the *sine qua non* for any move toward improved ties. This "shifting of the goalposts" was also driven by domestic political factors: As part

176

of a larger effort to establish his conservative credentials, Bush was prepared to embrace the outlook of the anti-Castro hardliners in the Cuban-American community and Congress, which translated into a full court economic, political, and propaganda offensive against the Castro regime.

Applying pressure on the Soviet Union to collaborate in this anti-Castro strategy was central to his approach and it set a pattern of bullying U.S. behavior that would eventually be applied to other countries as well. Between 1989 and 1991, the White House and the State Department leaned heavily on Mikhail Gorbachev to terminate all economic and military ties with Cuba as preconditions for large-scale U.S. assistance, which the Soviet leader viewed as critical to domestic economic recovery and, after the failed August 1991 coup, to continued political stability. This arm-twisting led the director of the Soviet Academy of Science's Institute on the U.S. and Canada, Georgi Arbatov, to caustically observe that "Americans have a good appetite and their appetite keeps growing; No matter how many good things they have had, they are asking for more and more."[1] Still, while Yeltsin completed the process set in place by Gorbachev to cut Cuba adrift economically, White House hopes for its swift collapse failed to eventuate.

As the November 1992 presidential election approached, Bush confronted a democratic opponent intent on making inroads into the historically republican Cuban-American vote by promising an even tougher sanctions policy if elected. Bill Clinton's advisers calculated that this tactic would neutralize Cuba as an election issue and thus allow the campaign to focus on social and economic policies that were the democratic candidate's strong points. Clinton himself threw down the gauntlet early in the contest, announcing he would support the Cuban Democracy Act (CDA), which mandated sanctions against U.S. subsidiaries doing business with Cuba, and aggressively cultivating Jorge Mas Canosa, head of the most influential and wealthiest exile community organization – the ferociously anti-Castro Cuban American National Foundation (CANF). Bush was initially reluctant to follow suit because of the almost certain tensions the CDA would provoke between the United States and its trade allies, but he eventually subordinated these and other concerns, including the possible adverse impact of the new sanctions measures on the worldwide operations of U.S. corporations, to the necessity of shoring up his Cuban-American electoral base. In October, Bush agreed to sign the legislation if it reached his desk.

The passage of the CDA into law had two profound consequences for Cuba policy. On the one hand, it promised to constrict the already limited political space available to dissidents and human rights groups on the island who refused to support the embargo precisely because it undermined the possibilities for the growth of a viable opposition movement. By signing the CDA, Bush sent a very sharp message about his order of priorities: The interests of the anti-Castroists in Cuba would take a back seat to the interests of the hardline exile community in Miami. On the other hand, it allowed the most virulent congessional antagonists of the Cuban regime to begin to seize the policy initiative.

Clinton's victory in the presidential election brought to the White House someone who had promised to "bring the hammer down" on the Castro regime. Yet if the new president linked fully normalized relations to a political transition, there was no necessary consensus among newly appointed foreign policy officials over how best to bring this about. For those who defined the embargo as the "cornerstone of our policy,"[2] it meant cracking down even harder economically via "one of the most severe set of sanctions that there is on the books anyplace"[3]; to others, it meant exploring opportunities at the margins to engage the Cubans in more productive arrangements, and using whatever U.S. leverage existed to shape the development of a civil society on the island that might ultimately facilitate the revolution's demise. During the first three years of the Clinton presidency, however, domestic political imperatives and periodic crises resulting from continuing disfunctions in the bilateral relationship severely checked efforts of the latter kind, and exhausted the enthusiasm of those officials most closely associated with them. The 1994–5 migration crisis best demonstrates the reasons why.

Although much smaller in scale, the mid-1994 exodus of Cubans was reminiscient of the Mariel boatpeople crisis of 1980 that contributed to Clinton's defeat in his bid for reelection as governor of Arkansas. As a result, the drastic short-term decision was taken to house this latest wave of rafters at the Guantánamo Naval Base pending a more permanent destination. By early 1995, this decision showed signs of backfiring and seriously embarrassing the administration. Reports reaching the Oval Office warned that tens of thousands of Cubans housed in overcrowded facilities at the base might riot by the summer and fuel another outflow if Washington bowed to their demands. In solving this dilemma, another factor that Clinton had to take into account was the growing nationwide opposition to further unregulated refugee flows into the United States. CANF and its legislative allies, who were bent on encouraging Cubans to leave the island, were no longer the only important constituency in the equation. After weighing its options, the White House settled on direct negotiations with Havana. The outcome of these talks was a decision to reverse the decades-old U.S. support of automatic asylum for Cuban refugees intercepted in the Florida Straits.

What the resolution of the crisis revealed was that given the right combination of pressing needs that extended beyond the interests of the exile community, long-held shibboleths of Cuba policy could, and would, be ditched. The migration agreement also raised the possibility of future, albeit limited, initiatives by those administration liberals disposed to test the limits of U.S. policy. Yet with the president's domestic policy advisers sensitive to the sustained influence that CANF alone among groups with an interest in Cuba policy exercised, not even minor new openings occurred during the latter half of 1995.

Clinton policy toward Cuba reflected both continuity and change with the Reagan–Bush era. Although operating on the basis of the same underlying Cold War assumptions that motivated his predecessors, hopes of the imminent demise of the Castro regime were no longer given serious consideration. "I don't think anyone thought it was about to collapse," observed a senior Cuba official in the State Department. "We felt that they would somehow muddle through [the economic crisis]."[4] In sync with the president's inward looking focus, Cuba policy was driven more than ever by the imperatives of domestic politics. If the ideological fixation of getting rid of Castro remained part of the broader policymaking context, on a day-to-day level what differentiated the Clinton approach was its sheer convictionless quality: the willingness to subordinate rational decision making in the national interest broadly defined to political calculations narrowly arrived at, the perception that this president had no fixed policy position other than one dictated by electoral concerns, and his desire not to alienate key voting constituencies in Florida and New Jersey or those legislators who did their bidding on Capitol Hill. Humanitarian, religious, and other critics of Cuba policy as well as moderate voices within the Cuban-American community who were being courted by some Clinton officials as a possible alternative constituency remained disorganized and unfocused, and offered few prospects of developing as a viable countervailing force. In its absence, the administration's political calculus was that it could not afford to risk any permanent rupture with the anti-Castro hardliners who were mobilizing support for new draconian measures to deepen the crisis of the Cuban economy. The U.S. business community, whose interests were about to be most directly affected by this pressure to toughen the Cuba embargo, was slow to appreciate the full implications of unfolding developments, especially in the Congress, and would soon regret it.

To the extent that the White House was willing to engage Havana during Clinton's first administration it was via the measured or calibrated response to reforms implemented by the Castro regime. Yet, as U.S. officials themselves conceded, this was "a never fully defined policy,"[5] and it came as little surprise that Havana was never able to meet the infinitely slippery conditions for any response on Washington's part. Clinton's timidity in exploring this much-touted option was reinforced by a general lack of enthusiasm on the Hill for making any concessions whatsoever to Castro and the outright hostility of the anti-Castro legislators. A Senate Foreign Relations Committee staff member put it succinctly: "It wasn't taken seriously by the Congress. Only the Cuban-Americans took it seriously, and they didn't like it."[6]

The February 1996 shootdown by Cuban jet fighters of two civilian planes piloted by anti-Castro Miami exiles was a defining moment in U.S.–Cuba relations: It ended the administration's reluctance to sign the punitive Helms–Burton legislation, which codified the plethora of embargo regulations into law, thus handing substantial authority over the future of bilateral ties to Congress. This development, in turn, effectively laid to rest the notion of the calibrated response as a way of encouraging major internal policy shifts by the Castro government; Havana was left with no incentive to seek some kind of permanent accommodation with its northern neighbor. In principally targeting America's allies around the world, Helms–Burton also reaffirmed the profoundly unilateral nature of U.S.–Cuba policy. Once more, good policy was sacrificed on the altar of good politics.

From the tone of Washington's response, observers could reasonably have concluded that the shootdown killed off some major U.S. initiative under consideration at the time. Such was not the case. The incident occurred against a background of prior provocations by the Brothers to the Rescue group, and warnings they received from the Cuban government and the State Department about the danger of their actions. The visit by European Commission (EC) Vice President Manual Marin to Cuba in early February to negotiate a development aid agreement was also part of this larger context against which the shootdown and its response must be judged. A U.S. diplomat met with Marin and conveyed the White House demand that any European Union (EU)–Cuban agreement must be conditioned on Castro's promise to improve security and freedom of movement for dissident groups on the island. Once the EC vice president had departed the island, having delivered the Clinton message during talks with the Cuban leader, a new round-up of dissidents took place. What explained this seemingly counterproductive act were the conditions Washington sought to attach to the agreement: they mirrored the thrust of parts of the Helms–Burton legislation the White House was reluctant to sign until the shootdown. Whereas the CDA had focused on people-to-people contacts as a way of encouraging the growth of civil society in Cuba, Helms–Burton proposed a much more overtly defined agenda of promoting internal opposition to the regime. The administration, in other words, had already begun to undermine a cental plank of its own policy *prior* to the shootdown in an attempt to hasten the demise of the Cuban Revolution. This failure on the part of U.S. officials to place specific events within a larger context undermined their repeated assertions that the Castro regime was simply being irrational or vindictive, or had no interest in improving bilateral ties.

With Clinton's reelection in November, Cuba became a low-priority foreign policy issue if nonetheless a continuing irritant for the administration. There were no perceived domestic political payoffs to be gained from taking any innovative steps to improve relations against a background of relentless demands from anti-Castro lawmakers to increase the pressure on Havana. When State Department officials were queried about Cuba's exclusion from the politics of détente the U.S. was pursuing with what remained of the socialist bloc, they typically responded that, "It was a matter of domestic politics. There [is] just no will to change the policy and there [is] nothing to be gained by doing it."[7] Off the record, however, some administration policymakers conceded that they were at a loss to fully understand the logic of the approach being taken, did not believe it worked, and failed to discern how it served any broader U.S. national interest.

Nonetheless, Clinton showed no interest in exploiting potential political opportunities that presented themselves during his second term and could have provided a way out of the mire created by Helms–Burton, and the basis for a reassessment of Cuba policy. One was the loosening of CANF's grip on the exile community as moderate Cuban-American groups began to make themselves heard in the public debate following the death of Jorge Mas Canosa Sr. in late 1997. Clinton's basic response was to take refuge in congressional obstructionism led by the Foundation's allies who advocated the toughest possible measures to force Castro from power. Another was the pope's decision to visit Cuba in January 1998, which could have been exploited to mobilize domestic political support for debating a policy shift within a noncrisis environment. Instead, senior administration officials lobbied the Vatican to take advantage of the papal trip to bolster opposition forces inside Cuba and sideline Castro as much as possible.

A third missed opportunity was the January 1999 bipartisan report of the Council of Foreign Relations that proposed a series of recommendations intended to position the White House to play a key role in shaping the inevitable post-Castro political transition. The president's enthusiasm extended only to those recommendations that could be embraced within the current policy approach. Finally, the Elián González affair handed Clinton a propitious circumstance to review Cuba policy. Its origins coincided with the emergence of politically eclectic forces in Congress, the business community, and the broader foreign policy establishment lobbying for changes; and its resolution forced the anti-Castro forces in Washington and Miami to assess the political damage to their cause from being on the wrong side of the debate. The White House once again preferred the cowardly, low-risk option, restating its support for the embargo and confining any changes to the margins.

Clinton responded similarly to a different kind of opportunity – the congressional groundswell during 1999–2000 for lifting the ban on food and medical exports to Cuba. He chose to stand by while the pro-CANF's forces mobilized sufficient votes to impose conditions, notably the ban on public or private financing of sales, that virtually ensured few, if any, transactions, would proceed. Frustrated antisanctions business organizations were dismayed over the White House stance. "Waiting for Fidel Castro to die of natural causes," USA Engage Chairman William Lane caustically observed, "is not an activist foreign policy."[8]

As his eight years in the Oval Office drew to a close, the bankrupt nature of Clinton's Cuba policy also extended to the global arena, where efforts to persuade or bludgeon Western governments into subordinating their own national interests to the exigencies of America's Cuba policy had triggered conflicts that were still unresolved. Key allies not only refused to acquiesce in the global reach of U.S. national laws, but they also actively retaliated with countervailing domestic measures, including antidote laws (Mexico), federal blocking orders (Canada), and trading interest protection legislation (Britain), and openly denounced and/or challenged the legality of these extraterritorial laws (Cuban Democracy Act, Helms–Burton) in global and regional forums – the United Nations, the Organization of American States, the North American Free Trade Association, the European Union, and, last but not least, the World Trade Organization. Ironically, most of these are institutions that the United States played a key role in helping to establish. Today, all of them are platforms for the opponents of its Cuba policy.

Like an increasing number of Americans themselves, few, if any, governments subscribe to the U.S. conviction that heightened economic warfare is the best way to force Havana to implement the kind of domestic changes that Washington demands as a precondition for normalizing bilateral relations. On the contrary, they place a much higher value on proliferating economic ties and political dialog as more likely to produce results. Amid the ensuing acrimony and conflict this dispute engendered between the United States and its allies, however, the core disagreement has always been over means, not ends – over how best to promote the common goal of political and economic changes in Cuba. Whereas London, Paris, Ottawa, and other capitals have viewed Cuba's opening to the world market as part of an internal reform process already underway, Washington's dismissive posture continues to link real reforms to the toppling of the Castro regime from power. This extremist stance remains the *sine qua non* for any U.S. move toward engagement.

White House attempts to disrupt trade between Cuba and the rest of the world sharply contradicts its vigorous advocacy of a level playing field for all of the globe's trading partners. From the ban on Cuba trade by subsidiaries of U.S. multinational corporations based in third countries to the unprecedented resort to the doctrine of extraterritoriality that violates the sovereignty of competing capitalist countries, U.S. economic warfare against the island nation has raised the possibility of a challenge to the authority of free trade agreements. Although politically and ideologically motivated sanctions have tended not to affect such agreements to date, the Bush–Clinton push to internationalize domestic laws was certainly perceived as having the potential to do so. Even when President George W. Bush Jr. announced his decision in July 2001 to suspend the implementation of Title III of Helms–Burton for a further six months, he acknowledged that "real differences remain between the United States and our allies concerning the best methods for pursuing change in Cuba."[9]

In these circumstances, America's senior alliance partners have steadfastly refused to be bullied or cajoled into doing Washington's bidding by falling into line on Cuba. Claims by U.S. officials that they have succeeded in encouraging the Europeans and others to pay greater attention to human rights in their dealings with Cuba ring hollow on close inspection. With modest exceptions – usually related to multilateral rather than bilateral ties – the Europeans pretend to share Washington's concerns about the level of repression in Cuba and the White House pretends to be impressed by their concerns to stave off congressional demands for a more vigorous enforcement of the extraterritorial provisions of Helms–Burton.

The return to the world of a single superpower has not meant the revival of a unipolar globe. Economic competition and the pursuit of market share have replaced the ideological divisions of the Cold War era and North–South conflict, and have created new schisms in the post–Cold War era. For most countries, the key to solving today's problems is multilateralism – negotiating collective interests and agreed-upon means to pursue them. However, the United States has yet to cast off its unilateralism and learn to play by the new agreed-upon rules of the international game. That Washington would persist in risking good relations with its most important political allies and economic partners over the relatively minor issue of Cuba trade and investment is clear evidence of this reluctance to change. Even its alleged greater engagement with the international community after the September 11, 2001, terrorist attacks on New York and Washington was more illusory than real. As one of George W. Bush Jr.'s policy advisers candidly put it, in its war on terrorism, the White House was pursuing "multilateralism a la carte" – that is, alliance building that served U.S. interests without constraining U.S. actions.[10]

What the dispute over Cuba demonstrates is that just as Washington expected a prostrate Soviet Union to buckle to its demands to rupture economic ties with the island at the end of the Cold War, so it now expects Europe, Canada, Latin America, and other capitalist bloc countries to automatically subordinate economic (and diplomatic) interests to U.S. foreign objectives. Yet what it also demonstrates is that, unlike the Soviet Union and irrespective of the pressures exerted, America's allies are less willing than ever to bow to such demands – and certainly not without a fight. Although prepared to compromise, they are not prepared to surrender. Throughout the conflict over the CDA and Helms–Burton, they have remained singularly unimpressed by a policy based on the "might makes right" principle and resolutely determined not to abandon their national economic interests or relinquish their rights under international law in order to accommodate U.S. policy imperatives.

At the beginning of the twenty-first century, the United States is still the dominant global hegemon, based largely on its continuing military and ideological superiority. Yet its economic, and, to a lesser extent, political power are no longer uncontested. The world of the grand coalition to confront communism has been transformed into a world of proliferating rivalries and challenges as Washington's European allies in particular seek to more aggressively pursue their own agendas. One clear signal of this new global rivaly was the statement by Swedish Prime Minister Goeran Persson at the June 2001 U.S.–EU summit in Gothenburg that Europe's new global mission was to serve "as a balance to U.S. domination."[11] In an era increasingly defined by global economic competition, U.S. diktats on the conditions of international trade and capital flows are more likely to be resisted than in the past. Although the United States currently remains able to gain its way in settling most of these conflicts, the allied response to its Cuba sanctions suggests that winning such battles will become more difficult in the future.

Postscript: Washington's Last Cold War

> The cavalry has arrived with respect to sanctions on Castro.
> Rep. Lincoln Díaz-Balart on the Bush administration

THE 2000 presidential election result came as a welcome relief to anti-Castro forces in the United States after the buffeting they had taken that year: first, in the court of public opinion over their handling of the Elián González affair, and second, in the Congress over the vote to exempt food and medicine sales from the embargo on Cuba. The return of a republican to the White House promised a reversal in their fortunes: at a minimum, George W. Bush could be expected to hold the line against the pressure from farm and business interests to ease sanctions and the debt he owed Cuban-American voters in Florida raised the possibility that he might consider harsh additional measures to bring about the downfall of the Castro regime. The new administration, said Cuban American National Foundation's (CANF) Dennis Hays, had a chance to "make a mark" on Cuba policy. To Ileana Ros-Lehtinen, that meant a halt to the "trickling, weakening of the U.S. embargo day-to-day during the Clinton administration."[1] Lincoln Díaz-Balart had made his position clear in an April 2000 memo to the Bush election campaign: Any move toward normalized relations must be predicated on political democratization and the release of political prisoners.[2] The ever-apocalyptic chair of the Senate Foreign Relations Committee (SFRC) Jesse Helms went further. "Like a cat with nine lives, Fidel Castro is about to survive his ninth U.S. president," he told a gathering hosted by the American Enterprise Institute. "I have a message for Mr Castro: The last of the cat's nine lives has begun."[3] He advocated a policy approach focused on channeling material support to Castro's internal opponents, which had been employed successfully by a republican White House in the 1980s to destabilize the communist regime in Poland.

185

Early signs from Bush policymakers suggested this kind of optimism was not unfounded. Although some high-level appointees questioned the number and effectiveness of sanctions or opposed them in principle, Cuba was a designated special case. At his confirmation hearing, incoming Secretary of State Colin Powell dismissed Castro as "an aging starlet who will not change in this life-time" and told the Senate Foreign Relations Committee (SFRC) that the new administration "will have to keep containing him, and it is President-elect Bush's intention to keep the sanctions in place."[4] Easing sanctions could only undercut efforts to achieve the historic strategic goal of terminating the Castro regime and its revolution. "We should continue to keep the sanctions in place," Powell told Capitol Hill lawmakers in mid-March, "because [Castro] has demonstrated previously that if you start to release those sanctions or if you try to cooperate with him, he will find a way to use those resources to enhance and strengthen the regime." The only exception, echoing Helms, were funds that directly benefit the Cuban people and "opportunities to have some interchanges."[5]

Vice President Richard Cheney delivered much the same message only days after Bush's inauguration. His belief that "unilateral economic sanctions... don't work very well" did not apply to Cuba. "I don't think that there's any prospect of lifting those sanctions as long as Fidel Castro is there."[6] Meanwhile, Condoleezza Rice, Bush's choice to head the National Security Council, was busy reassuring exile hardliners that there would be no changes in Cuba policy until the island had made a transition to democracy.

The most prominent anti-Castro legislators were intent on ensuring this hard-line language was not empty rhetoric. With the February deadline for the publication of Commerce Department draft regulations governing food and medicine sales fast approaching, Helms and the new chair of the House International Relations Committee (HIRC) Henry Hyde (R-Ilinois) wrote to Secretary Donald Evans objecting to his department's support for a broad definition of the regulations that included a license exception for agricultural trade with Cuba. They received strong backing from Treasury officials who also argued for a stringent application of the regulations based on a case by case review of every license submission.[7] While the administration procrastinated on a final decision, Senators Chuck Hagel (R–Nebraska) and Christopher Dodd introduced a Cuba Food and Medicine Access Bill into Congress to free up Cuba trade by closing some of the loopholes in the Nethercutt amendment. Their measure would provide normal export financing for U.S. private sector exporters to Cuba, lift the ban on American ships carrying agricultural and medicine supplies to the island, and restore presidential flexibility on the issue of travel restrictions. The administration response was swift and emphatic. "We are not reviewing our policies with respect to exports to Cuba," Secretary Powell assured the SFRC.[8]

A number of key foreign policy appointments were powerful indicators that Cuba policy was more likely to be toughened than eased. Foremost among these was Bush's choice to be Assistant Secretary of State for Inter-American Affairs. Cuban exile Otto Reich had a formidable reputation in the 1980s as an anti-Communist ideolog and, in charge of the Office of Public Diplomacy, had played a leading role in the Reagan administration's covert anti-Sandinista program. A Washington lobbyist since 1994, his clients included Bacardi–Martini and a gaggle of anti-Castro Cuban groups whose interests he had worked hard to include in the drafting of the Helms–Burton legislation. Reich's strongest advocates included Lincoln Díaz-Balart (who called the choice "brilliant,"[9]) Jesse Helms and, last but not least, the president's brother, Florida Governor Jeb Bush.

Three other Cold War "warrior" appointments also boded ill for any moderation in Cuba policy: Elliott Abrams, named Senior Director of the NSC Office of Democracy, Human Rights and International Operations, had been an active participant in the covert war against Nicaragua as the State Department's highest ranking Latin Americanist; the newly appointed United Nations Ambassador John Negroponte, who, as U.S. Ambassador to Honduras between 1981 and 1985, ignored major human rights abuses by that country's armed forces while acting as a "point man" in Reagan efforts to topple the Nicaraguan government from power; and Roger Noriega, nominated to serve as the U.S. Ambassador to the Organization of American States, who had earned his stripes in the anti-Castro cause as the senior foreign policy adviser to Senator Helms during the 1990s.

With Bush and Cheney pontificating on the administration's unwavering commitment to keep the Cuba sanctions in place and ignoring overtures from Havana to open negotiations and the nomination of former Reagan hardliners to key Latin American posts, the message sent to the foreign policy bureaucracy was clear and unmistakable: It was business as usual when it came to Fidel Castro's government. The annual State Department report on narcotics control, for instance, did not list Cuba as a major drug transit country, but referred to it as "a country of concern."[10] That Cuban authorities had adopted a relatively tough approach in dealing with the problem – seizing more than 7.5 tons of drugs in 1995, 8.8 tons in 1999, and 13 tons in 2000[11] – seemed of little consequence to Washington, which once again failed to respond to Havana's call for a pact to fight drug trafficking in the subregion. In a speech at Georgetown University in August, former Clinton White House drug policy director, General Barry McCaffrey criticized Bush for letting such opportunities pass and Congress for repeatedly obstructing efforts to increase cooperation with Cuba on drug interdiction activities. "Our current policy is mistaken," he said, "and we do need to engage [the Cubans] on this issue."[12]

The department's annual Patterns of Global Terrorism, released in April, continued to list Cuba as a terrorist state on the still tenuous grounds that it provided a safe haven for Basque ETA terrorists and American fugitives and because of its ties to Colombia's two largest guerrilla movements. Washington, however, remained content to leave Afghanistan and Pakistan off the list, even though the report accused the Taliban of providing refuge for international terrorists, and Karachi of direct links to Kashmiri and other terrorist groups[13] – connections that would soon prove far more lethal to U.S. interests.

Meanwhile, efforts to isolate Cuba diplomatically intensified in the lead-up to the annual Geneva United Nations Human Rights Commission (UNHRC) vote on a resolution condemning Havana over its treatment of dissidents. Although Assistant Secretary of State Michael Parmly had described Cuba's human rights record as comparable with those of Burma and North Korea, Secretary Powell – again singling out Cuba for special attention – told House lawmakers that passage of the UNHRC resolution was "a priority" of the administration.[14] As it happened, there was another priority: to secure the deletion of a statement in the resolution, inserted by several European Union (EU) countries, criticizing the U.S. embargo of Cuba. Washington was successful on both counts: the offending words were removed and the amended resolution passed but by a narrow margin of twenty-two to twenty, with ten abstentions, including Brazil, Colombia, Ecuador, Mexico, and Peru. Given what one senior administration official termed "a real pressure strategy from the president to the embassies" to gain the votes of UNHCR members, the result was not the decisive outcome the White House sought.[15] To compound its frustration, the resolution's sponsor, the Czech Republic, gave an undertaking to Havana that it would not do Washington's bidding in the UNHRC again; only weeks later, the United States was voted off this international body for the first time since 1947 by governments (enemies and allies alike) who had become increasingly angered by its continued resort to unilateralism in pursuit of foreign policy goals.

Bush nevertheless applauded the UNHCR vote from Quebec, where he was attending another Cuba-free Summit of the Americas meeting. While there, he again highlighted the contradiction between Washington's approach to Cuba and its resolute defense of trade ties with China, despite the latter's inclusion on the State Department's list of major drug transiting countries and its record of large-scale human rights violations. "I still think we ought to trade with China," Bush told reporters, "because I think trade will not only help our economy and help people in our economy, like farmers, for example, I also know by spreading trade in the marketplace, it will enhance freedom."[16]

America's rice farmers could not have agreed more with that philosophy, or understand why their government refused to include an all but guaranteed market for them in a country that imported 400,000 tons of rice in 1999 and 450,000 tons in 2000. "We need help," complained an industry lobbyist. "We hear the administration is pro-trade . . . and here we have a country [Cuba] that is willing to help us move our product, and we have seen no movement at all [from the White House]."[17] Nor were they likely to in the foreseeable future. Opposing Cuba trade, declared one administration official, was a position from which the president would not budge: "[He] hopes that trade benefits all sectors of the economy, including the farming sector. But when it comes to Cuba . . . there won't be any changes."[18]

On another front, pressures from the Cuba lobby in Congress and its CANF allies to increase U.S. aid to antigovernment forces on the island under the program established by the Helms–Burton Act and administered by the Agency for International Development (AID) were steadily building. In May, Senators Helms and Lieberman dusted off their Cuban Solidarity Act legislation that proposed a four-year, $100 million program of direct assistance to anti-Castro groups and individuals. One congressional staffer argued that such a proposal did not fall under the authority of AID as it was "basically a covert aid program for Cuba." Just as concerning, he said, "We don't even know who the final recipients are [and] the host government doesn't accept it. It's nuts."[19] The bill provided for a modest increase in the programming budgets of Radio and TV Martí and instructed Attorney General John Ashcroft to investigate high-level official Cuban involvement in the 1996 shootdown with a view to prosecution. CANF was also busy seeking to lift its profile in the aftermath of the Elián González affair. In February, it opened a "Free Cuban Embassy" in Washington as part of what new executive director, Joe García, had earlier called an effort to "reengage America's conscience." Three months later, Dennis Hays implicitly acknowledged the growing antisanctions mood in Congress when he said it was time to change the debate on Cuba. "The argument should not be about our embargo," Hays said. "It should be how do we promote peaceful, democratic change in Cuba."[20]

Against the background of these legislative activities and the shift in CANF tactics, Bush made his first comprehensive Cuba policy statement. In a May 18 Cuban Independence Day address, he described the Cuba sanctions as "not just a policy tool, [but also] a moral statement" and emphasized that his administration would oppose any attempt to weaken the embargo until the regime frees political prisoners, permits freedom of speech, and holds democratic elections. "The policy of our government is not merely to isolate Castro, but to actively support those working to bring about democratic change in Cuba," Bush told the assembled guests.[21] For this reason, he supported the Helms–Lieberman bill as well as a new version of the Cuban Internal Opposition Assistance Act first introduced into the House by Lincoln Díaz-Balart and Robert Menéndez in 1999. Where the Clinton administration had toyed with encouraging the development of civil society in Cuba, the hallmark of Bush's approach would be a concerted attempt to fuel internal opposition while maintaining maximum external pressure on the regime.

Dissidents on the island wasted no time in condemning this approach. To Elizardo Sánchez, the president of the Cuban Commission on Human Rights, it was a "mistaken policy" that would only increase tensions across the Florida Straits, lead to more attacks on prodemocracy activists, and hamper the transition to democracy. Ohalys Victores, a journalist with Cuba Voz Agency, observed that genuine dissidents do not benefit from this kind of aid, and his organization was "unaware of the destination" of any such assistance.[22] In June, two independent Cuban trade union activists, writing in the *New York Times*, argued that the proposed legislation would only divide the antiregime activitists "into haves and have nots" and stunt democratic political initiatives.[23] Even among State Department officials doubts about the strategy persisted. "We are committed to doing more to encourage human rights activists and other dissidents, but we're finding it difficult to find ways," said one. "The problem is how to encourage dissidents," said another. "It's very difficult. Cuba's a police state; they're very good at thwarting our efforts down there, and it doesn't make much sense to do anything that is going to get people thrown in jail." What constituted effective assistance also had to be considered carefully. "There's no point in sending down information people won't take. There is no point in sending polemical information."[24]

Yet the White House confronted a more pressing problem – growing dissatisfaction among segments of the anti-Castro camp that its policy practice did not match its rhetoric. Inviting Cuban-Americans to the White House for Independence Day celebrations, appointing them to key posts in the administration, promised support for the pending Helms–Lieberman bill, and a sharp increase in the number of fines levied on U.S. citizens defying Cuba travel restrictions were "greatly appreciated," said one republican congressional staffer, "but they are symbols. Title III [of Helms–Burton that enabled American citizens to take legal action against foreign companies found trafficking in confiscated Cuban properties] is the meat."[25] Anti-Castro lawmakers led by Robert Menéndez were still urging the White House to make an example of Spain's Sol Melia hotel group. Bush, however, was being subjected to precisely the same contradictory pressures that Clinton faced over implementing Title III: The EU provided guarantees to Sol Meliá that it would not tolerate U.S. sanctions against the group over its Cuba investments and threatened a WTO challenge if Washington took such a step. Spanish officials and those of one other major European government visited Washington and "raised the issue at extremely high levels" of the administration."[26] No doubt aware of Europe's view on this matter, Secretary of State Powell had earlier told the HIRC that a waiver would be considered "only when we believe there are serious, great, overriding national interests for which waiver authority is provided."[27]

As the actual decision neared, however, it seemed only a substantive trade-off would convince proponents of a Title III determination that those conditions had been met. For one thing, there was still an expectation that this White House would implement Helms–Burton more aggressively than had its predecessor, especially in view of the Act's limited success so far in deterring foreign investment in Cuba. Then, when Fidel Castro momentarily almost collapsed during an outdoor speech in Havana at the end of June, CANF leaders and other opponents of the revolution felt more confident than they had since the early 1990s that the regime was fast approaching its nadir.[28] One last major initiative by the White House might be all that was required to push it into oblivion. No such optimism flourished within the foreign policy bureaucracy – or at least not for long. "There's nobody that I talk to around anymore who talks like that," said one official in the State Department. "People say Castro could last another ten years. He may fall over tomorrow, but nobody [in this administration] is going to say that Castro's on his last legs."[29]

The eventual release of the regulations governing food and medicine sales to Cuba on July 12 disappointed those hoping to keep maximum pressure by authorizing the narrowest possible interpretation of what Congress intended when it originally passed the law: a midcourse had been struck between Commerce and Treasury. More promising was the president's announcement twenty-four hours later of new measures to strengthen the embargo and assist the "democratic opposition" inside Cuba. Dissidents and human rights activists would receive an undetermined increase in funds; the newly appointed director of the Office of Cuba Broadcasting, Salvador Lew, was authorized to "use all available leads to overcome the jamming" of TV Martí; Treasury was instructed to provide more funds to enforce restrictions on remittances to Cuba, to be accompanied by a crackdown on unlicensed travel to the island; and Bush committed his administration to "oppose any attempt to weaken sanctions against the Castro regime" in the absence of political redemocratization.[30]

The sanctions reference was a scarcely disguised challenge to the recently introduced Bridges to the Cuban People Act, sponsored by a bipartisan group of legislators in both the House and Senate, that would eliminate restrictions on food and medicine exports to Cuba, and repeal codification of the embargo under Helms–Burton. Repeating his Independence Day remarks, Bush defended the existing sanctions regime as "not just a policy, but a moral statement."[31] Soon after, he formally nominated Otto Reich to run inter-American relations at State; Elliot Abrams to take charge of democracy and human rights issues at the NSC; Mauricio Tamargo, a Cuban-American and former legal counsel to Ros-Lehtinen, to chair the Federal Claims Settlement Commission; and Rogelio Pardo-Maurer, a Washington lobbyist for the Nicaragua contras, to be Deputy Assistant Secretary of Defense for Western Hemisphere Affairs.[32] At Treasury's Office of Foreign Assets Control, officials were now charged with rigorously enforcing travel laws to Cuba, safe in the knowledge that "the letter of the law *is* the letter of the law."[33] On July 16, against this background of a trade-off in harsher measures against Cuba, the president announced that Title III of Helms–Burton would be waivered for another six months.

Although leading members of the Cuban-American community in Miami and Washington regretted the decision, most concurred with CANF's Joe García, that "nonetheless, we feel that this administration is moving forward to bring about democracy in Cuba."[34] Diaz-Balart understood the president's desire to avoid a trade war with Europe in the WTO "over a single title of Helms–Burton at this time, [which] would dangerously strengthen the coalition of those seeking to eliminate the entire embargo." He praised Bush as the "strongest and truly indispensible factor standing between the Clinton-created anti-embargo coalition and the elimination of the embargo."[35] Jesse Helms cautioned against being "overly critical of the decision today [because] President Bush's posture toward Castro is very clear, whereas his predecessor's was fuzzy." Critics, he said, failed to appreciate that the president "is, in fact, taking a very tough line, which is certain to make Fidel Castro squirm."[36] One of the few discordant voices was Robert Menéndez, who accused Bush of reneging on his promise to get tough with Castro: "On his first opportunity to show his true colors, the president was dishonest and weak and has failed the Cuban people."[37] Yet, while CANF Vice President Dennis Hays affirmed the community's trust in Bush's judgment that the "timing was not quite right,"[38] the latter's decision to exercise the Clinton waiver made it increasingly unlikely that such a time would ever arrive.

To the antisanctions lobby, another Title III waiver was small comfort. All it signified to USA Engage Chairman William Lane was that "Helms–Burton is a dead letter in the sense that no change is expected [from the Clinton strategy]."[39] Nonetheless, it remained the law of the land, and as one U.S. official commented, "There was a lot of relief among the Europeans with the waiver decision and the extent of relief has led people to forget that there's a Title IV [barring senior executives of companies trafficking in confiscated property from entry to the United States]. That could still come up."[40] The Clinton White House had invoked this provision to deny visas to executives of Canada's Sherritt International, Mexico's Grupo Domos, and the Israeli-owned citrus company BM.

Those business organizations leading the fight against the sanctions regime in general viewed Bush's commitment to stay tough on Cuba as unshakeable. "There is absolutely no sign in the administration of any shift away from a hardline on Cuba," said one prominent lobbyist, "and we have no expectation that there is going to be any change."[41] This pessimism elicited no denial from State Department officials: "Business doesn't talk to us because they know what the policy is, and if they come to us they know we'll tell them what the policy is."[42] Yet an intransigent White House is not the only formidable obstacle to mustering support for a new business assault on the sanctions in place. The community itself is "divided and does not speak with one voice" and, with the exception of agricultural groups, "is not going to lead the charge for changes. A lot of companies are not going to be against [Cuba trade]. It's a question of the amount of energy and political capital they're prepared to put in."[43] To the extent that there exists a community consensus, it is confined to an in-principle opposition to sanctions in general or what William Lane termed "a lazy man's foreign policy."[44] Firms with a specific interest in the Cuba market, observed another antisanctions business lobbyist, have resigned themselves to "waiting for Fidel to die."[45]

Other developments, however, suggested that the latest Title III waiver might well be the high-water mark on Cuba sanctions. In Miami, the CANF leadership had begun to fracture seriously. In late July, Ninoska Pérez Castellon, a spokesperson and foundation board member, resigned from the organization, accusing Jorge Mas Jr. of betraying its traditional hardline anti-Castro stance in favor of a greater willingness to compromise on key issues. Within weeks, another twenty CANF board members quit as well, citing a variety of complaints against Jorge Mas ranging from a dictatorial leadership style based on alleged efforts to take full control of the Foundation's finances to his support for Miami hosting the Latin Grammy Awards as proof that he and his allies had gone soft on Castro's regime.[46]

Still, CANF's implosion at this time had less implications for Cuba policy than might have been the case a decade earlier. Not only had the epicenter of anti-Castro policy influence shifted to Capitol Hill, especially since the 1996 shootdown, but with the election of George W. Bush Jr., exile hardliners now had a powerful ally and a direct link to the White House in the person of Florida Governor Jeb Bush. At a February 24 meeting with leaders of the Cuban-American community, Jeb Bush reassured the group that he would do all in his power to press on the White House the necessity for maintaining a hardline Cuba policy. One of his first initiatives was to lobby his brother in support of the Reich appointment. The interconnected political fates of the Bush brothers had created a new dynamic in the domestic politics of Cuba policy that more than counterbalanced the turmoil within CANF ranks. "Jeb Bush is very close to Díaz-Balart and Ros Lehtinen, and the administration listens to them on issues pertaining to Cuba," explained a State Department Cuba official. "CANF plays a less important role because there is this much more important channel to the White House." Yet another department regional affairs specialist was quick to dismiss any notion that the Foundation had ceased to be an important player in the Cuba policy equation. It is, he said, "still the biggest [Cuban-American] organization by miles."[47] According to a former senior Clinton Commerce Department official now active in the anti-sanctions movement, CANF's relations with the Bush administration are as tight as ever: "Clinton saw the demographics of South Florida changing. He saw the cracks in CANF. He was driven by political expediency, but in a more sophisticated way. On the republican side there is not the same kind of probing for cracks, looking for dissent, trying to take the temperature of the Cuban-American community. They're locked in step."[48]

A second development with potentially far-reaching implications for Cuba policy was the decision in late May by Vermont Senator James Jeffords to leave the Republican Party – a move that returned control of that Chamber to the Democrats. Delaware's Joseph Biden replaced Jesse Helms as chair of the Committee on Foreign Relations, and Christopher Dodd took charge of the Sub-committee on Western Hemisphere Affairs. Both were political moderates not imbued with the kind of visceral or ideological hostility toward Castro that had characterized the Helms's stewardship. Anti-sanctions business leaders were pleased that Helms had been replaced by someone who was "less predictable, more moderate, and a more thoughtful voice. Biden won't prevent things from being considered like Helms would."[49] Nor was Cuba a front-burner issue for the new chair as it had been for Helms. Scheduled hearings on the Helms–Lieberman legislation, according to a committee staffer, were unlikely anytime soon.[50]

Coinciding with this shift in the balance of power was the appearance of a more broad-based support for at least some limited changes in Cuba policy. On July 25, the House of Representatives approved for the second year running an amendment to the 2002 Treasury Department appropriations bill, "strongly op-pose[d]" by the administration, blocking funds to enforce restrictions on travel to Cuba. Of the 240 (to 186) votes in favor of the amendment, introduced by Jeff Flake (R–Arizona), 67 were Republicans, many of whom had consistently sided with CANF in the past on issues related to Cuba. The antisanctions forces called it an "unexpected victory,"[51] while CANF interpreted the vote as sending a very clear message to its constituency: "As you can see with that vote," said Dennis Hays, "the embargo is not a winning issue for us." Secure in his belief that the president was firmly committed to maintaining the embargo in the absence of major changes in Cuba, Jorge Mas Jr. agreed: "We [now] need to talk about different things."[52]

Although Bush threatened a veto if the Senate approved the travel measure, another potential confrontation beckoned in the form of amendments to appropriations bills prepared by Bryon Dorgan (D–North Dakota) to repeal all restrictions on export finance and travel to Cuba. However, the administration was not doing battle only with Congress as it sought to reaffirm its credentials with Cuba hardliners. In early August, the White House bowed to intense lobbying by the exile community and its lawmakers to exempt twenty Cuban rafters intercepted at sea by the U.S. Coast Guard from the "wet foot/dry foot" policy and allow them to be landed on American territory. Ostensibly, these rafters were material witnesses in an Immigration and Naturalization Service investigation into people-smuggling operations on the island. Coast Guard officials believed that during the previous twelve months, those Cubans reaching the mainland were "almost exclusively" being smuggled across the Florida Straits at fees of up to $10,000 per person.[53] Although Bush dismissed any suggestion of a shift away from the "wet foot/dry foot" policy, a precedent had been set, and there was no reason to doubt that opponents of the 1994 migration agreement would seek to exploit it in the future.

Globally, Bush maintained Cuba's exclusion from his policy of détente or efforts at rapprochement with virtually all other Third World countries with which the United States had serious outstanding disagreements. Ignoring the passage of a resolution by the European Parliament opposing China's bid to host the 2008 Olympic games, the White House announced that it would not actively lobby against Beijing's candidacy. Awarding the games to China on this occasion, said a State Department official, would be a "powerful but tangible incentive" for the Asian giant to improve its human rights record.[54] The case of North Korea was equally revealing of the contradictions in U.S. policy. Testifying before a House Committee in mid-June, Assistant Secretary of State James Kelly referred to a scheduled meeting between officials of both countries to renew discussions over security and economic issues: "We have some important interests to pursue and we're going to do so *without any preconditions.*"[55] In Seoul two weeks later, Secretary Powell said that the United States was ready to begin a dialog with North Korea at a time of its choosing and "without preconditions."[56] The White House subsequently put a damper on Powell's apparent eagerness.[57] Even so, the general approach still contrasted sharply with the wall of silence that greeted Cuban overtures to Washington.

America's solution to the problem of Cuba continued to dismay its major allies. They failed to comprehend the logic of a policy approach based on the proposition that of all the countries that were part of the Cold War socialist bloc, only Cuba was immune from engagement as a step toward normalizing bilateral relations. The European and Canadian governments remained committed to precisely the same kind of formula that Powell articulated for dealing with North Korea, notwithstanding the sensitivities of the Cuban leadership to international criticism of its human rights record and its domestic political arrangements. Castro's angry responses might lead to a temporary downward spiral in diplomatic ties, but neither the Europeans nor the Canadians have been sufficiently discouraged to the extent that they are willing to stop persisting and acknowledge that the U.S. punitive approach works. In late August, for instance, a delegation of EU officials led by its president Louis Michel arrived in Havana to iron out problems in the relationship. Bitter at a number of Western European nations for supporting the American-sponsored UNHCR resolution condemning the government's treatment of dissidents in April 2000, Cuba had canceled an EU ministers' visit and withdrew its application for membership of the multilateral trade and aid pact between the EU–African, Caribbean, and Pacific group of nations. Now, said Michel, it was important to resume the political dialog "as fast as possible [and] without one side imposing conditions on the other."[58]

The September 11 terrorist attacks on New York and Washington reduced all such developments at home and abroad in the debate over Cuba policy to mere curiosities. Dorgan's amendments to repeal all U.S. travel restrictions to Cuba were an immediate casualty, dropped to facilitate the rapid passage of antiterrorist legislation through the Senate. Castro denounced this "atrocious and insane terrorist act,"[59] offered material assistance in the effort to track down the perpetrators, and Cuba's cooperation in the global war against terrorism. The White House summarily rejected the former but remained open to any useful intelligence information the Cubans might be able to provide. Its reluctance to actively pursue cooperation with Havana was partly bound up in domestic politics – what one American official termed "the political firestorm such an arrangement would cause among Cuban-Americans."[60] U.S. officials also doubted Cuba could provide helpful intelligence about the world of Islamic fundamentalists in contrast to other countries (Iran, Syria, Libya, Sudan) on the State Department's list of sponsors of international terrorism.

A sensitive subject at the best of times, possible intelligence cooperation was further complicated by the arrest of the Defense Intelligence Agency's senior

Cuba analyst, Ana Belen Montes, less than two weeks after the September attacks, on charges of providing classified defense information to the Castro government. This development was guaranteed to make it more difficult for those on the American side who would be responsible for taking the initiative in this area. A cooling in the atmosphere soon followed, reflected in the Bush administration decision to impose travel restrictions on the Cuban diplomats in Washington.[61]

The administration's hastily crafted antiterrorist legislation had the potential to inflict collateral damage on Cuba. In its original form, the bill proposed to suspend the 2000 Trade Sanctions Reform Act (TSRA) and grant the president broad new powers to impose unilateral food and medicine sanctions against a nation deemed complicit in terrorist actions, drug trafficking, or the spread of weapons of mass destruction. Negotiations with the Senate Judiciary Committee finally produced slight modifications of the TSRA that minimized any significant repercussions for food and medicine sales to Cuba.[62] Nevertheless, the Castro government remained vulnerable to U.S. retaliation, despite announcing it would sign twelve U.N. treaties aimed at fighting international terrorism, merely by dint of the State Department's refusal to delete it from the list of terrorist states.

A senior State official dismissed calls from critics of the embargo, including prominent Cuban-Americans, that Cuba be removed from the list, as nothing but an attempt to take advantage of the events of September 11 "to scrub the list of countries which were placed on it for political reasons. This logic is painfully contrived, and the effort has *no, no* chance of success whatever."[63] This sentiment meshed perfectly with the views of the Cuban-American leadership. CANF's Dennis Hays argued that Cuba's "long history" of support for terrorism dictated that it stay on the list.[64] Reportedly in "close touch" with Bush officials,[65] lawmakers Lincoln Díaz-Balart and Ileana Ros-Lehtinen demanded additional measures be taken; combatting terrorism worldwide required more pressure on the Castro regime, in particular, a strengthening of the embargo.

For Cuba, however, the worst was yet to come. On October 18, Russian President Vladimir Putin abruptly announced that Moscow was closing its electronic surveillance base at Lourdes, from which Havana benefited to the tune of at least $200 million a year in rent, and was withdrawing an estimated 1,500 Russian troops and technicians based on the island. The Clinton administration had resisted the efforts of anti-Castro lawmakers to get the White House to cut annual U.S. economic assistance and credits to Russia by an equivalent amount to that Moscow paid the Cubans on the grounds that Lourdes contributed to the management of the nuclear strategic balance, and that its closure would in turn threaten U.S. signals intelligence facilities elsewhere that perform a similar function. Now Moscow was buckling for reasons of its own – according to the Russians, high costs and budgetary issues loomed large in the decision.[66] Irrespective of Putin's motivation, however, the Lourdes closure was consistent with Moscow's renewed interest in forging a new strategic understanding with a Bush White House determined to pursue a nuclear missile defense system. The decision also reflected a desire to capitalize on the post–September 11 improvement in relations as a result of Putin's extraordinarily active support for the U.S. war against terrorism. While attending the APEC summit in Shanghai, U.S. Secretary of State Powell met with his Russian counterpart the same day Putin announced the Lourdes closure and praised the decision as ushering in a new era of cooperation. "Not only is the Cold War over," declared Powell, "the post–Cold War period is also over."[67] The temperature of U.S.–Cuba relations, however, was as chilly as ever.

The first commercial transactions between Cuba and the United States in four decades did little to lower the temperature. Washington's decision to allow this sale of food and medicines to Cuba had its origins in the worst hurricane (Michelle) to hit the island in almost half a century and largely replicated the Clinton White House response to Hurricane Lilli in October 1996. On that occasion, the President waived a ban on flights to the island and licensed a one-off shipment of supplies under pressure from the Cuban-American community. This time, the Cuban government refused the offer of disaster relief but agreed to pay hard currency for up to $40 million worth of goods purchases directly from American companies – which was made possible by legislation passed by the Congress in 2000. However, the Bush White House refused Havana's demand that the strict regulations it had attached to such sales be lifted as well as Castro's proposal that Cuban vessels transport the purchased items from the mainland to the island.[68]

Not surprisingly, Cuban Vice President Carlos Lage dismissed any notion that the sales were the precursor of a fundamental shift in U.S. policy.[69] Senior Bush policymakers could not agree more. In early December, then Acting Secretary of State for Inter-American Affairs Lino Gutiérrez – himself a Cuban-American hardliner – assured a Miami gathering that the embargo remained firmly in place. "The United States has not changed any rules," he insisted, "*or moved in any way to encourage these sales.*"[70] That same day, the White House issued a statement reiterating the President's strong opposition to a Senate Agriculture Committee proposal to allow private U.S. financing of food sales to Cuba.

Twelve years after the collapse of the Soviet Union, the U.S. government remained wedded as firmly as ever to a Cold War approach to Cuba. At home, it denied American companies and agricultural producers the opportunity to realize the full potential of a small but lucrative market in the Caribbean. Abroad,

Washington's policy almost totally isolated it from the rest of the international community. In the hemisphere, all but two countries had reestablished full diplomatic relations with the island; at the global level, the November 2001 annual U.N. General Assembly nonbinding resolution calling on the U.S. to end the trade embargo was carried by a vote of 167 to 3. Major American allies in Europe, Canada and Latin America fail to comprehend the logic of a policy approach still based on the notion that Cuba remains the only member of the Cold War socialist bloc immune from "engagement" as a step toward normalizing bilateral ties.

As the Bush administration began its second year, prospects for any shift in Washington's hardline policy toward Cuba appeared bleak. To mollify potential critics of its decision to waive implementation of Title III of Helms–Burton for another six months, the White House announced the recess appointment of Otto Reich as Assistant Secretary of State for Inter-American Affairs (whose nomination had been blocked by Senate Democrats during 2001) and the choice of Cuban-American Army colonel, Emilio Gonzalez, as NSC Western Hemisphere Director for the Caribbean and Central America.[71] Castro's support for bilateral drug interdiction efforts, cooperation in the war against terrorism, and offer to help facilitate the housing of Taliban and Al Qaeda prisoners at the Guantánamo Naval Base (by providing medicine supplies and sanitation programs) were summarily dismissed in language reminiscent of the Clinton years. "Cuba has not taken any of the steps necessary to make improvement of relations possible," insisted the State Department's Richard Boucher."[72] In Havana, Vicki Huddleston, the principal officer of the U.S. Interest Section labelled the Cuban overtures "a façade [and] all cosmetic."[73] It was unlikely that the Castro government would, or more importantly could, take 'steps' deemed worthy of a positive Bush White House response in the foreseeable future.

Notes

INTRODUCTION

1. Quoted in Youssef M. Ibrahim, "U.N. Votes, 157-2, in Nonbinding Referendum Against U.S. Embargo of Cuba," *New York Times*, October 15, 1998, p. 9.
2. President George Bush, "America Must Remain Engaged," in U.S. Department of State, *Dispatch*, December 21, 1992, pp. 893–95.
3. Anthony Lake, "From Containment to Enlargement," in U.S. Department of State, *Dispatch*, September 27, 1993, pp. 658–64.

CHAPTER 1

1. Patrick J. Kiger, *Squeeze Play: The United States, Cuba and the Helms–Burton Act*. Washington DC: Center for Public Integrity, 1997, p. 25.
2. On the economic mobility of Cuban-Americans, see Miguel González-Pando, *The Cuban Americans*. Westport CT: Greenwood Press, 1998, pp. 116–39.
3. Quoted in Peter H. Stone, "Cuban Clout," *National Journal*, February 20, 1983, p. 450.
4. Quoted in Lourdes Meluza, "La Causa: Exiles Redirect Their Efforts," *Miami Herald*, April 13, 1986. [Reprinted in Information Services on Latin America, hereafter ISLA].
5. Quoted in González-Pando, *The Cuban-Americans*, p. 158. Also see Mariá Cristina García, *Havana USA: Cuban Exiles and Cuban Americans in South Florida, 1956–1994*. Berkeley: University of California Press, 1996, pp. 146–7.
6. William M. LeoGrande, *Our Own Backyard*. Chapel Hill: University of North Carolina Press, 1998, p. 146.
7. George Gedda, "The Cuba Lobby," *Foreign Service Journal*, June 1993, p. 26.
8. Quoted in Susan Epstein and Mark P. Sullivan, *Radio and Television Broadcasting to Cuba: Background and Current Issues*. Congressional Research Service, August 5, 1994, p. 3.
9. Gaeton Fonzi, "Who Is Jorge Mas Canosa?" *Esquire*, January 1993, p. 122.
10. John Spicer Nichols, "The Power of the Anti-Fidel Lobby," *The Nation*, October 24, 1988, pp. 389–91.
11. Kiger, *Squeeze Play*, p. 30.

12. Ann Louise Bardach, "Our Man in Miami," *New Republic*, October 3, 1994, p. 22.
13. Gedda, "The Cuba Lobby," p. 26.
14. Interview with Andrew Semmel, Washington DC, May 14, 1999. Foreign affairs adviser to Senator Richard Lugar since 1987.
15. Interview with Vicki Huddleston, Washington DC, May 17, 1999. Deputy Coordinator and Coordinator/Director, Office of Cuban Affairs, Department of State, mid-1989 to June 1993.
16. Interview with Michael Skol, Washington DC, May 6, 1999. Deputy Assistant Secretary of State for South America, 1990; Principal Deputy Secretary of State for Inter-American Affairs, 1993 to 1995.
17. Stone, "Cuban Clout," pp. 450–1.
18. Scott Sleek, "Mr. Mas Goes to Washington," *Common Cause Magazine*, January/February 1991, p. 37.
19. See Phil Brenner and Saul Landau, "Passive Aggression," *NACLA Report on the Americas*, November 1990, pp. 19–20.
20. Quoted in Kiger, *Squeeze Play*, p. 33.
21. Interview with Richard Nuccio, Falls Church, Virginia, May 20, 1999. Staff aide to congressman Robert Torricelli, summer 1991 to July 1993, with special responsibility for Cuba affairs; Department of State Cuba official and White House Special Representative on Cuba, July 1993 to April 1996.
22. Fonzi, "Who Is Jorge Mas Canosa?" p. 119; Larry Rohter, "A Rising Cuban-American Leader," *New York Times*, October 29, 1992, p. 18.
23. Quoted in Carla Anne Robbins, "Dateline Washington: Cuban-American Clout," *Foreign Policy*, Fall 1992, p. 163.
24. Quoted in Bill Gertz, "Castro Still Backing Subversives but Wants to Shed 'Violent' Image," *Washington Times*, February 14, 1989, p. A4.
25. Telephone interview with Robert Morley, Washington DC, May 19, 1999. Coordinator, Office of Cuban Affairs, Department of State, mid-1988 to mid-1991; Latin American Director, National Security Council Staff, summer 1991 to June 1993.
26. Gillian Gunn, *Cuba in Transition*. New York: Twentieth Century Fund, 1993, p. 18.
27. Quoted in Linda Feldmann, "Why Castro Is Freeing Prisoners," *Christian Science Monitor*, January 12, 1989, p. 7.
28. Quoted in "No Thaw with Cuba, Baker Says," *Miami Herald*, March 29, 1989 [ISLA] [our emphasis]. During his confirmation hearings, Baker stated that "Castro's continuing support for subversion and instability in [Latin America] make it extremely difficult for us to talk about normalizing relations at this stage of the game." U.S. Congress, Senate, Committee on Foreign Relations, *Nomination of James A. Baker III*, 101st Cong., 1st sess., January 17 and 18, 1989, p. 85.
29. Quoted in David Remnick and Julia Preston, "Gorbachev Attacks U.S. Regional Roles," *Washington Post*, April 5, 1989, p. A1.
30. See Claes Brundenius, *Revolutionary Cuba: The Challenge of Economic Growth with Equity*. Boulder: Westview Press, 1984; Andrew Zimbalist and Susan Eckstein, "Patterns of Cuban Development: The First Twenty-Five Years," *World Development*, Vol. 15, No. 1, January 1987, pp. 10–17; "Cuba Warns Creditors on

Loans and Trade Squeeze," *Latin American Regional Reports: Caribbean*, May 9, 1986, p. 1; Andrew Zimbalist, "Cuban Political Economy and Cubanology: An Overview," in Zimbalist, ed., *Cuban Political Economy*. Boulder: Westview Press, 1998, p. 11; A.R.M. Ritter, "Cuba's Convertible Currency Debt Problem," *Cepal Review*, No. 36, December 1988, especially pp. 127–33; Andrew Zimbalist, "Teetering on the Brink: Cuba's Current Economic and Political Crisis," *Journal of Latin American Studies*, Vol. 24, Part 2, May 1992, pp. 407–18.

31. See Joseph B. Treaster, "Castro Scorning Gorbachev Model," *New York Times*, January 11, 1989, p. 10.

32. Quoted in Remnick and Preston, "Gorbachev Attacks U.S. Regional Roles," p. A22.

33. Quoted in David Remnick and Julia Preston, "Soviet in Cuba Criticizes Export of Revolution," *Washington Post*, April 4, 1989, p. A1.

34. Quoted in Remnick and Preston, "Gorbachev Attacks U.S. Regional Roles," p. A1.

35. See Raymond L. Garthoff, *The Great Transition: American–Soviet Relations and the End of the Cold War*. Washington DC: Brookings Institution, 1994, p. 742.

36. Quoted in Remnick and Preston, "Gorbachev Attacks U.S. Regional Roles," p. A22.

37. See Gillian Gunn, "Will Castro Fall?" *Foreign Policy*, No. 79, Summer 1989, pp. 137–8; "Cuba Kicks Off Plan to Export Medical Supplies," *Times of the Americas*, May 29, 1991, p. 14; Economist Intelligence Unit, *Quarterly Economic Review of Cuba*, May 1989, p. 17; Howard W. French, "Castro Flirts with Capitalism to Stave Off Collapse," *New York Times*, December 5, 1990, p. 18; Michael White, "Castro Courts International Visitors," *Christian Science Monitor* (International Weekly Edition), July 13–19, 1990, p. 10B; "Betting on Tourism as Exchange Earner," *Latin American Weekly Report*, June 13, 1991, p. 8.

38. U.S. Congress, House, Committee on Foreign Affairs, Subcommittee on Western Hemisphere Affairs, *Cuba and the United States: Thirty Years of Hostility and Beyond*, 101st Cong., 1st sess., August 1, 2, September 20, 21, 27, 1989, pp. 90–1.

39. Ibid., pp. 90, 153.

40. See Brenner and Landau, "Passive Aggression," p. 14.

41. U.S. Congress, House, *Cuba and the United States*, p. 91.

42. Quoted in Morris H. Morley, *Imperial State and Revolution: The United States and Cuba, 1952–1986*. New York: Cambridge University Press, p. 277.

43. Michael Kozak, in U.S. Congress, House, *Cuba and the United States*, p. 167.

44. Quoted in Paul Bedard, "Bush Says Castro Is Out of Touch with Rest of World," *Washington Times*, August 17, 1989, p. A3.

45. Quoted in Leogrande, *Our Own Backyard*, p. 554.

46. Aronson and Baker, quoted in Michael R. Beschloss and Strobe Talbott, *At the Highest Levels*. London: Warner Books, 1993, p. 57.

47. Quoted in Ibid.

48. Quoted in Don Oberdorfer, *From Cold War to a New Era*. Baltimore: Johns Hopkins University Press, 1998, pp. 40–1.

49. Quoted in Beschloss and Talbott, *At the Highest Levels*, p. 105.

50. Quoted in Ibid., p. 156.
51. George Bush and Brent Scowcroft, *A World Transformed*. New York: Alfred A. Knopf, 1998, pp. 163, 165. In the case of El Salvador, administration officials charged that the Cubans were still channeling weapons to the FMLN guerrillas; all that had changed was the primary transit point for deliveries, from Nicaragua to Mexico. See "U.S. Says Cuba Sends Arms to Salvadorans via Mexico," *Washington Post*, December 26, 1989 [ISLA].
52. Quoted in Beschloss and Talbott, *At the Highest Levels*, p. 156.
53. Bush and Scowcroft, *A World Transformed*, p. 166.
54. See Walter LaFeber, *Inevitable Revolutions*. New York: WW Norton, 1993, pp. 347–8.
55. Quoted in Brenner and Landau, "Passive Aggression," p. 14.
56. Paul Bedard, "US Putting Cuba in a Vise, Quayle Tells Vets," *Washington Times*, March 6, 1990, p. A3.
57. Interview with Dan Fisk, Washington DC, May 20, 1999. Staff aide to Assistant Secretaries of State for Inter-American Affairs, Elliot Abrams, 1986 to 1988, and Bernard Aronson, 1989 to 1991; Office of Inter-American Affairs (ISA), Department of Defense, 1991 to 1992; staff member, House International Relations Committee, November 1992 to June 1994, and Senate Foreign Relations Committee, July 1994 to July 1997.
58. Quoted in Bedard, "US Putting Cuba in a Vise, Quayle Tells Vets," p. A3.
59. State Department official quoted in Rowan Scarborough and Bill Gerts, "Left Nearly Alone, Cuba Faces a Crisis," *Washington Times*, March 1, 1990, p. A6; Quayle and Bush quoted in Ann Devroy, "U.S. Employs 'Verbal Policy' in Attempt to Isolate Castro," *Washington Post*, April 3, 1990 [ISLA].
60. See Gil Klein, "Bush Lays Down His Conditions for Normal Relations with Cuba," *Washington Post*, March 20, 1990, p. A4. For an excellent discussion of this shift, see H. Michael Erisman, "US–Cuban Relations: Moving Beyond the Cold War to the New International Order?" in Ransford W. Palmer, ed., *The Repositioning of US–Caribbean Relations in the New World Order*. Westport, CT: Praeger, 1997, pp. 53–8.
61. Kenneth N. Skoug, Jr., Director, Office of Cuban Affairs, "Cuba's Growing Crisis, May 27, 1987, in *Department of State Bulletin*, September 1987, p. 89.
62. Telephone interview with Bernard Aronson, Washington DC, May 17, 1999. Assistant Secretary of State for Inter-American Affairs, 1989–1993; co-chair, Council on Foreign Relations Cuba Task Force, 1998–2000.
63. Quoted in Gunn, "Will Castro Fall?" p. 148.
64. See Sandra Dibble, "Dissident's Call for Dialogue Ignites Exiles," *Miami Herald*, June 22, 1990 [ISLA]. On the U.S. response, see *CubaINFO*, July 19, 1990, p. 2.
65. Interview with Vicki Huddleston.
66. Quoted in Mimi Whitefield, "Cuba Seeks Course for the '90s Amid Communist World Crisis," *Miami Herald*, January 22, 1990 [ISLA].
67. Confidential Interview 10, Washington DC, May 12, 1999. Department of State Cuba official, Bush administration; senior Latin American official with Cuba responsibilities in the first and second Clinton administrations.
68. See *CubaINFO*, March 20, 1990, p. 7; *CubaINFO*, April 6, 1990, p. 2.
69. Telephone interview with Robert Morley.

70. Interview with Vicki Huddleston.
71. Telephone interview with Bernard Aronson.
72. Quoted in *CubaINFO*, October 5, 1990, p. 2.
73. Quoted in *CubaINFO*, June 19, 1991, p. 3.
74. Confidential Interview 10.
75. Interview with Richard Nuccio.
76. Peter Slevin, "Amnesty Finds Abuse on Decline in Cuba," *Miami Herald*, September 6, 1988 [ISLA]; "U.N. Finds Some Gains in Cubans' Rights," *New York Times*, February 26, 1989, p. 3. Also see Aryeh Neier, "In Cuban Prisons," *New York Review of Books*, June 30, 1988, pp. 21, 22.
77. See Paul Lewis, "U.S. to Press U.N. Chief on Human Rights in Cuba," *New York Times*, January 27, 1990, p. 8; Lewis, "Move by U.N. Chief on Cuba Irks U.S.," *New York Times*, January 30, 1990, p. 11; Lewis, "Rights Panel Scolds Cuba, Not China," *New York Times*, March 7, 1990, p. 3.
78. U.S. Congress, House Committee on Foreign Affairs, and Senate Committee on Foreign Relations, *Country Reports on Human Rights Practices for 1989*, 101st Cong., 2nd Sess., February 1990, p. 529.
79. Telephone interview with Robert Morley.
80. Lawyers Committee for Human Rights, *Critique: Review of the Department of State's Country Reports on Human Rights Practices for 1989*. New York, July 1990, p. 46; Human Rights Watch, *Human Rights Watch World Report 1992*. New York, December 1991, p. 194; Human Rights Watch, *Cuba: "Perfecting" the System of Control: Human Rights Violations in Castro's 34th Year*. New York, February 25, 1993, p. 24.
81. Human Rights Watch, *Human Rights Watch World Report 1990*. New York, January 1991, p. 142.
82. Quoted in David Hoffman, "Bush Urges Support for TV Martí," *Washington Post*, April 3, 1990, p. A15.
83. Quoted in *CubaINFO*, August 7, 1990, p. 1.
84. Quoted in Epstein and Sullivan, *Radio and Television Broadcasting in Cuba*, pp. 9–10.
85. Interview with Vicki Huddleston.
86. Confidential Interview 1, Washington DC, May 10, 1999. Staff member of the Senate Foreign Relations Committee, 1989–2000.
87. Quoted in Devroy, "U.S. Employs 'Verbal Policy' in Attempt to Isolate Cuba."
88. See Mimi Whitefield, "Improved U.S.–Cuba Phone Service Put on Hold," *Miami Herald*, February 14, 1990 [ISLA].
89. ABC was ultimately permitted to broadcast the Games from Havana, but only on the condition that the host country was paid nothing for the television rights.
90. See Mimi Whitefield, "U.S. Hooks Bass Angler Who Led Groups to Cuba," *Miami Herald*, January 28, 1990 [ISLA].
91. *CubaINFO*, May 31, 1991, p. 2.
92. Quoted in *CubaINFO*, September 13, 1991, p. 5.
93. Laura Brooks, "Cuban Economic Woes Reduce Trade with Panamanians," *Christian Science Monitor*, November 9, 1990 [ISLA].
94. Quoted in Martin McReynolds, "Bush Urges Raising Ante Against Castro," *Miami Herald*, March 21, 1990 [ISLA].

95. See Thomas L. Friedman, "Baker Braves the Gauntlet in the Moscow Parliament," *New York Times*, February 11, 1990, p. 20.
96. Telephone interview with John Christiansen, Washington DC, May 10, 1999. Assistant Country Director for the Caribbean (ISA), Office of the Secretary, Department of Defense, March 1990 to April 1993.
97. Quoted in *CubaINFO*, June 4, 1990, p. 5.
98. Quoted in Beschloss and Talbott, *At the Highest Levels*, p. 225.
99. Quoted in David Hoffman, "Bush Holds Off on Economic Aid to Soviets," *Washington Post*, June 30, 1990, p. A23.
100. Quoted in Martin McReynolds, "U.S. Says It Urged Soviets to Seek Cuba Reforms," *Miami Herald*, June 7, 1990 [ISLA].
101. Telephone interview with Bernard Aronson.
102. See, for example, Sandra Dibble, et al., "Exiles Press Soviets for Change in Cuba," *Miami Herald*, May 27, 1990 [ISLA].
103. *CubaINFO*, October 19, 1990, p. 2.
104. Quoted in Anne-Marie O'Connor, "Soviets Tell Cubans They'll Give Aid Until U.S. Drops Embargo," *Cox News Service*, December 5, 1990.
105. Quoted in Ibid.
106. *CubaINFO*, August 7, 1990, p. 5.
107. Quoted in *CubaINFO*, July 22, 1990, p. 4.
108. See Lee Hockstader, "Castro's Cuba at 32, Faces Stiffest Economic Test," *Washington Post*, January 1, 1991, p. A18; Carmelo Mesa-Lago, ed. *Cuba: After the Cold War*. Pittsburgh: University of Pittsburgh Press, 1993, pp. 59–97, 133–96; Richard F. Kaufman, "The Cuban Economy: Crises and Change in the 1990s," in U.S. Congress, Joint Economic Committee, *The Caribbean Basin: Economic and Security Issues*, 102nd Cong., 2nd Sess., January 1993, pp. 134–5.
109. Quoted in *CubaINFO*, December 14, 1990, p. 1.
110. "Spain–Cuba Venture to Make Energy Savings in Cuban Industry," November 11, 1991, *Reuters News Service*; Andrew Zimbalist, "Dateline Cuba: Hanging On in Havana," *Foreign Policy*, No. 92, Fall 1993, p. 154.
111. Quoted in *CubaINFO*, May 31, 1991, p. 1; Andrew Rosenthal, "Bush Overture to Cuban Leader," *New York Times*, May 21, 1991, p. 6.
112. Aronson and CANF quoted in Alfonso Chardy and Christopher Marquis, "U.S. Offers New Initiative on Cuba," *Miami Herald*, May 21, 1991, pp. 1A, 19A.
113. Quoted in Beschloss and Talbott, *At the Highest Levels*, p. 389.
114. U.S. Congress, House, Committee on Foreign Affairs, Subcommittee on Western Hemisphere Affairs, *Cuba in a Changing World: The United States–Soviet–Cuban Triangle*, 102nd Cong., 1st Sess., April 30, July 11 and 31, 1991, p. 131.
115. See Garthoff, *The Great Transition*, p. 744.
116. Quoted in *CubaINFO*, September 13, 1991, p. 5.
117. Gershman quote and NED figures in Alfonso Chardy, "Pro-Democracy Group Doubles Cuba Funds," *Miami Herald*, December 22, 1991 [ISLA].
118. U.S. Congress, House, *Cuba in a Changing World*, p. 95.
119. Quoted in Clifford Krauss, "U.S. Taking Steps to Bar New Wave of Cuban Emigres," *New York Times*, August 4, 1991, pp. 1, 18.
120. Quoted in Mimi Whitefield, "New Restrictions on Travel to Cuba Imposed by US," *Miami Herald*, September 28, 1991 [ISLA].

121. U.S. Congress, House, *Cuba in a Changing World*, p. 127.
122. Quoted in Guy Gugliotta, "Moscow's Aid to Cuba: A Persistent Irritant in U.S.–Soviet Relations," *Washington Post*, July 28, 1991 [ISLA].
123. U.S. Congress, House, *Cuba in a Changing World*, pp. 155, 176.
124. Interview with Richard Nuccio.
125. "Trade with Cuba Booms for US MNC's Foreign Subs," *Business International*, December 16, 1991, p. 426.
126. Kiger, *Squeeze Play*, p. 34.
127. Interview with Richard Nuccio.
128. Christopher Marquis, "Embargo Bill's Success Testifies to Exile's Clout," *Miami Herald*, September 28, 1992, p. 11A.
129. Quoted in "Trade with Cuba Booms for US MNC's Foreign Subs," p. 426.
130. James A. Baker III, *The Politics of Diplomacy*. New York: G.P. Putnam's Sons, 1995, pp. 528, 529.
131. Quoted in Thomas L. Friedman, "Gorbachev Says He's Ready to Pull Troops Out of Cuba and End Castro's Subsidies," *New York Times*, September 12, 1991, pp. 1, 12.
132. Quoted in Norman Kempster, "US Adopts Hands-Off Cuba Policy," *Los Angeles Times*, September 14, 1991 [ISLA].
133. Quoted in *CubaINFO*, October 4, 1991, p. 1. Statements such as these reflected more of a hope than anything else. According to the State Department's Office of Cuban Affairs Coordinator, a more realistic appraisal of Castro's ability to retain power continued to predominate in the bureaucratic debate: "Our feeling in ARA [American Republic Affairs], and I think we pretty much carried the day with the rest of the policy community, was that Fidel Castro would probably not be removed from government until he died. There was no institutional position that Castro was on his last legs." Telephone Interview with Robert Morley.
134. Quoted in Robbins, "Dateline Washington: Cuban-American Clout," p. 180.
135. Quoted in *Latin American Regional Reports: Caribbean*, April 2, 1992, p. 12.
136. Quoted in John E. Yang, "Bush Moves to Tighten Trade Embargo Against Cuba," *Washington Post*, April 19, 1992, p. A23.
137. U.S. Congress, House, Committee on Foreign Affairs, *Consideration of the Cuban Democracy Act of 1992*, 102nd Cong., 2nd Sess., March 18, 25, April 2, 8, May 21, June 4, 5, 1992, pp. 403, 359.
138. Canadian Embassy officials, Washington DC, quoted in *CubaINFO*, October 2, 1992, pp. 1–2.
139. Quoted in Gillian McGillivray, *Trading with the "Enemy": Canadian–Cuban Relations in the 1990s*. Georgetown University: Center for Latin American Studies, December 1997, p. 10.
140. Quoted in *CubaINFO*, October 27, 1992, p. 2.
141. Quoted in "UK Rejects Trade Ban on Cuba by US," *Financial Times*, October 21, 1992, p. 5.
142. U.S. Congress, House, *Consideration of the Cuban Democracy Act of 1992*, p. 359.
143. Ibid., pp. 358, 402–3.
144. See Christopher Marquis and Paul Anderson, "Bush to Sign Cuba Bill in Miami," *Miami Herald*, October 23, 1992, p. A1.

145. Interview with Richard Nuccio. Robert Torricelli acted as Clinton's Latin American adviser during the 1992 election campaign.
146. Quoted in Kiger, *Squeeze Play*, p. 35.
147. U.S. Congress, Senate, Committee on Foreign Relations, Subcommittee on Western Hemisphere and Peace Corps Affairs, *The Cuban Democracy Act of 1992, S.2918*, 102nd Cong., 2nd Sess., August 5, 1992, pp. 27, 29.
148. Ibid., pp. 40–1.
149. Interview with Andrew Semmel.
150. See "House Joins Senate in Backing Bills to Tighten Embargo," *Congressional Quarterly Weekly Report*, September 26, 1992, p. 2964; Marquis, "Embargo Bill's Success Testifies to Exile's Clout," p. 11A.
151. Confidential Interview 1.
152. Telephone Interview with Bernard Aronson.
153. Interview with Kirby Jones, Washington DC, May 12, 1999. President, Alamar Associates, a consultancy working with U.S. corporations interested in pursuing trade and business opportunities in Cuba.
154. Interview with Willard Workman, Washington DC, May 12, 1999. Vice President, International, U.S. Chamber of Commerce.
155. See Howard W. French, "Cuba, Long Forbidden, Wins Major Attention Abroad," *New York Times*, April 19, 1992, p. F5; Charles W. Thurston, "Executives Opposed to Cuba Embargo Grow More Vocal in Criticism of Bush," *Journal of Commerce*, July 6, 1992 [ISLA]; Jane Bussey, "U.S. Companies Say Torricelli Bill will Cost Their Subsidiaries Millions," *Miami Herald*, September 23, 1992 [ISLA].
156. Interview with Andrew Semmel.
157. Quoted in *CubaINFO*, October 27, 1992, p. 2.
158. Quoted in Larry Rohter, "Clinton Sees Opportunity to Break G.O.P. Grip on Cuban-Americans," *New York Times*, October 31, 1992, p. 6.
159. Quoted in *CubaINFO*, November 13, 1992, p. 2.
160. Telephone Interview with Robert Morley.
161. Telephone Interview with Bernard Aronson [our emphasis].
162. Quoted in *CubaINFO*, September 14, 1992, p. 2.
163. Quoted in Peter Slevin, "Bush Signs Law Aimed at Castro," *Miami Herald*, October 24, 1992, p. 1A.
164. Quoted in Tom Fiedler and Ivan Roman, "Clinton–Mas Meeting Shocks Cuban Miami," *Miami Herald*, October 29, 1992, p. 1A.

CHAPTER 2

1. Quoted in *CubaINFO*, February 8, 1993, p. 1
2. Wayne Smith, *Our Cuban Diplomacy*. Washington DC: Center for International Policy, October 1994, p. 3; *CQ's Politics in America 2000*. Washington DC: Congressional Quarterly, 1999, p. 295.
3. Quoted in Pascal Fletcher, "Try Lifting Embargo, Cuba Urges U.S.," April 27, 1993, *Reuters News Service*; *CubaINFO*, December 18, 1992, p. 2.
4. Human Rights Watch, *Human Rights Watch World Report 1994*. New York, 1993, p. 88.
5. Confidential Interview 10.

6. Quoted in Guy Gugliotta, "Exiles Urge Moderation Toward Cuba," *Washington Post*, January 19, 1993 [ISLA].
7. Quoted in *CubaINFO*, April 30, 1993, p. 3.
8. Quoted in *CubaINFO*, February 8, 1993, p. 2. Also see John M. Goshko, "Controversy Erupts on Latin American Post," *Washington Post*, January 23, 1993 [ISLA].
9. Quoted in *CubaINFO*, March 19, 1993, p. 2.
10. U.S. Congress, Senate, Committee on Foreign Relations, *Nomination of Warren M. Christopher to be Secretary of State*, 103rd Cong., 1st Sess., January 13–14, 1993, p. 140.
11. May 27 press conference, quoted in *CubaINFO*, June 18, 1993, p. 2.
12. "March 23, 1993," *United States Policy Toward Cuba: The Clinton Administration's First Year – A Chronology*, Washington DC: National Security Archive, 1994.
13. Quoted in Pamela Constable, "Clinton Is Urged to Lift Cuban Embargo but Firm Policy Still in Place," *Boston Globe*, May 13, 1993, p. 2; *CubaINFO*, May 21, 1993, p. 2.
14. "February 19, 1993," *United States Policy Toward Cuba.*
15. Interview with Michael Skol.
16. Quoted in *CubaINFO*, May 21, 1993, p. 3.
17. See Jeff Leen and Andres Oppenheimer, "Clinton Caught Off Guard by Proposed Cuba Charges," *Miami Herald*, April 9, 1993 [ISLA].
18. Quoted in *CubaINFO*, June 18, 1993, p. 11. Also see Nancy Klingener, "Nine Alpha 66 Members Plead Innocent to Weapons Charge," *Miami Herald*, May 27, 1993 [ISLA].
19. Interview with Alexander Watson, Arlington, Virginia, May 13, 1999. Assistant Secretary of State for Inter-American Affairs, 1993–1996.
20. Interview with Richard Nuccio.
21. Interview with Michael Skol.
22. Interview with Alexander Watson.
23. Ibid.
24. Interview with Richard Nuccio.
25. Interview with Dennis Hays, Washington DC, May 14, 1999. Director, Office of Cuban Affairs, Department of State, summer 1993 to May 1995.
26. Telephone Interview with John Christiansen; Telephone Interview with Raimundo Ruga, Washington DC, May 12, 1999. Cuba Desk officer, Department of Defense, August 1993 to August 1996, February to July 1997. He chaired the Secretary's Cuba Task Force, summer 1994.
27. Confidential Interview 5, Washington DC, May 18, 1999. Department of State, senior Inter-American Affairs official with Cuba responsibilities, late 1996 to 2000.
28. Confidential Interview 10.
29. Interview with Michael Ranneberger, Washington DC, May 17, 1999. Coordinator, Office of Cuban Affairs, Department of State, July 1995 to 2000.
30. Quoted in Andres Oppenheimer and Mimi Whitefield, "OAS Warms to Possibility of Cuba's Return to Group," *Miami Herald*, June 18, 1994, p. 13A.
31. Quoted in *CubaINFO*, April 30, 1993, p. 1.
32. Quoted in John M. Kirk and Peter McKenna, *Canada–Cuba Relations*. Gainesville: University Press of Florida, 1997, pp. 154–5.

33. "April 15, 1993," *United States Policy Toward Cuba.*
34. Quoted in José De Cordoba, "Cuba Is Selling What It Usurped and Original Owners Are Fuming," *Wall Street Journal*, October 21, 1993, p. 14.
35. Quoted in Andres Viglucci, "Flights to Cuba Okd, but Restrictions Apply," *Miami Herald*, September 1, 1993, p. 7A. Also see Daniel Williams, "U.S. Rejects Cuba's Demand that Exiles Buy Tour Packages," *Washington Post*, September 17, 1993, p. A2.
36. Quoted in *CubaINFO*, January 28, 1994, p. 2.
37. Quoted in Epstein and Sullivan, *Radio and Television Broadcasting to Cuba*, p. 14; Mark P. Sullivan, *Cuba: Issues for Congress*. Congressional Research Service, September 6, 1994, p. 13.
38. Quoted in *CubaINFO*, April 29, 1994, p. 1.
39. U.S. Congress, House, Committee on Foreign Affairs, Subcommittee on Western Hemisphere Affairs, *Recent Developments in Cuba Policy: Telecommunications and Dollarization*, 103rd Cong., 1st Sess., August 4, 1993, p. 14.
40. Quoted in Tom Carter, "Cuban Relations Won't Warm Soon, State Official Says," *Washington Times*, October 27, 1993, p. A12.
41. Interview with Alexander Watson.
42. Quoted in Tom Fiedler, "Clinton: Cuba Embargo 'Right,'" *Miami Herald*, September 1993, p. 6A.
43. Quoted in Douglas Farah, "U.S.–Cuban Ties: Slight Warming, but Both Sides Doubt Massive Shift," *Washington Post*, July 31, 1993 [ISLA].
44. U.S. Congress, Senate, Select Committee on Intelligence, *Prospects for Democracy in Cuba*, 103rd Cong., 1st Sess., July 20, 1993, p. 7.
45. By 1994, EU nations accounted for 38 percent of Cuba's imports and 29 percent of its exports, up from around 6 percent of the island's total global trade in 1989 – again, in the context of Cuba's overall trade contraction. See Joaquin Roy, *Cuba, the United States, and the Helms–Burton Doctrine*. Gainesville: University Press of Florida, 2000, p. 108; Gabriel A Ondetti, *Western European and Canadian Relations with Cuba After the Cold War*. Georgetown University: Center for Latin American Studies, 1995, p. 4. For figures on the growth in Latin American trade, see *Latin American Monitor: Caribbean*, May 1995, p. 6; James Brooke, "Latin America Now Ignores U.S. Lead in Isolating Cuba," *New York Times*, July 8, 1995, pp. 1, 15.
46. U.S. Congress, Senate, *Prospects for Democracy in Cuba*, p. 11.
47. Quoted in Daniel Williams, "U.S. Stands Its Ground on Cuba," *Washington Post*, December 21, 1993, p. A11.
48. Interview with Dennis Hays.
49. Confidential Interview 10.
50. Interview with Dennis Hays.
51. Interview with Richard Nuccio.
52. See Thomas W. Lippman, "U.S.–Cuba Accord Limited to Convicts," *Washington Post*, October 2, 1993, p. A14.
53. See Carla Ann Robbins, "CIA Tells Clinton He Could Face a Crisis in Cuba if 'Serious Instability' Develops," *Wall Street Journal*, November 22, 1993, p. 10.
54. Quoted in Lippman, "U.S.–Cuba Accord Limited to Convicts," p. A14.
55. Both officials quoted in Williams, "U.S. Stands Its Ground on Cuba," p. A11.

56. Interview with Alexander Watson.
57. Confidential Interview 10.
58. Confidential Interview 1.
59. Interview with Andrew Semmel.
60. See "Tens of Thousands March Against Castro," October 10, 1993, *Reuters News Service*.
61. See *CubaINFO*, November 24, 1993, p. 4.
62. Quoted in Ibid., p. 6.
63. Quoted in *CubaINFO*, December 17, 1993, p. 1.
64. Quoted in *CubaINFO*, April 8, 1994, p. 13.
65. U.S. Congress, House, Committee on Foreign Affairs, Subcommittee on Western Hemisphere Affairs, *U.S. Policy and the Future of Cuba: The Cuban Democracy Act and U.S. Travel to Cuba*, 103rd Cong., 1st Sess., November 18, 1993, pp. 21–4.
66. Ibid., pp. 33–6.
67. Ibid., pp. 16–20; Correspondence with Alexander Watson, December 5, 1999.
68. U.S. Congress, House, *U.S. Policy and the Future of Cuba*, pp. 16–20.
69. See Christopher Marquis and Mimi Whitfield, "Limits on Cuba Trips Will Remain," *Miami Herald*, February 5, 1994, p. 29A.
70. Quoted in *CubaINFO*, November 24, 1993, p. 2.
71. Quoted in *CubaINFO*, March 19, 1993, p. 4.
72. U.S. Congress, House Committee on Foreign Affairs and Senate Committee on Foreign Relations, *Country Reports on Human Rights Practices for 1993*, 103rd Cong., 2nd Sess., February 1994, p. 409.
73. Human Rights Watch, *Cuba: Stifling Dissent in the Midst of Crisis*. New York, February 1994, p. 3.
74. Interview with Dennis Hays.
75. U.S. Congress, House, Committee on Ways and Means, Subcommittee on Selective Revenue Matters and Trade, *H.R. 2229, Free Trade With Cuba Act*, 103rd Cong., 2nd Sess., March 17, 1994, pp. 185, 186.
76. Interview with Dennis Hays.
77. Interview with Michael Skol.
78. U.S. Congress, House, Committee on Foreign Affairs, *The Free and Independent Cuba Assistance Act of 1993*, 103rd Cong., 2nd Sess., March 24, 1994, p. 32.
79. Interview with Alexander Watson.
80. Interview with Michael Skol.
81. Interview with Dan Fisk.
82. Interview with Richard Nuccio.
83. See *Cuban and Haitian Asylum Seekers: Recent Trends*. Congressional Research Service, September, 1, 1994.
84. President Clinton, "The Crisis in Haiti," in U.S. Department of State, *Dispatch*, September 1994, p. 605. For an extended analysis, see Morris Morley and Chris McGillion, " 'Disobedient' Generals and the Politics of Redemocratization: The Clinton Administration and Haiti," *Political Science Quarterly*, Vol. 112, No. 3, Fall 1997, pp. 1–21.
85. Quoted in Human Rights Watch, *Cuba: Repression, the Exodus of August 1994, and the U.S. Response*. New York, October 1994, p. 8.
86. Sullivan, *Cuba: Issues for Congress*, September 6, 1994, p. 14.

87. Interview with Richard Nuccio. Following the June 1980 riot, Clinton could barely contain his anger at the Carter White House over being saddled with this explosive refugee problem. See David Maraniss, *First in His Class*. New York: Simon & Schuster, 1995, pp. 379–80.

88. Telephone Interview with Leon Panetta, San Francisco, October 13, 2001. White House Chief of Staff, mid-1994 to January 1997.

89. Confidential Telephone Interview 1, San Francisco, December 20, 1999. Senior foreign policy official during the first and second Clinton administrations.

90. Telephone Interview with Raimundo Ruga.

91. Quotes in Walter Pincus and Roberto Suro, "Ripple in Florida Straits Overturned U.S. Policy," *Washington Post*, September 1, 1994, p. A34.

92. Quoted in *CubaINFO*, September 1, 1994, p. 5.

93. Quoted in Ibid., p. 4.

94. Quoted in Ibid.

95. Quoted in Jon Nordheimer, "Cuban Group Forges Link to Clinton," *New York Times*, August 26, 1994, p. 12.

96. Interview with Richard Nuccio.

97. Human Rights Watch, *Cuba: Repression, the Exodus of August 1994, and the U.S. Response*, p. 11; Douglas Jehl, "President Moves to Punish Castro for Cuban Exodus," *New York Times*, August 21, 1994, pp. 1, 28.

98. *CubaINFO*, September 1, 1994, pp. 3–4.

99. Quoted in Ann Devroy, "Panetta Hints at Blockade of Cuba," *Washington Post*, August 22, 1994, p. A11.

100. Quoted in Susanne Schafer, "Pentagon Plays Down Cuban Blockade Threat," *The Australian*, August 24, 1998, p. 8.

101. Quoted in Steven Greenhouse, "U.S. Promises to Respond if Castro Offers Reforms," *New York Times*, August 29, 1994, p. 10.

102. Confidential Telephone Interview 1.

103. Interview with Alexander Watson.

104. Interview with Dennis Hays.

105. Quoted in Schaffer, "Pentagon Plays Down Cuban Blockade Threat," p. 8; Daniel Williams, "U.S. Policy on Cuba Awash in Contradictions," *Washington Post*, August 25, 1994, p. A25.

106. Quoted in Ibid., p. A1.

107. See, for example, *CubaINFO*, September 22, 1994, p. 22; Tom Kenworthy, "U.S. Rejects Expansion of Talks With Castro," *Washington Post*, August 29, 1994, p. A14.

108. Editorial, "Cuba: Time to Talk," *New York Times*, August 26, 1994, p. 28.

109. Tarnoff and Christopher quoted in Kenworthy, "U.S. Rejects Expansion of Talks with Castro," p. A14.

110. Interview with Michael Skol; Correspondence with Michael Skol, December 7 and 9, 1999.

111. Quoted in Vernon Silver, "Cuban-Americans Caution on Talks," *New York Times*, September 3, 1994 [ISLA].

112. *CubaINFO*, September 22, 1994, p. 12; Alfonso Chardy, "U.S. Officials Visit Miami in Effort to Calm the Cuban Community," *Miami Herald*, September 3, 1994, p. 22A.

113. Quoted in Christopher Marquis, "U.S.–Cuba Discussion Hits Snag," *Miami Herald*, September 3, 1994, p. 22A.
114. See Robert Suro, "U.S., Cuba Agree on Stemming Raft Tide," *Washington Post*, September 10, 1994, pp. A1, A18; Daniel Williams, "U.S., Cuba Interrupt Migration Discussions," *Washington Post*, September 8, 1994, p. A32.
115. Quoted in Suro, "U.S., Cuba Agree on Stemming Raft Tide," p. A1.
116. Interview with Dennis Hays.
117. Quoted in *CubaINFO*, September 22, 1994, pp. 5–6.
118. Interview with Richard Nuccio.
119. Claiborne Pell and Lee H. Hamilton, "The Embargo Must Go," *Washington Post*, September 8, 1994, p. A19.
120. Kiger, *Squeeze Play*, p. 45.
121. U.S. Congress, House, Committee on International Relations, Subcommittee on the Western Hemisphere, *Cuba and U.S. Policy*, 104th Cong., 1st Sess., February 23, 1995, p. 14.
122. Quoted in Tim Golden, "Prospects Now for U.S.–Cuban Thaw Are Fading," *New York Times*, December 5, 1994, p. 3.
123. See *CubaINFO*, February 7, 1995, pp. 13–14.
124. Telephone Interview with Leon Panetta.
125. See Mark P. Sullivan, *Cuba–U.S. Relations: Should the United States Increase Sanctions on Cuba?* Congressional Research Service, May 16, 1995, pp. 2–5.
126. Quoted in *CubaINFO*, February 23, 1995, p. 2.
127. Interview with Alexander Watson.
128. Interview with Dennis Hays.
129. Interview with Kirby Jones.
130. Interview with Dan Fisk.
131. Ibid.
132. Ibid. For a discussion of the aggressive and lavishly funded lobbying campaign mounted by CANF and Jorge Mas Canosa in support of Helms–Burton, see Kiger, *Squeeze Play*, pp. 52–4.
133. Confidential Interview 2, Washington DC, May 11, 1999. Congressional Cuba specialist, monitored the legislative debate over Cuba policy between 1993 and 2000.
134. U.S. Congress, House, Committee on International Relations, Subcommittee on the Western Hemisphere, *The Cuban Liberty and Democratic Solidarity (Libertad) Act of 1995*, 104th Cong., 1st Sess., March 16, 1995, pp. 22, 61–2.
135. Quoted in Steven Greenhouse, "Clinton Opposes Move to Toughen Embargo on Cuba," *New York Times*, May 5, 1995, pp. 1, 8.
136. Quoted in *CubaINFO*, April 6, 1995, pp. 2–3.
137. Confidential Interview 7, Washington DC, May 18, 1999. Department of State official directly involved with Cuba policy between 1995 and 2000.
138. Interview with Dennis Hays. Canada was also particularly critical of Helms–Burton, and not without good reason. It denounced key aspects of the legislation, including the provision that countries (such as Canada) importing Cuban sugar would be unable to sell sugar, molasses, or syrup products in the U.S. market, terming it a clear violation of international trade agreements. If translated into law, Ottawa policy makers warned, it could trigger a trade war putting at risk nearly

$1 billion in bilateral trade. Other provisons of concern were Title III, which raised the possibility of Canadian investors in Cuba being sued for damages in U.S. courts for "trafficking" in properties confiscated from American owners after 1959, and Title IV denying entry into the U.S. to any senior executive of these multinationals deemed to have "benefited" from the expropriated property venture.

139. Quoted in *CubaINFO*, April 27, 1995, p. 5.
140. See Daniel Williams and Ann Devroy, "Clinton May Ease Sanctions on Cuba," *Washington Post*, March 7, 1995, pp. A1, A7; Scott Armstrong and Saul Landau, "Adrift Off Cuba," *Washington Post*, April 2, 1995, pp. C1, C4.
141. Interview with Michael Skol.
142. Confidential Telephone Interview 1.
143. All quotes in Daniel Williams, "Continued Cuba Sanctions Pressed by GOP Leaders," *Washington Post*, March 8, 1995, p. A22; *CubaINFO*, March 16, 1995, pp. 12–13.
144. All quotes in Ann Devroy and Daniel Williams, "Serious Alarm Bells Led to Talks with Cuba," *Washington Post*, May 5, 1995, p. A4; Steven Greenhouse, "How the Clinton Administration Reversed U.S. Policy on Cuban Refugees," *New York Times*, May 21, 1995, p. 8.
145. Interview with Richard Nuccio.
146. Quoted in Devroy and Williams, "Serious Alarm Bells Led to Talks with Cuba," p. A14. Also see Steven Greenhouse, "U.S. Will Return Refugees to Cuba in Policy Switch," *New York Times*, May 3, 1995, p. 14.
147. Confidential Telephone Interview 1.
148. U.S. Congress, House, Committee on International Relations, *The Clinton Administration's Reversal of U.S. Immigration Policy Toward Cuba*, 104th Cong., 1st Sess., May 18, 1995, pp. 14, 25, 32, 34, 41–2. On Tarnoff's perception of Hays's reliability, see Devroy and Williams, "Serious Alarm Bells Led to Talks with Cuba," p. A14; U.S. Congress, Senate, Committee on Foreign Relations, Subcommittee on Western Hemisphere and Peace Corps Affairs, *Cuban Liberty and Democratic Solidarity Act*, 104th Cong., 1st Sess., May 22 and June 14, 1995, p. 19.
149. Interview with Ricard Nuccio.
150. U.S. Congress, House, *The Clinton Administration's Reversal of U.S. Immigration Policy Toward Cuba*, p. 15.
151. Quoted in Ann Devroy and Daniel Williams, "In Reversal, U.S. to Accept Cubans Held at Navy Base," *Washington Post*, May 3, 1995, p. A8.
152. Interview with Richard Nuccio.
153. Quoted in Greenhouse, "U.S. Will Return Refugees to Cuba in Policy Switch," p. 1.
154. Confidential Interview 6, Washington DC, May 14, 1999. Senior official, Office of Cuban Affairs, Department of State, July 1995 to July 1998.
155. Interview with Dan Fisk.
156. Quoted in *CubaINFO*, June 29, 1995, p. 11.
157. Quoted in Ibid., pp. 9–10.
158. Quoted in *CubaINFO*, August 28, 1995, p. 1.
159. Quoted in David E.Singer, "Real Politics: Why Suharto Is In and Castro Is Out," *New York Times*, October 31, 1995, p. 3. Also see William M. LeoGrande, "From Havana to Miami: U.S. Cuba Policy as a Two Level Game," *Journal of Inter-American Studies and World Affairs*, Vol. 40, No. 1, Spring 1998, pp. 75, 81.

160. Quoted in *CubaINFO*, August 28, 1995, p. 6.
161. Interview with Richard Nuccio.
162. U.S. Congress, Senate, *Cuban Liberty and Democratic Solidarity Act*, pp. 17–18, 41.
163. Interview with Richard Nuccio.
164. Confidential Telephone Interview 1.
165. Interview with Richard Nuccio.
166. Ibid.
167. Interview with Michael Skol.
168. Confidential Interview 1.
169. Interview with Richard Nuccio.
170. Interview with Willard Workman.
171. Interview with Andrew Semmel.
172. Interview with Willard Workman.
173. U.S. Congress, House, Committee on Agriculture, Subcommittee on Foreign Agriculture and Hunger, *Agricultural Implications of Renewed Trade with Cuba*, 103rd Cong., 2nd Sess., May 19, 1994, pp. 32–4.
174. Sam Dillon, "Companies Press Clinton to Lift Embargo on Cuba," *New York Times*, August 27, 1995, p. 1.
175. All quotes in Ibid, pp. 1, 6.
176. Editorial, "Confronting Castro," *Journal of Commerce*, September 27, 1995, p. 6A.
177. "U.S. Business Isn't Afraid to Shout, 'Cuba Si!' " *Business Week*, November 6, 1995, p. 39; Pamela S. Falk, "Eyes on Cuba," *Foreign Affairs*, March/April 1996, p. 16.
178. Quoted in Ibid., p. 18. For discussions of generational shifts, see Mariá de Los Angeles Torres, *In the Land of Mirrors*. Ann Arbor: University of Michigan Press, 1999, especially pp.159–61; Mireya Navarro, "Miami's Generations of Exiles, Side by Side, Yet Worlds Apart," *New York Times*, February 11, 1999 [Online Edition, hereafter OE].
179. Interview with Michael Ranneberger.
180. Confidential Telephone Interview 1. Also see Michael Dobbs, "U.S. Weighs Eased Cuba Travel Rules," *Washington Post*, July 6, 1995, p. A15.
181. Quoted in David E. Singer, "Real Politics: Why Suharto Is In and Castro Is Out," *New York Times*, October 31, 1995, p. 3 [our emphasis]. When next the two leaders were in the same room at the 2000 United Nations Millenium Summit in New York, the White House reversed its Castro "handshake" policy and Clinton did shake hands with the Cuban leader. See David E. Sanger, "It's a Handshake and Small Talk for Clinton and Castro," *New York Times*, September 8, 2000, p.10.
182. Interview with Roberto Robaina, Sydney, Australia, November 22, 1995.
183. Confidential Interview 7.
184. Interview with Richard Nuccio.
185. Interview with Stuart Eizenstat, Washington DC, September 16, 2001. U.S. Ambassador to the European Union, 1993 to 1996; President's Special Representative for the Promotion of Democracy in Cuba, 1996 to 1998; Deputy Treasury Secretary, Under Secretary of State for Economic, Business and Agricultural Affairs, Undersecretary of Commerce for International Trade 1998–2000.
186. Interview with Richard Nuccio.

187. Confidential Interview 7.
188. See Richard A. Nuccio, "Cuba: A U.S. Perspective," in Richard N. Haass, ed., *Transatlantic Tensions*. Washington DC: Brookings Institution, 1999, p. 16. Marin later told Eizenstat that he was "very angry" about Castro's actions. Interview with Stuart Eizenstat.

CHAPTER 3

1. Transcript, White House, Office of the President, "Statement by the President," February 26, 1996.
2. See Andres Oppenheimer and Christopher Marquis, "Missile Attack Weighed After Shoot-Down," *Miami Herald*, October 1, 1996, p. 25A.
3. Telephone Interview with Leon Panetta.
4. Telephone Interview with Raimundo Ruga.
5. Interview with Richard Nuccio.
6. Quoted in *CubaINFO*, February 29, 1996, p. 13.
7. Telephone Interview with Leon Panetta. One school of thought accused the Cuban government of deliberately ordering the shootdown "to freeze the situation with the United States for a while and give itself some breathing room." See, for example, David Reiff, "Cuba Refrozen," *Foreign Affairs*, July/August 1996, pp. 73–4. Such assertions were not backed up by any evidence.
8. Quoted in Arthur Golden, "Relations with Cuba Key Topic of Forum," *San Diego Union–Tribune*, May 13, 1996, p. B3.
9. Confidential Interview 3, Washington DC, May 17, 1999. Department of State official involved with Cuba since 1995; Office of Cuban Affairs, mid-1997 to 2000.
10. Interview with Richard Nuccio.
11. Telephone Interview with Leon Panetta.
12. Quoted in John F. Harris and Paul Blustein, "Hill GOP Rules Out Compromise on Cuba," *Washington Post*, February 28, 1996, p. A14.
13. Interview with Richard Nuccio.
14. Quoted in Harris and Blustein, "Hill GOP Rules Out Compromise on Cuba," p. A14.
15. Quoted in Jerry Gray, "President Agrees to Tough New Set of Curbs on Cuba," *New York Times*, February 29, 1996, p. 4.
16. Interview with Andrew Semmel.
17. Quoted in Harris and Blustein, "Hill GOP Rules Out Compromise on Cuba," p. A14.
18. U.S. Congress, House, Committee on International Relations, *Shoot Down of U.S. Civilian Aircraft by Castro Regime*, 104th Cong., 2nd Sess., February 29, 1996, p. 7.
19. Transcript, White House, Office of the Press Secretary, "Background Briefing by Senior Administration Official," February 26, 1996.
20. See "Cuba Trade: This Hornets' Nest Is Really Buzzing," *Business Week*, November 25, 1996, p. 58.
21. Interview with Dan Fisk.
22. Quoted in *CubaINFO*, March 4, 1996, p. 3.

23. Telephone Interview with Raimundo Ruga.
24. See Gillian Gunn Clissold, "Cuban–U.S. Relations and the Process of Transition," in Miguel Angel Centeno and Mauricio Font (eds.), *Toward a New Cuba*. Boulder: Lynne Rienner, 1997, pp. 82–3.
25. Interview with Richard Nuccio.
26. Quoted in "High Seas Turn Back Cuban Exiles' Flotilla," March 3, 1996, *Reuters News Service*.
27. Confidential Interview 4, Washington DC, May 17, 1999. Washington-based Cuba specialist and participant in the executive branch policy debate during the Clinton presidency.
28. Interview with Richard Nuccio.
29. Elizardo Sanchez, quoted in *CubaINFO*, May 2, 1996, p. 8.
30. See U.S. General Accounting Office, *U.S. Information Agency: Issues Related to Reinvention Planning in the Office of Cuba Broadcasting*, May 1996, p. 21.
31. *CubaINFO*, May 2, 1996, p. 5.
32. U.S. Congress, House, Committee on International Relations, Subcommittee on the Western Hemisphere, *Enforcement of Penalties Against Violations of the U.S. Embargo on Cuba*, 104th Cong., 2nd Sess., March 5, 1996, pp. 8, 11.
33. Quoted in *CubaINFO*, June 13, 1996, p. 4.
34. Mark P. Sullivan et al., *Cuba–U.S. Relations: A Chronology of Key Events, 1959–1966*. Congressional Research Service, February 18, 1997, p. 27.
35. Quoted in *CubaINFO* July 11, 1996, p. 2; U.S. Congress, House, Committee on International Relations, Subcommittees on International Operations and Human Rights, and on the Western Hemisphere, *Human Rights Violations in Castro's Cuba: The Repression Continues*, 104th Cong., 2nd Sess., June 27, 1996, p. 8.
36. U.S. Congress, House, Committee on International Relations, Subcommittee on the Western Hemisphere, *The Implementation of the Cuban Liberty and Democratic Solidarity (Libertad) Act of 1996*, 104th Cong., 2nd Sess., July 11, 1996, p. 19.
37. William M. Leogrande, "Enemies Evermore: US Policy Towards Cuba After Helms–Burton," *Journal of Latin American Studies*, Vol. 29, Part 1, February 1997, p. 213.
38. Quoted in Alexander M. Sullivan, "Clinton Launches Campaign to Pressure Castro on Democracy," July 16, 1996, U.S. Information Agency [hereafter USIA] Wireless File, Washington DC.
39. Quotes in *CubaINFO*, August 1, 1996, p. 4; Sullivan, "Clinton Launches Campaign to Pressure Castro on Democracy."
40. Quoted in *CubaINFO*, August 1, 1996, p. 4.
41. Chretien quoted in Anne Swardson, "Allies Irked by Bill to Deter Their Trade with U.S. Foes," *Washington Post*, March 7, 1996, p. A20.
42. Quoted in Clyde H. Farnsworth, "Canada Warns U.S. on Law Penalizing Cuba Commerce," *New York Times*, June 18, 1996, p. D6. Also see Charles Trueheart, "Neighbors Slam U.S. on Cuba," *Washington Post*, June 14, 1996, p. A38.
43. Quoted in Bernard Simon and Guy de Jonquieres, "Canada Retaliates Against U.S. Law," *Financial Times*, June 18, 1996, p. 6.
44. Quoted in Juliet O'Neill, "Clinton Relaxes Anti-Cuba Stategy," *Vancouver Sun*, July 17, 1996, p. A1.

45. Interview with Michael Ranneberger.
46. Quoted in *Foreign Broadcast Information Service: Latin America* 96-048, March 11, 1996 [hereafter FBIS].
47. Larry Rohter, "Latin American Nations Rebuke U.S. For the Embargo on Cuba," *New York Times*, June 6, 1996, p. 6.
48. Quoted in "OAS Vote Should Not Be Seen as Pro-Cuba – Chile," June 7, 1996, *Reuters News Service.*
49. Quoted in Rohter, "Latin American Nations Rebuke U.S. for the Embargo on Cuba," p. 6.
50. Confidential Interview 6.
51. Quoted in Steven Lee Myers, "Clinton Troubleshooter Discovers Big Trouble from Allies on Cuba," *New York Times*, October 23, 1996, p. 1.
52. Quoted in "Europeans Agree on Steps to Retaliate for U.S. Cuba Curbs," *New York Times*, July 16, 1996, p. 9.
53. Quoted in Lionel Barber, "Europe Vows to Act on U.S. Anti-Cuba Law," *Financial Times*, July 16, 1996, p. 1.
54. Interview with R. Roger Majak, Washington DC, May 11, 1999. Assistant Secretary of Commerce for Export Administration, 1995–2000.
55. All quotes in John F. Harris, "Clinton Delays Law Allowing Cuba Suits," *Washington Post*, July 17, 1996, p. A22; Craig R. Whitney, "Europe Gives Clinton Stand on Cuba Law Cold Shoulder," *New York Times*, July 18, 1996, p. 15; Ian Black and John Palmer, "Europe Reacts Coolly to Clinton Delaying Tactics," *The Guardian*, July 18, 1996, p. 13; Guy de Jonquieres et al., "EU Unites Over U.S. Measures Against Cuba," *Financial Times*, July 18, 1996, p. 6.
56. Quoted in "France to Hit Back if Hurt by Helms–Burton," July 25, 1996, *Reuters News Service.*
57. U.S. Congress, House, *The Implementation of the Cuban Liberty and Democratic Solidarity (Libertad) Act of 1996*, p. 21.
58. Confidential Interview 8, Washington DC, May 11, 1999. Senior Clinton administration official involved with economic aspects of Cuba policy.
59. Interview with Stuart Eizenstat.
60. Ibid.; quoted in Thomas W. Lippman, "U.S. Allies to Seek Reform in Cuba," *Washington Post*, August 19, 1996, p. A19.
61. Interview with R. Roger Majak.
62. Brittan and Rexrodt quoted *CubaINFO*, September 19, 1996, p. 2.
63. Confidential Interview 7.
64. Interview with Stuart Eizenstat.
65. Quoted in *CubaINFO*, September 19, 1996, p. 1. Also see Laura Eggerton, "Eggleton Ready for Fight Over Cuba," *Toronto Globe & Mail*, January 4, 1997, p. 2.
66. Quoted in *CubaINFO*, October 10, 1996, p. 7.
67. Confidential Interview 10.
68. See *CubaINFO*, November 5, 1996, p. 1.
69. U.S. Congress, Senate, Committee on Foreign Relations, *Nomination of Secretary of State*, 105th Cong., 1st Sess., January 8, 1997, p. 67.
70. Transcript, "Eizenstat Briefing on Clinton's Libertad Extension," USIA Washington File, January 3, 1997.

71. Quoted in *CubaINFO*, January 15, 1997, p. 4.

72. Quoted in Ibid., p. 3.

73. Quoted in *CubaINFO*, February 6, 1997, p. 4.

74. Quoted in *CubaINFO*, January 15, 1997, p. 5.

75. Transcript, *Helms–Burton: A Loose Canon*? Center for International Policy Conference, Washington DC, February 9–11, 1997.

76. Interview with Willard Workman.

77. Interview with Ian Baird, Washington DC, May 11, 1999. Deputy Assistant Secretary of Commerce for Export Administration, late 1980s to 2000.

78. See National Association of Manufacturers, *A Catalog of New U.S. Unilateral Economic Sanctions for Foreign Policy Purposes 1993–96*. Washington DC, March 1997, 30 pp.

79. Interview with William Lane, Washington DC, May 18, 1999. Chairman of USA Engage, formed by American corporations in 1997 to lobby against unilateral economic sanctions; Washington Director of Governmental Affairs, Caterpillar, Inc.

80. See "Congress Considers Revoking Title III Waiver of Helms–Burton Act," *Inside US Trade*, May 16, 1997.

81. Quoted in *CubaINFO*, August 21, 1997, pp. 4–5.

82. Quoted in *CubaINFO*, September 11, 1997, pp. 1–2.

83. See Ann Louise Bardach and Larry Rohter, "Key Cuba Foe Claims Exiles' Backing," *New York Times*, July 12, 1998, pp. 1, 10; Bardach and Rohter, "Life in the Shadows, Trying to Bring Down Castro," *New York Times*, July 13, 1998, pp. 1, 6–7.

84. Following the eighth round of talks in December, Deputy Assistant Secretary of State John Hamilton acknowledged Havana's continuing complaints about the U.S. response to Cuban citizens using force to enter the United States, but argued, "We are complying with our obligations [and there is] no way that we condone, acquiesce in, or accept, the use of violence in the migration relationship." Transcript, "Hamilton Briefing on U.S.–Cuban Migration Talks," U.S. Information Service [hereafter USIS] Washington File, December 4, 1997.

85. Quoted in *CubaINFO*, February 27, 1997, p. 7.

86. Transcript, "U.S. Government Seriously Considering Exemptions for Travel to Cuba," USIS Washington File, August 19, 1997.

87. Confidential Interview 5.

88. Quoted in *CubaINFO*, October 23, 1997, p. 4.

89. Quoted in Laurence McQuillan, "Clinton Seeking Sign of Change in Cuba," October 17, 1997, *Reuters News Service*; Christopher Marquis, " 'The Ball Is in Cuba's Court,' Clinton Says," *Miami Herald*, October 17, 1997, p. 22A.

90. Transcript, White House, Office of the Press Secretary, "Interview with the President, 'NBC's Meet the Press,' " November 7, 1997.

91. Quoted in *CubaINFO*, July 10, 1997, p. 1.

92. Transcript, "Representative Hamilton on Sanctions Reform Proposal," USIS Washington File, October 24, 1997.

93. Transcript, "Senator Lugar on Bill to Reform Use of Sanctions," USIS Washington File, October 24, 1997.

94. See Juan O. Tamayo, "U.S. Funds Efforts Aiming to Build Democracy in Cuba," *Miami Herald*, October 25, 1998 [OE]; *CubaINFO*, January 8, 1998, p. 1.

95. Quoted in *CubaINFO*, January 8, 1998, p. 3.

96. Telephone Interview with John Merrill, Washington DC, May 11, 1999. Director for Caribbean and Central American Affairs, Department of Defense, 1997–1999. Merrill recalled that in late 1998, "I began watching Cuba myself and, in effect, became Country Desk officer for Cuba."

97. Quoted in Thomas W. Lippman, "Business-Led Coalition Urges U.S. to Relax Embargo on Cuba," *Washington Post*, January 14, 1998, p. A16.

98. Quoted in Jim Wolf, "Broad U.S. Coalition Urges Food Sales to Cuba," January 14, 1998, *Reuters News Service*.

99. Quoted in "Coalition Calls for Change in U.S. Policy for Aid to Cuba," USIA Washington File, January 15, 1998.

100. Quoted in Christopher Marquis, "Plan for Food Aid to Cuba in Works to Help Poor," *Miami Herald*, January 28, 1998 [OE].

101. Transcript, White House, Office of the Press Secretary, "Press Briefing by Mike McCurry," January 13, 1998.

102. Testimony before the House Ways and Means Committee, in "Kantor Says WTO Does Not Infringe U.S. Sovereignty," USIA Wireless File, Washington DC, March 13, 1996.

103. Peter Guilford, quoted in Paul Lewis, "Cuba Trade Law: Export of U.S. Ire and Politics," *New York Times*, March 15, 1996, p. D3.

104. Quoted in Thomas W. Lipmann, "Europeans Assail U.S. Trade Curbs," *Washington Post*, June 13, 1996, p. A20.

105. Quoted in Paul Blustein and Thomas W. Lippman, "Allies Angered by U.S. Boycott Policy," *Washington Post*, May 10, 1996, p. A31.

106. Quoted in Bruce Clark et al., "Rifkind Hits at Cuba Trade Curb," *Financial Times*, May 30, 1996, p. 4.

107. Confidential Interview 5.

108. Quoted in *CubaINFO*, June 13, 1996, p. 3.

109. Quoted in Harris, "Clinton Delays Law Allowing Cuba Suits," p. A22.

110. Quoted in David E. Sanger, "Talk Multilaterally, Hit Allies With Stick," *New York Times*, July 21, 1996, p. E3.

111. Quoted in Steven Erlanger and David E. Sanger, "On Global Stage, Clinton's Pragmatic Turn," *New York Times*, July 29, 1996, p. 17.

112. Confidential Interview 3.

113. Confidential Interview 7.

114. Confidential Interview 6.

115. Confidential Interview 5.

116. Quoted in Wendy Lubetkin, "EU Brings Helms–Burton Law Before World Trade Organization," USIA Wireless File, Washington DC, October 16, 1996 [our emphasis].

117. Quoted in Gail Russell Chaddock, "U.S. Puts World Trade at Risk in Cuba Fight," *Christian Science Monitor*, October 22, 1996, p. 14.

118. Gardner quoted in Wendy Lubetkin, "WTO Accepts EU Request for Panel on Helms–Burton Act," USIA Wireless File, Washington DC, November 20, 1996; Eizenstat quoted in Warner Rose, "Taking Helms–Burton to WTO Seen Inciting Protectionism in U.S.," USIA Wireless File, Washington DC, November 21, 1996.

119. Quoted in David E. Sanger, "Europe Postpones Challenge to U.S. on Havana Trade," *New York Times*, February 13, 1997, p. 9.
120. Quoted in Francis Williams and Nancy Dunne, "EU Forces Dispute Panel on Cuba Trade," *Financial Times*, November 21, 1996, p. 1.
121. Quoted in *CubaINFO*, February 27, 1997, pp. 5–6.
122. See Peter Kornbluh, "From Here to Cuba," *New York Times*, May 17, 1995, p. 19.
123. Quoted in Lippman, "Europeans Assail U.S. Trade Curbs," p. A20.
124. Quoted in John Palmer and Jonathan Freedland, "Europe Poised for Trade War with U.S. over Cuba," *The Guardian*, July 16, 1996, p. 3.
125. Quoted in Guy de Jonquieres, "Showdown on Cuba Trade," *Financial Times*, February 3, 1997, p. 1.
126. Confidential Interview 3.
127. Jonathan Freedland, "Clinton Likely to Hold Fire on Cuba Bill," *Guardian Weekly*, November 17, 1996, p. 3.
128. Quoted in *CubaINFO*, December 12, 1996, pp. 6–7.
129. See Roy, *Cuba, the United States, and the Helms–Burton Doctrine*, pp. 123–4.
130. Transcript, *Helms–Burton: A Loose Canon?*, p. 24.
131. Quoted in David Fox, "EU Warns WTO Facing 'Immeasurable Damage' from U.S.," February 12, 1997, *Reuters News Service*.
132. Nicholas Burns, quoted in "U.S. Disappointed by EU Move over Cuba Law," February 13, 1997, Reuters News Service.
133. Quoted in David E. Sanger, "U.S. Rejects Role for World Court in Trade Dispute," *New York Times*, February 21, 1997, p. 1; Paul Blustein and Anne Swardson, "U.S. Vows to Boycott WTO Panel," *Washington Post*, February 21, 1997, p. A12.
134. Interview with Michael Ranneberger.
135. Quoted in Sanger, "U.S. Rejects Role for World Court in Trade Dispute," p. 7.
136. Interview with Michael Ranneberger.
137. Quoted in Paul Blustein and Thomas W. Lippman, "Trade Clash on Cuba Is Averted," *New York Times*, April 12, 1997, p. 1.
138. "Eizenstat Statement on U.S.–EU Helms/Burton Agreement," USIA Wireless File, Washington DC, April 11, 1997 [our emphasis].
139. "Europe Backs Down on Helms–Burton," *Latin American Weekly Report*, April 15, 1997, p. 170.
140. Quoted in "Europeans Disavow Tough U.S. Stance on Cuba," April 19, 1997, *Reuters News Service*.
141. Quoted in "Germany Welcomes Pact With U.S. on Cuba Trade," April 18, 1997, *Reuters News Service*.
142. Quoted in "Canada Says Cuba Compromise Only a First Step," April 11, 1997, *Reuters News Service*.
143. Quoted in Blustein and Lippman, "Trade Clash on Cuba Trade Is Averted," p. 20.
144. Burns quoted in "U.S. Criticizes Franco–Cuban Investment Pact," April 24, 1997, *Reuters News Service*; Borotra quoted in Marcel Michelson "Focus-France Signs Cuba Deal, Warns U.S.," April 25, 1997, *Reuters News Service*.
145. *CubaINFO*, October 23, 1997, p. 2.
146. Quoted in "EU's Brittan-Working Hard to End Spat with US re Cuba/Libya," September 24, 1997, *Reuters News Service*.

147. See, for example, Assistant Secretary of State Alan Larson, "Transcript of Press Conference," Brussels, October 14, 1997, USIS Washington File.
148. Quoted in "Franco-American Ties Tense Once More," October 4, 1997, *Reuters News Service*. On ILSA, see George E. Shambaugh, *States, Firms and Power*. Albany: State University of New York Press, 1999, pp. 184–6.
149. Jospin and EU officials quoted in "Jospin Defends Total, Rebuffs US Sanctions," September 29, 1997, *Reuters News Service*; Roger Cohen, "France Scoffs at U.S. Protest over Iran Deal," *New York Times*, September 30, 1997, p. 12.
150. Quoted in "EU, U.S. on Collision Course over Total Contract," September 30, 1997, *Reuters News Service*.
151. Quoted in Carol Giacomo, "U.S., EU Discuss Total Deal with Iran," October 2, 1997, *Reuters News Service*.
152. Quoted in Thomas W. Lippman, "U.S. Delays Sanctions on Iran Gas Deal," *Washington Post*, October 4, 1997, p. A18.
153. Quoted in William Drozdiak, "Even Allies Resent U.S. Dominance," *Washington Post*, November 4, 1997, p. A13.
154. Quoted in Douglas Hamilton, "EU Rejects U.S. Bid to Talk Round Anti-Cuba Law," October 17, 1997, *Reuters News Service*.
155. Quoted in *CubaINFO*, November 13, 1997, p. 5.
156. U.S. Congress, House, Committee on International Relations, Subcommittee on International Economic Policy and Trade, *WTO–Dispute Settlement Body*, 105th Cong., 2nd Sess., March 30, 1998, p. 12.
157. Quoted in "EU Welcomes U.S. Review of Sanctions Policy," January 9, 1998, *Reuters News Service*.
158. Paeman and Eizenstat quoted in Carol Giacomo, "US Reviewing Its Sanctions Policy," January 7, 1998, *Reuters News Service*.
159. "EU Plans to Increase Investment in Cuba," *CUBANEWS*, March 1998, p. 6.
160. Quoted in *CubaINFO*, February 26, 1998, p. 7.

CHAPTER 4

1. Quoted in "Clinton Deflects Pope's Call to Relax Cuba Embargo," January 21, 1998, *Reuters News Service*.
2. Interview with Michael Ranneberger.
3. Interview with Stuart Eizenstat. Also see "Transcript of White House Press Briefing by Mike McCurry," January 23, 1998, *Reuters News Service*.
4. Quoted in Christopher Marquis, "U.S. Officials Are Faintly Hopeful that Pope Could Aid Freedom in Cuba," *Philadelphia Inquirer*, January 20, 1998 [OE]; Interview with Stuart Eizenstat.
5. Confidential Interview 5.
6. Quoted in Anthony Boadle, "U.S. Sees Little Change in Cuba with Pope's Visit," January 21, 1998, *Reuters News Service*.
7. Quoted in Tim Weiner, "Pope vs. Embargo: Still a Sharp Divide in U.S.," *New York Times*, January 21, 1998, p. 8.
8. Quoted in Tracey Eaton and Alfredo Corchado, "Pope Brings a Message of Hope to Cuba," *Dallas Morning News*, January 22, 1998 [OE].

9. Quoted in *CubaINFO*, February 26, 1998, p. 2. In March 1997, the American Association for World Health issued a damning report on the repercussions of Clinton's policy for bringing about change in Cuba. Based on a year-long investigation, it concluded that the U.S. embargo had dramatically harmed the health and nutrition of a large part of the island population. This it attributed largely to the consequences of the CDA: The ban on U.S. subsidiary trade had limited Cuba's access to medicines and medical supplies; the extraordinarily cumbersome and time-consuming Treasury and Commerce licensing procedures for individual humanitarian sales of these goods to Cuba "actively discouraged any medical commerce"; the U.S. shipping embargo not only dissuaded the transfer of medical equipment to the island, but also forced Cuban companies to pay millions of dollars in extra travel costs, leading to further cutbacks in imports of basic medical goods and foodstuffs; and humanitarian aid from American NGOs and international organizations had been completely inadequate to the task of compensating for the losses sustained by a "relatively sophisticated and comprehensive public health system [that has been] systematically stripped of essential resources." Only the Cuban government's commitment to "maintain[ing] a high level of budgetary support for a health care system designed to deliver primary and preventative health to all its people [averted a] humanitarian catastrophe."

The report challenged a fundamental tenet of Clinton policy – that humanitarian considerations had been quarantined from other embargo provisions – and it undermined much of the administration rhetoric about reaching out on a people-to-people basis to support ordinary Cubans against their government. See American Association for World Health, *The Impact of the U.S. Embargo on Health & Nutrition in Cuba*. Washington DC: March 1997, 301 pp.

10. Quoted in *CubaINFO*, February 26, 1998, pp. 9, 11.

11. Transcript, Department of State, "Daily Press Briefing," by James P. Rubin, February 20, 1998.

12. U.S. Congress, House, Committee on International Relations, Subcommittee on the Western Hemisphere, *The Visit of His Holiness Pope John Paul II to Cuba: An Assessment of Its Impact on Religious Freedom in Cuba*, 105th Cong., 2nd Sess., March 4, 1998, p. 22.

13. Quoted in Thomas W. Lippman, "U.S. to Ease Some Curbs Against Cuba," *Washington Post*, March 20, 1998, p. A16.

14. Quoted in Steven Erlanger, "U.S. to Ease Curbs on Relief to Cuba and Money to Kin," *New York Times*, March 20, 1998, p. 8.

15. Transcript of address and question session by Undersecretary of Commerce for International Trade Stuart Eizenstat, U.S. Chamber of Commerce, Washington DC, November 20, in *U.S. *Cuba Policy Report*, November 27, 1996, pp. 5–6.

16. Confidential Interview 6.

17. Quoted in Mark P. Sullivan, *Cuba: Issues for Congress*. Congressional Research Service, April 9, 1998, p. 9.

18. "Text: State Department Statement on March 20 Cuban Measures," USIS Washington File, May 13, 1998.

19. Quoted in Richard Whittle, "Albright: Cuba Will Remain Under Tight Economic Embargo," *Dallas Morning News*, March 21, 1998 [OE]. Albright also wanted to

avoid "any show of softness on Castro [that] would have torpedoed [her] carefully nurtured relationship with [Jesse] Helms." Thomas W. Lippman, *Madeleine Albright and the New American Diplomacy*. Boulder: Westview Press, 2000, p. 47.

20. Quoted in Richard Whittle, "House Panel Debates Whether to Continue Cuban Embargo," *Dallas Morning News*, May 8, 1998 [OE].
21. Transcript, "The Cuba Decision," *The NewsHour with Jim Lehrer*, March 20, 1998. Also see Carol Rosenberg, "Miami Lawmakers Warn Against Easing Sanctions on Cuba," *Miami Herald*, March 19, 1998 [OE].
22. Quoted in Ginger Thompson, "Pressured by Vatican, Clinton to Ease Sanctions Against Cuba," *Chicago Tribune*, March 20, 1998 [OE].
23. Quoted in "Business Ad Urges U.S. Change in Cuba Policy," January 15, 1998, *Reuters News Service*.
24. Interview with William Lane.
25. Telephone Interview with Raimundo Ruga.
26. Christopher Marquis, "Pentagon Calls Cuban Forces Weak," *Miami Herald*, March 29, 1998 [OE].
27. Quoted in Ibid.
28. Quoted in Andres Oppenheimer, "Cuban Forces Cut in Half, General Says," *Miami Herald*, February 21, 1998 [OE].
29. Quoted in Marquis, "Pentagon Calls Cuban Forces Weak."
30. Transcript, "DIA Report on Cuban Threat to U.S. National Security," USIS Washington File, May 6, 1998.
31. "Text: Defense Secretary's Letter to Thurmond on Cuban Threat," USIS Washington File, May 6, 1998.
32. "Text: DIA Report on Cuban Threat to U.S. National Security."
33. Transcript, "Ranneberger Worldnet-TV Interview," USIA, May 13, 1998.
34. Confidential Interview 5. Discussing the UNHRC's favorable vote on the Cuban human rights resolution at its 1999 meeting, the Coordinator of State's Office of Cuban Affairs admitted that "we put a lot of pressure on" Ecuador, Argentina, Chile, and Uruguay, who supported the resolution on this occasion. Interview with Michael Ranneberger.
35. U.S. Congress, House, Committee on International Relations, Subcommittee on the Western Hemisphere, *Latin America and the Caribbean: An Update and Summary of the Summit of the Americas*, 105th Cong., 2nd Sess., May 6, 1998, pp. 18–19.
36. Quoted in Christopher Marquis, "Lawmakers: U.S. Must Aid Cuban Dissidents," *Miami Herald*, April 24, 1998 [OE].
37. See *CubaINFO*, March 20, 1998, pp. 1, 3; *CubaINFO*, April 9, 1998, p. 6.
38. See Christopher Marquis, "Helms–CANF Bill Would Send Federal Aid to Cuba," *Miami Herald*, May 13, 1998 [OE].
39. Quoted in *CubaINFO*, April 30, 1998, p. 2.
40. Quoted in Christopher Marquis and Jodi A. Enda, "Miami Lawmakers Cool to New Rules," *Miami Herald*, May 19, 1998 [OE]; U.S. Congress, House, Committee on International Relations, *Economic Sanctions and U.S. Policy Interests*, 105th Cong., 2nd Sess., June 3, 1998, pp. 11, 17.

41. Quoted in Dan Balz, "U.S. Eases Stand on Cuba, Iran Sanctions," *Washington Post*, May 19, 1998, p. A15.
42. Quoted in Jeffrey Ulbrich, "U.S. Agrees to Ease Trade Sanctions," *Washington Post*, May 18, 1998 [OE].
43. Confidential Interview 3.
44. Confidential Interview 2.
45. Interview with Andrew Semmel.
46. Quotes in Balz, "U.S. Eases Stand on Cuba, Iran Sanctions," p. A15.
47. Interview with Stuart Eizenstat.
48. Quoted in "U.S. Lawmakers See Loopholes in US–EU Cuba Pact," June 18, 1998, *Reuters News Service*; "White House, Congress Spar Over Deal with E.U.," *CUBANEWS*, July 1998, p. 8.
49. Quoted in *CubaINFO*, August 4, 1998, p. 4. Reflecting on the 1998 May understanding a year later, a senior Department of Commerce official described it as full of "smoke and mirrors" such as the EU's commitment to take arms export controls into account in dealing with Cuba. "We haven't seen much of that," he conceded. "I live in dread and fear of being called up to the Hill and asked about that." Interview with R. Roger Majak.
50. Quotes in *CubaINFO*, July 30, 1998, p. 3.
51. Quoted in Juan O. Tamayo, "Treasury Scrutinizes Washington Company's Cuba Trip," *Miami Herald*, August 7, 1998 [OE].
52. Interview with William Lane, Washington, D.C., September 12, 2001.
53. Quotes in Kevin Hall, "U.S. Quietly Making it Easier for Some Business to Be Done with Cuba," *Journal of Commerce*, August 6, 1998, reprinted in *Reuters News Service*; Tamayo, "Treasury Scrutinizes Washington Company's Cuba Trip."
54. Quoted in Linda Robinson, "An Opening to Cuba?" *U.S. News & World Report*, September 28, 1998, p. 45.
55. Quoted in Marc Selinger, "Treasury Denies Washington, D.C. Firm's Business Trip to Cuba," *Washington Times*, September 5, 1998, reprinted in Reuters News Service.
56. Transcript of statement by Kirby Jones, president, Alamar Associates, on the U.S.–Cuba Business Summit, September 9–12, 1998, Cancun, Mexico, September 30, 1998.
57. Interview with Kirby Jones.
58. Transcript of statement by Kirby Jones.
59. Quoted in *CUBANEWS*, September 1998, p. 8.
60. Quotes in Carol Rosenberg, "Foundation Leaders Cut Short in Discussion with State Department," *Miami Herald*, August 26, 1998 [OE].
61. Confidential Interview 6.
62. *CubaINFO*, September 10, 1998, p. 2.
63. See Barbara Leitch LePoer et al., *India–Pakistan Nuclear Tests and U.S. Response.* Congressional Research Service, November 24, 1998, pp. 6–7, 20–1.
64. Letter in *Congressional Record: Senate*, October 20, 1998, pp. S12681–S12683.
65. Quoted in "Kissinger, Eagleburger Seek Review of Cuba Policy," *Miami Herald*, October 13, 1998 [OE].

66. Quoted in Frank Davies, "White House Considers Plan for Commission to Carry Out a Bipartisan Review," *Miami Herald*, November 24, 1998 [OE].
67. Quotes in *CubaINFO*, December 16, 1998, pp. 1, 2.
68. Quoted in Pascal Fletcher, "U.S. Senator Proposes 'New Conversation' With Cuba," December 7, 1998, *Reuters News Service*; Mark Fineman, "2 Democrats Seek a New Cuba Policy," *Los Angeles Times*, December 12, 1998 [OE].
69. Quoted in Jonathan Wright, "U.S. Decides Against Cuba Policy Review," January 5, 1999, *Reuters News Service.*
70. Quoted in Frank Davies, "Initiative Rejects Plan for Full Policy Review," *Miami Herald*, January 5, 1999 [OE].
71. Quoted in Jim Mann, "Clinton Takes a Weak Cut at Baseball Diplomacy," *Los Angeles Times*, January 13, 1999 [OE].
72. Confidential Interview 7.
73. Quoted in Juan O. Tamayo, "How Battle on Policy Toward Cuba Led to Easing," *Miami Herald*, January 19, 1999 [OE]. Also see Tim Weiner, "Anti-Castro Exiles Won Limit on Changes," *New York Times*, January 6, 1999 [OE].
74. Quoted in Tom Carter, "Castro Scores with Baseball Exchange," *Washington Times*, May 8, 1999, p. A14. Also see Davies, "Initiative Rejects Plan for Full Policy Review."
75. "Text: Clinton Announces New Steps to Help Cuban People," USIA Washington File, January 5, 1999.
76. Confidential Interview 7.
77. Editorial, "Changes Terrain on Cuba," *New York Times*, January 6, 1999 [OE]. Tolman quoted in *CubaINFO*, February 1, 1999, p. 2. Once again, editorial support for this sentiment extended well beyond the major "papers of record." The *San Francisco Examiner* (January 6) described Clinton's measures as a "few slight relaxations" that pointed in the right direction but "not far enough." The *Fort Worth Star–Telegram* (January 6) argued that U.S. policy toward Cuba "stopped making sense the day the Cold War ended" and expressed the hope that the January 5 steps would be the beginnings of a move to "eliminate the embargoes on trade with Cuba." The *Philadelphia Inquirer* (January 6) thought it was "about time" Clinton reassessed an "increasingly pointless embargo," while the *St. Louis Post–Dispatch* (January 7) urged the president to abolish the entire embargo and craft a Cuba policy "that reflects the interests of the whole country, not just a special-interest group" [all OE].
78. Interview with Willard Workman.
79. Charles Abbott, "Farm Group Asks U.S.Talks to Open Cuba Trade," January 14, 1999, *Reuters News Service.*
80. Quoted in Juan O. Tamayo, "Eased Cuba Sanctions Questioned," *Miami Herald*, January 7, 1999 [OE].
81. Quoted in "Clinton Eases Restrictions on Cuba but Stops Short of Reviewing Embargo," *Congressional Quarterly Weekly Report*, January 9, 1999, p. 69.
82. Quoted in Tim Weiner, "U.S. Ready to Ease Some Restrictions in Policy on Cuba," *New York Times*, January 5, 1999, p. 4.
83. Interview with Robert Philippone, Washington DC, May 13, 1999. National Security adviser to Senator Bob Graham, including responsibility for advising the Florida Democrat on Cuba policy, 1996–2000.

84. "Text: Albright on Promoting U.S.–Cuban Exchanges," USIA Washington File, January 5, 1999; Transcript, "Interview with Secretary Albright," *The NewsHour with Jim Lehrer*, January 5, 1999.
85. Interview with R. Roger Majak.
86. "Transcript: Senior U.S. Officials Speak on Cuba Policy," USIA Washington File, January 5, 1999.
87. Ibid.
88. Confidential Interview 10.
89. Council on Foreign Relations, Report of an Independent Task Force, *U.S.–Cuban Relations in the 21st Century*. New York, 1999.
90. Confidential Interview 4.
91. Confidential Interview 7.
92. "Transcript: Senior U.S. Officials Speak on Cuba Policy."
93. See Peter Kornbluh, "Baseball Diplomacy," *In These Times*, May 16, 1999, p. 16; Kornbluh, "U.S.–Cuba: Extra Innings," *The Nation*, May 10, 1999, p. 6.
94. Interview with Thomas Quigley, May 14, 1999, Washington, D.C. Latin American Adviser to the U.S. National Catholic Conference of Bishops.
95. Quoted in Tim Johnson, "Cuban Church Speaking Out on Sensitive Issues," *Miami Herald*, January 31, 1999 [OE].
96. Confidential Interview 4.
97. Quoted in Juan O. Tamayo, "U.S. Study Blasts Radio Martí," *Miami Herald*, February 11, 1999 [OE].
98. *CubaINFO*, February 22, 1992, p. 2.
99. Quoted in Pascal Fletcher, "Cuba: Telecom Threat Problem for US," *Financial Times*, February 9, 1999 [OE].
100. U.S. Congress, Senate, Committee on Foreign Relations, *Castro's Crackdown in Cuba: Human Rights on Trial*, 106th Cong., 1st Sess., March 10, 1999, p. 1.
101. Quoted in *CubaINFO*, March 22, 1999, p. 2.
102. Quoted in Serge F. Kovaleski, "For U.S. and Cuba, It was Just a Game," *Washington Post*, March 30, 1999, p. A8.
103. U.S. Congress, House, Committee on International Relations, Subcommittee on the Western Hemisphere, *U.S.–Cuba Relations: Where Are We and Where Are We Heading?* 106th Cong., 1st Sess., March 24, 1999, pp. 1, 5, 27, 32.
104. Quoted in "That Elusive Chinese Spring," *The Economist*, March 6, 1999, pp. 33–4.
105. See Frank Davies, "U.S. Cites China, Cuba Political Repression," *Miami Herald*, February 27, 1999 [OE]. Also see Human Rights Watch, *Cuba's Repressive Machinery: Forty Years After the Revolution*. New York, June 1999.
106. Quoted in Frank Davies, "Officials Speaks Up for Cuba," *Miami Herald*, March 16, 1999 [OE].
107. Quoted in Jim Mann, " 'Rogue' White House Terms Require a Little Explaining," *Los Angeles Times*, February 24, 1999 [OE].
108. Quoted in "Stoked by Farm Interests, Anti-Sanctions Movement Builds in Both Chambers," *Congressional Quarterly Weekly Report*, March 27, 1999, p. 767.
109. Transcript, "A New Conversation About Cuba," delivered to the Seventeenth Annual Journalists and Editors Workship on Latin America, April 23, 1999.

110. Quoted in Philip Shenon, "U.S. To Ease Policy on Some Sanctions," *New York Times*, April 29, 1999, p. 1.
111. Quoted in Juan O. Tamayo, "U.S. Fine-Tunes Cuba Trade," *Miami Herald*, May 13, 1999, p. 12A.
112. Interview with R. Roger Majak.
113. Confidential Interview 10.
114. Quoted in Karen DeYoung, "U.S. Businesses Eye Trade with Cuba," *Washington Post*, July 28, 1999 [OE].
115. U.S. Congress, House, Committee on Agriculture, *Economic Sanctions and the Effect on U.S. Agriculture*, 106th Cong., 1st Sess., June 9, 1999, pp. 40–3, 47.
116. U.S. Congress, Senate, Committee on Banking, Housing, and Urban Affairs, *Review of the Export Control Authorities*, 106th Cong., 1st Sess., June 17, 23, 24, 1999, pp. 121, 158.
117. Quoted in Ana Radelat, "Farmers Seeking Exports to Cuba, Other Nations," *Miami Herald*, July 5, 1999 [OE].
118. U.S. Congress, House, *U.S.–Cuba Relations: Where Are We and Where Are We Heading?* p. 30.
119. Quoted in Christopher Marquis, "U.S. Eyes Spanish Firm's Cuba Holdings," *Miami Herald*, August 12, 1999 [OE]. Ranneberger's nomination was confirmed by the full Senate in November 2000. However, Burton actively lobbied to block Peter Romero's career, writing to Helms as early as mid-May "to hold firm in your resolve not to see Romero confirmed." Quoted in Al Kamen, "Romero Nomination Gets More Flak," *Washington Post*, May 17, 1999, p. A17. Helms never allowed a vote on Romero's nomination. As a consequence, he served as Acting Secretary until Clinton made a recess appointment toward the end of his presidency. In July 2001, Romero stepped down from the position.
120. Quoted in Juan O. Tamayo, "U.S. Poised to Bar Execs of Firm Operating in Cuba," *Miami Herald*, July 3, 1999 [OE].
121. Christopher Marquis, "U.S. Eyes Spanish Firm's Cuba Holdings," *Miami Herald*, August 12, 1999 [OE].
122. CEMEX's decision to sever a number of technical agreements with the Cuban Cement Producers Association days before it was due to receive an official State Department warning that its agreements covered a plant formerly owned by the U.S. Lone Star Industries, Inc. "was more than a coincidence," according to one U.S. policymaker privy to a series of meeting between department and Cemex lawyers. Quoted in "Cemex Quits Cuba to Avoid U.S. Sanctions," May 29, 1996, *Reuters News Service*. Grupo Domos only terminated its business operations in Cuba because it could not meet its financial obligations to the Cuban government. Sherritt remained the single largest foreign investor in Cuba. See John Schreiner, "Fidel Castro's Canadian Friend," *Financial Post*, December 12, 1998 [OE].
123. Juan O. Tamayo, "U.S. Re-examines Cuban Connections to Ilegal Drug Smugglers," *Miami Herald*, July 23, 1999 [OE].
124. Quoted in Douglas Farah, "Cuba Wages a Lonesome Drug War," *Washington Post*, May 25, 1999 [OE]. Also see "Cuba Cooperating to Combat Drug Trade, U.S. Official Says," *New York Times*, May 8, 1999, p. 3.

125. Quoted in Juan O. Tamayo, "U.S. Officials to Visit Cuba, Discuss Cooperative Efforts in Drug War," *Miami Herald*, June 19, 1999 [OE]. Also see Peter Kornbluh, *Cuba, Counternarcotics and Collaboration: A Security Issue in U.S.–Cuban Relations*. Georgetown University: Center for Latin American Studies, December 2000, pp. 8–9.

126. Interview with Michael Ranneberger. Also see Tim Golden, "U.S., Avoiding Castro, Relaxes Rules on Cuba," *New York Times*, July 7, 1999, pp. 1, 8.

127. Quoted in DeYoung, "U.S. Business Eye Trade with Cuba."

128. See Christopher Marquis, "Proposal to Lift Sanctions on Cuba Defeated in Senate," *Miami Herald*, August 5, 1999 [OE]; "U.S. Wants More Contacts with Cuban People," September 30, 1999, *Reuters News Service*; Mark P. Sullivan, *Cuba: Issues for Congress*. Congressional Research Service, November 19, 1999, p. 11.

129. Quoted in *CubaINFO*, November 23, 1999, p. 3.

130. Press Release, House International Relations Committee, October 19, 1999. Also see U.S. Congress, House, Committee on International Relations, *The Cuban Program: Torture of American Prisoners by Cuban Agents*, 106th Cong., 1st Sess., November 4, 1999.

131. Quoted in Tracey Eaton, "Possible U.S.–Cuba Anti-Drug Agreement Is Mired in Politics," *Dallas Morning News*, October 24, 1999 [OE].

132. Quotes in Juan O. Tamayo, "Despite Concern, Clinton Omits Cuba as Major Drug-Transit Point," *Miami Herald*, November 11, 1999 [OE].

133. U.S. Congress, House, Committee on Government Reform, Subcommittee on Criminal Justice, Drug Policy and Human Resouces, *Cuban Link to Drug Trafficking*, 106th Cong., 1st Sess., November 17, 1999, pp. 11, 15, 25, 31; transcript reprinted in *Reuters News Service*, November 17, 1999. Also see opening statements by Burton and Ben Gilman in U.S. Congress, House, Committee on Government Reform, *Drug Trafficking in the Caribbean*, 106th Cong., 2nd Sess., January 3, 4, 2000, pp. 1–7.

134. See Karen DeYoung, "Can Elián Case Alter U.S.–Cuban Dynamics? Custody Fight Renews Debate on Relations," *Washington Post*, May 2, 2000 [OE].

135. Quoted in Juan O. Tamayo, "U.S. Rebuffs Castro on His Demand for Return of 6-Year-Old Rafter," *Miami Herald*, December 7, 1999 [OE].

136. Quoted in Steven Mufson "Clinton Warns Against Politics in Cuban Boy's Case," *Washington Post*, December 9, 1999, p. A41.

137. See Frank Newport, "Americans Say it is in Elián González' Best Interests to Return to Cuba with His Father," *The Gallup Poll Monthly*, April 2000, p. 26.

138. Ibid.

139. See Karen DeYoung and Juliet Eilperin, "Elián to Meet with His Grandmothers Today," *Washington Post*, January 26, 2000 [OE]; Peter Wallsten, "Elián Case Forces a Fresh Look at Cuban-American Influence," *Congressional Quarterly Weekly Report*, April 8, 2000, pp. 827–8.

140. Quoted in Francine Kiefer and James N. Thurman, "Race, Pardons and a Small Boy from Cuba," *Christian Science Monitor*, January 20, 2000, [OE].

141. Quoted in Mary Leonard, "Congress Readies Bill to Make Cuban Boy a U.S. Citizen," *Boston Globe*, January 25, 2000 [OE].

142. Quoted in John M. Broder and Elaine Sciolino, "Legal Process on Cuban Boy Winds Toward a Close, Its Way Complicated by Politics," *New York Times*, March 31, 2000 [OE].

143. Alfonso Chardy et al., "Grass-Roots Support for Elián Takes on a Defiant Tone," *Miami Herald*, March 28, 2000 [OE].

144. Alex Veiga, "Mayor: No Aid to Help Feds in Showdown with Elián's Relatives," *Miami Herald*, March 29, 2000 [OE].

145. Quoted in Sue Anne Presley and John F. Harris, "Gore Backs Bill on Elián Status," *Washington Post*, March 31, 2000 [OE].

146. Quotes in Katherine Q. Seelye, "Gore Supporting Residency Status for Cuban Child," *New York Times*, March 31, 2000; Ceci Connolly, "Candidates Are Critical of U.S. Handling of Elián," *Washington Post*, April 23, 2000 [OE].

147. Quoted in Wallsten, "Elián Case Forces a Fresh Look at Cuban-American Influence," p. 828.

148. See John F. Harris and Davis A. Vise, "White House Wants Frustrating Elián Drama to Close," *Washington Post*, April 15, 2000 [OE]; Mary Leonard, "White House Relieved Reno Acted," *New York Times*, April 23, 2000 [OE].

149. See Ibid.

150. See Robert A. Jordan, "Gore Trod Unwisely in Florida and Could Yet Pay the Toll," *Boston Globe*, April 9, 2000 [OE]; John Donnelly, "Cuban Vote in Florida, Often Crucial, Is Likely to Opt for Bush," *Boston Globe*, April 25, 2000 [OE].

151. Quoted in Juan O. Tamayo, "Crisis Shook Exile Lobby," *Miami Herald*, April 25, 2000 [OE].

152. The preliminary results of a poll conducted by the Florida International University's Cuba Research Institute showed that although 78.5 percent of Miami–Dade County's Cuban-Americans believed that Elián should have stayed in the United States, only 28.3 percent of national respondents shared this view. However, more than 80 pecent of both samples agreed that the case had hurt the Cuban-American community. See Florida International University, Cuban Research Institute, Institute for Public Opinion Research, *October 2000 Cuba Poll* (IPOR Website).

153. Quoted in De Young, "Can Elián Case Alter U.S.–Cuban Dynamic? Custody Fight Renews Debate on Relations."

154. See Edward Wong, "Miami Raid Is Criticized after Reno Meets with Lawmakers," *New York Times*, April 25, 2000 [OE]; Lizette Alvarez, "Republicans Back Away from Their Indignation Over Seizure of Cuban Boy," *New York Times*, May 3, 2000 [OE].

155. Quoted in Alfredo Corchado, "Saga Seen as Hope for Cuba Ties," *Dallas Morning News*, April 23, 2000 [OE].

156. Quoted in John Donnelly, "Policy Review Likely on Cuba, U.S. Officials Say," *Boston Globe*, April 9, 2000 [OE].

157. Quoted in Tamayo, "Crisis Shook Exile Lobby."

158. Quoted in "US Official Terms Castro's Actions 'Cynical,'" *Boston Globe*, April 27, 2000 [OE].

159. See Christopher Marquis, "Despite U.S. Restrictions Against Cuba, Door Opens Wider for Visits by Americans," *New York Times*, June 19, 2000 [OE].

160. Quoted in Ana Radelat, "U.S. Business Eyes Havana," *Miami Herald*, June 27, 2000 [OE]. That the administration was prepared to ignore CANF complaints when it suited its purpose was demonstrated only days earlier, when Cuban baseball player Andy Morales was repatriated after being intercepted in the Florida Straits as he attempted to reach U.S. territory. Morales was ineligible for asylum under Clinton's "wet foot/dry foot" policy, but he was nevertheless the first prominent Cuban athlete in memory to be sent back to the island. See Christopher Marquis, "United States Sends Cuban Athlete Home," *New York Times*, June 8, 2000 [OE].

161. See David González, "On Show in Cuba: Marvels of American Medicine," *New York Times*, January 28, 2000 [OE].

162. Quoted in "Helms Relents; Panel Votes to Allow Sale of Food to Cuba," *Miami Herald*, March 24, 2000 [OE].

163. During 1999–2000, Nethercutt received more than $92,000 in PAC campaign contributions from an agribusiness determined to break the embargo wall blocking its access to the Cuban market. Center for Responsive Politics data, Open Secrets.org website, October 1, 2001.

164. See Mary McGrory, "Trade Imbalance," *Washington Post*, May 4, 2000 [OE].

165. Extracts from State Department Country reports on both countries quoted in Karen DeYoung and Eric Painin, "Congressional Mood Shifts on Cuba Trade Ban," *Washington Post*, May 23, 2000 [OE]. Also see the comments on Cuba by Assistant Secretary of State Harold Hongju Koh, in U.S. Congress, House, Committee on International Relations, Subcommittee on International Operations and Human Rights, *Country Reports on Human Rights Practice for 1999*, 106th Cong., 2nd Sess., March 8, 2000, pp. 37–8.

166. U.S. Department of State, *Patterns of Global Terrorism 1998*, April 1999, p. 30. Also see *CubaINFO*, May 21, 1998, p. 7, and March 4, 1996, pp. 1–2.

167. Interview with Michael Ranneberger.

168. Confidential Interview 5.

169. Confidential Interview 6.

170. Quoted in Judith Miller, "South Asia Called Major Terror Hub in Survey by U.S.," *New York Times*, April 30, 2000 [OE]. Also see Barry Schweid, "Cuba on List of Terrorism Sponsors," *Miami Herald*, May 2, 2000 [OE].

171. Quoted in Tamayo, "Crisis Shook Exile Lobby."

172. See John P. Hardt, *Russia's Paris Club Debt: U.S. Interests*. Congressional Research Service, July 18, 2000, p. 4; Neil C. Sorrells, "Bill Targets Russia's Cuban Listening Post," *Congressional Quarterly Weekly Report*, May 6, 2000, p. 1060; Christopher Wilson, "U.S. House Uses Debt to Hit Russia Over Cuba Spy Station," July 19, 2000, *Reuters News Service*. Companion legislation introduced into the Senate by Connie Mack never got out of committee.

173. Quoted in "Russian Official Protests U.S. Vote Restricting Aid Over Cuba Spy Station," *Miami Herald*, May 6, 2000 [OE].

174. Ana Radelat, "GOP Divided on Easing Sanctions," *Miami Herald*, May 22, 2000 [OE].

175. Quoted in Eric Pianin and Karen DeYoung, "GOP Leaders Appear Ready to Ease Cuba Embargo," *Washington Post*, June 21, 2000 [OE].

176. Quotes in John Burgess, "Cuban Entrepreneurs to Visit U.S.," *Washington Post*, June 3, 2000 [OE].

177. Quoted in Mary Beth Warner, "Cuba Vote Signals Change for Cuban-American Lobby," June 14, 2000, *Reuters News Service*. On Cuba's market potential, see Kimberly L. Waldner and Wayne S. Smith, *Conference Probes Potential for U.S.– Cuba Farm Trade*. Washington DC: Center for International Policy, March 2001, pp. 1–3.

178. Quoted in Jim Lobe, "Cuba: U.S. Food Exporters Could Earn $400 million a Year," June 15, 2000, *Reuters News Service*.

179. Quoted in Justin Brown, "U.S. Backing Away from Sanctions," *Christian Science Monitor*, June 23, 2000 [OE].

180. All quotes in Juan O. Tamayo, "Farmers Fuel Drive to Repeal Sanctions," *Miami Herald*, June 25, 2000 [E].

181. Quoted in Pianin and DeYoung, "GOP leaders Appear Ready to Ease Cuba Embargo."

182. Nethercutt and Ros-Lehtinen quoted in "Lawmakers Back Easing Cuba Embargo for Food Sales," *Miami Herald*, June 27, 2000 [OE].

183. See Eric Pianin, "House GOP Agrees to Relax Cuba Trade Embargo," *Washington Post*, June 27, 2000 [OE].

184. Quotes in "Senate Pushes More Cuba Trade," *Miami Herald*, July 7, 2000 [OE]; Ana Radelat, "Support Ebbs for Proposal to Soften Cuba Embargo," *Miami Herald*, July 14, 2000 [OE]; "Support for Cuba Trade Compromise Continues to Wane," July 19, 2000, *Reuters News Service*.

185. Quoted in Jodi A. Enda, "Clinton 'Inclined' to Sign Bill That Eases Embargo," *Miami Herald*, June 29, 2000 [OE].

186. See Christopher Marquis, "House Approves Easing of Embargo on Cuba Trade and Travel," *New York Times*, July 21, 2000 [OE]. For an informative discussion of the travel restrictions issue, see Mark P. Sullivan, *Cuba: U.S. Restrictions on Travel and Legislative Initiatives in the 106th Congress*. Congressional Research Service, August 11, 2000, 6 pp.

187. Norman Kempster, "U.S. Accuses Cuba of Inhibiting Emigration," *Los Angeles Times*, August 29, 2000, p. A4; Scott Wilson, "Feud Threatens Pact on Cuba–U.S. Migration," *Washington Post*, August 30, 2000, pp. A1, A19.

188. See Frank Davies, "Cuban Official Bared from D.C.," *Miami Herald*, September 12, 2000 [OE].

189. Transcript, White House, Office of the Press Secretary, "Press Briefing by Jake Siewert," October 10, 2000.

190. See Frank Davies, "U.S. to Pay Victims of Terror Using Assets of Cuba, Iran," *Miami Herald*, October 7, 2000 [OE]; "Clinton Administration Strikes Deal on Brothers to the Rescue," *CUBANEWS*, October 5, 2000, p. 5.

191. See "Condoleeza Rice, Rep. Lincoln Díaz-Balart Agree on Blueprint for Bush's Cuba Policy," *Cuba Trader*, December 4, 2000 [OE].

192. Quoted in Frank Davies, "Party Adopts Pro-Embargo Platform," *Miami Herald*, August 1, 2000 [OE]. Also see "Party Platforms on Cuba," *Miami Herald*, August 14, 2000 [OE].

193. Text, "Texas Governor George W. Bush on U.S. Policy for Latin America," Miami,

Florida, August 25, 2000, U.S. Department of State, International Information Programs.

194. Quoted in Mark Silva, "Bush Backs Cuban Refugee Policy," *Miami Herald*, September 12, 2000, p. A1; Carol Rosenberg, "Bush Signals Shift on Immigration," *Miami Herald*, September 15, 2000, p. 16A.

195. Quoted in Mark Silva and Lesley Clark, "Dade Supporters Hear Tough Talk on Castro," *Miami Herald*, November 6, 2000 [OE].

196. Quoted in David E. Sanger, "World Views: Rivals Differ on U.S. Role in the World," *New York Times*, October 29, 2000 [OE].

197. Quoted in Luisa Yanez and Mark Silva, "Lieberman Salutes Founder of CANF," *Miami Herald*, October 24, 2000 [OE].

198. Quoted in Laurence Arnold, "Cuban Group Torn on Candidates," *Washington Post*, October 4, 2000 [OE]; Yanez and Silva, "Lieberman Salutes Founder of CANF."

199. Quoted in Juan O. Tamayo, "Exile Group Hires Ex-U.S. Official to Lead Image Effort," *Miami Herald*, June 30, 2000 [OE].

200. Quoted in Scott Wilson, "In Miami, Cuba Exile Group Shifts Focus," *Washington Post*, September 14, 2000, p. A3.

201. Marry Beth Warner, "Cuba Vote Signals Change for Cuban-American Lobby," June14, 2000, *Reuters News Service*.

202. Quoted in Christopher Marquis, "Cuban-American Lobby on the Defensive," *New York Times*, June 30, 2000 [OE].

203. Quoted in Ana Radelat, "Deal Reached in Congress for U.S.–Cuba Food Sales," *Miami Herald*, October 6, 2000 [OE].

204. See Juan O. Tamayo, "Relaxing Sanctions Could Yield Little in Short Run," *Miami Herald*, June 26, 2000 [OE]; Economist Intelligence Unit, *Country Report: Cuba*, June 2000, p. 30.

205. "Text of Clinton's Serbia Talks," *New York Times*, October 7, 2000 [OE].

206. Quoted in "Clinton Says 1996 Incident Undercut Plan to Weaken Castro," *Miami Herald*, November 9, 2000 [OE].

207. See Steven A. Holmes and Lizette Alvarez, "Senate Approves Easing Sanctions on Food to Cuba," *New York Times*, October 19, 2000 [OE]. Despite the "caveats" attached to the legislation, USA Engage Chairman William Lane interpreted the business community response "a positive one" and termed the new law "another validator that the U.S. sanctions policy in general was gradually reflecting greater sanity." He noted the absence of new unilateral sanctions during 1999 and 2000 that he attributed to the effectiveness of the business lobby in "moving the needle away from a lazy man's foreign policy that imposed sanctions for a quick political gain to a smart sanctions policy that kept high technology away from rogue regimes and tried to direct all attention at the elites and not at the masses." Interview with William Lane, September 12, 2001.

208. Council on Foreign Relations, Report of an Independent Task Force, *U.S.–Cuban Relations in the 21st Century: A Follow-On Report*, New York, 2001.

209. Quoted in "Clinton Says U.S., Vietnam Open New Chapter," *New York Times*, November 17, 2000 [OE] [our emphasis].

210. Mark Silva, "Seniors, Cuban Exiles Key Forces," *Miami Herald*, November 9,

2000 [OE]. Another study reported that appoximately 60,000 more Cuban-Americans voted for Bush than had voted for Robert Dole, the 1996 republican presidential candidate. James W. Ceaser and Andrew E. Busch, *The Perfect Tie.* Lanham: Rowman & Littlefield, 2001, p. 119.

211. Quoted in "Albright Regrets Castro's Still Around," *Miami Herald*, January 10, 2001 [OE].

CONCLUSION

1. Quoted in *CubaINFO*, June 22, 1990, p. 4.
2. Principal Deputy Secretary of State Robert Gelbard, in U.S. Congress, Senate, *Prospects for Democracy in Cuba*, p. 11.
3. Secretary of State Warren Christopher, in U.S. Congress, House, Committee on Foreign Affairs, *Middle East Peace and Other Vital Interests*, 103rd Cong., 2nd Sess., July 28, 1994, p. 15.
4. Confidential Interview 6.
5. Confidential Interview 10.
6. Confidential Interview 1.
7. Confidential Interview 6.
8. Interview with William Lane.
9. "Text: Bush Extends Suspension of Title III of Helms–Burton Act," U.S. Department of State, International Information Programs, Washington File, July 17, 2001.
10. Quoted in Howard LaFranchi, "New US Foreign Policy Very Much Like Old," *Christian Science Monitor*, October 3, 2001 [OE].
11. Quoted in Ambrose Evans-Pritchard, "Europe Mounts Challenge to Global Cop," *Sydney Morning Herald*, June 16, 2001, p. 19.

POSTSCRIPT

1. Ros-Lehtinen and Díaz-Balart quoted in Carol Rosenberg, "Hardening of Cuba Policy is expected from Bush," *Miami Herald*, December 19, 2000 [OE].
2. See Ibid.
3. Quoted in "Helms Predicts Castro Will Fall During Bush Presidency," January 12, 2001, *Reuters News Service*. Also see Tracey Eaton, "Battle Over Cuba Heating Up Again," *Dallas Morning News*, January 14, 2001 [OE].
4. U.S. Congress, Senate, Committee on Foreign Relations, *Nomination of Colin L. Powell to Be Secretary of State*, 107th Cong., 1st Sess., January 17, 2001, p. 61.
5. Quoted in "Sanctions Needed on Castro's Cuba, Powell Says," March 14, 2001, *Reuters News Service*. This position was consistent with the Bush administration's response to the International Trade Commission report on the economic embargo that concluded that unilateral sanctions only served to strengthen the Castro regime and increase the hardships on ordinary Cubans. Bush officials, however, preferred to stress the report's findings that the benefits to the U.S. economy of lifting the embargo would be marginal. See United States International Trade Commission, *The Economic Impact of U.S. Sanctions with Respect to Cuba*, February 2001.
6. Quoted in Miles A. Pomper, "GOP Drive to Roll Back Sanctions Promises to Be

a Case by Case Struggle," *Congressional Quarterly Weekly Report*, February 10, 2001, p. 339; "U.S. Cuba Sanctions to Continue with Castro–Cheney," January 8, 2001, *Reuters News Service.*

7. See "Rules for Cuba Sales Stalled by Congress, State Department," *CUBANEWS*, March 2001, p. 7.

8. U.S. Congress, Senate, Committee on Foreign Relations, *Overview of Foreign Policy Issues and Budget*, 107th Cong., 1st Sess., March 8, 2001, p. 34. For a summary of the various legislative initiatives to ease export and travel restrictions to Cuba during Bush's first year in office, see Mark P. Sullivan and Maureen Taft-Morales, *Cuba: Issues for Congress*. Congressional Research Service, August 31, 2001, pp. 15–18.

9. Quoted in Karen DeYoung, "Anti-Castro Figure Named to State Dept," *Washington Post*, April 15, 2001 [OE].

10. Quoted in "U.S. Summaries of Key Nations in Drug Report," CNN.com/U.S., March 1, 2001.

11. Tracey Eaton, "Cuba: Smuggle and You'll Die," *Dallas Morning News*, June 27, 2001 [OE].

12. Quoted in Anne Usher, "Ex-Drug Czar: U.S., Cuba Should Cooperate Against Trafficking," *Miami Herald*, August 29, 2001 [OE].

13. U.S. Department of State, *Patterns of Global Terrorism*, April 2001 [OE]; Marc Lacey, "Attacks Were Up Last Year, U.S. Terrorism Report Says," *New York Times*, May 1, 2001 [OE]. Also see Paul R. Pillar, *Terrorism and U.S. Foreign Policy*. Washington DC: Brookings Institution, 2001, pp. 45, 181–3. Retaining Cuba on the list of terrorist states was interpreted by the business community as another obstacle to the easing of sanctions. During talks with State Department officials in early September, one of the community's principle lobbyists found that although the administration was reviewing its sanctions policies toward countries such as North Korea, Cuba was placed "in a different category. I sensed that any change is a long, long way off. From a sanctions point of view, Cuba is listed as a terrorist state and a lot of controls and limitations grow out of that." Confidential Interview C, Washington DC, September 13, 2001. Senior official of a high-profile business organization active in the antisanctions campaign.

14. Quoted in "Powell Says UN Rights Censure of Cuba a Priority," March 7, 2001, *Reuters News Service.*

15. Quoted in Pablo Alfonso, "U.N. Panel Condemns Cuba for Rights Abuses," *Miami Herald*, April 19, 2001 [OE]. Other participants in the phone calling 'offensive' included Vice President Cheney, NSC Adviser Rice, and Deputy Secretary of State Richard Armitage. See *U.S. ˙Cuba Policy Report*, April 2001, p. 2.

16. Quoted in Rhonda Schaffler, "Tough Call – Economic Sanctions Against Cuba," April 26, 2001, *Reuters News Service.*

17. Quoted in Mark Fineman, "China President's Tour Underscores Shifts in Latin American Landscape," *Los Angeles Times*, April 15, 2001 [OE]. Also see Tom Hargrave, "Cuba's Rice Imports Will Increase in 2002," PlanetRice.Net, September 19, 2001.

18. Quoted in Alfredo Corchado, "Delayed Traders," *Dallas Morning News*, May 12, 2001 [OE].

19. Quoted in Karen DeYoung, "More U.S. Aid Sought for Cuban Dissidents," *Washington Post*, March 8, 2001 [OE].

20. Quoted in Christopher Marquis, "Helms and Lieberman Seek to Aid Dissidents in Cuba," *New York Times*, May 16, 2001 [OE].

21. White House, Office of the Press Secretary, "Remarks by the President in Recognition of Cuba Independence Day," May 18, 2001.

22. Quoted in Marc Frank, "Dissident Scorns U.S. Plan to Bankroll Castro Foes," May 17, 2001, *Reuters News Service*; "Cuba's Internal Dissidents Rejects U.S. Bill Granting Them Economic Aid," *FBIS: LAT*-2001-0517, May 17, 2001.

23. Pedro Pablo Álvarez Ramos and Héctor Palacios Ruiz, "Aid We'd Rather Not Receive," *New York Times*, June 18, 2001 [OE].

24. Confidential Interview A, Washington DC, September 14, 2001. Office of Cuban Affairs, Department of State; Confidential Interview B, Washington DC, September 14, 2001, Bureau of Western Hemisphere Affairs, Department of State.

25. Quoted in Tom Carter, "Bush Weighs Helms–Burton Law," *Washington Times*, June 11, 2001 [OE].

26. Confidential Interview A. Also see "EU Assures Spanish Hotel Group of Support over U.S. Sanctions Against Cuba," *FBIS: WEU*-2001-0321, March 17, 2001.

27. Transcript of Hearings, March 7, 2001, in *Reuters News Service*.

28. See, for example, Dana Canedy, "On Land and Sea, Florida Plans for Turmoil After Castro's Death," *New York Times*, July 2, 2001 [OE].

29. Confidential Interview A.

30. Quoted in "Bush Vows Crackdown on Travel to Cuba," *Miami Herald*, July 14, 2001 [OE].

31. Quoted in James Gerstenzang, "U.S. Gets Tough on Its Cuba Restrictions," *Los Angeles Times*, July 14, 2001 [OE].

32. Almost five months later, the democratic chair of the Senate Foreign Relations Committee, Joseph Biden, was not only still refusing to schedule Reich's confirmation hearings but also signaling that the nomination was "not likely to go anywhere." Interview with CNN, quoted in *Bloomberg News Service Online*, October 29, 2001.

33. Janice O'Connell, staff member, Senate Foreign Relations Committee, "U.S.–Cuban Relations: Is the Cold War in the Caribbean Thawing?" Session at Latin American Studies Association XXIII International Congress, Washington DC, September 6, 2001.

34. Quoted in Jay Hancock, "Sanctions Decision Near, Bush Appeases Anti-Castro Cubans," *Baltimore Sun*, July 14, 2001 [OE].

35. Quoted in Tim Johnson, "Bush Suspends Law Enabling Lawsuits over Property Confiscated by Cuba," *Miami Herald*, Juy 17, 2001 [OE]; Karen DeYoung, "Bush Continues a Clinton Policy on Cuba," *Washington Post*, July 17, 2001 [OE].

36. Quoted in G. Robert Hillman, "Bush Suspends Suits Over U.S. Property in Cuba," *Dallas Morning News*, July 17, 2001 [OE]; Christopher Marquis, "Bush Forgoes Trying to Bar Cuba Deals by Foreigners," *New York Times*, July 17, 2001 [OE].

37. Quoted in Tim Johnson and Nancy San Martin, "Bush: Ban on Cuba Lawsuits Remains," *Miami Herald*, July 17, 2001 [OE].

38. Quoted in DeYoung, "Bush Continues a Clinton Policy on Cuba."

39. Interview with William Lane, September 12, 2001.

40. Confidential Interview A.
41. Confidential Interviews C.
42. Confidential Interview B.
43. Confidential interview C.
44. Interview with William Lane, September 12, 2001.
45. Confidential Interview D, Washington DC, September 13, 2001. Senior official of a high-profile business organization active in the antisanctions campaign.
46. Dana Canedy, "Official in a Cuban Exile Group Resigns, Exposing a Rift," *New York Times*, July 24, 2001 [OE]; Luisa Yanez and Nancy San Martin, "20 on CANF Board Resign," *Miami Herald*, August 8, 2001 [OE].
47. Confidential Interview A; Confidential Interview B.
48. Confidential interview C. Also see Shawn Zeller, "The Bush Brothers' Cuban Connection," *National Journal*, March 10, 2001, pp. 716–18.
49. Confidential Interview C.
50. See John Maggs, "New President, Same Old Cuba Policy," *National Journal*, June 16, 2001, p. 1823.
51. Confidential Interview C.
52. Hays and Mas Santos quoted in Rafael Lorente, "Anti-Castro Group's Moderation Makes Waves," *Chicago Tribune*, July 29, 2001 [OE].
53. Quoted in Nancy San Martin, "Traffic of Cubans Multiplying," *Miami Herald*, August 2, 2001 [OE]. Also see Alfonso Chardy et al., "Cubans Found at Sea Are Coming to the U.S.," *Miami Herald*, August 3, 2001 [OE].
54. Quoted in Steven Mufson, "U.S. Decides to Stay Neutral on Beijing's Olympic Bid," *Washington Post*, June 25, 2001 [OE]. Also see Jane Perlez, "U.S. Won't Block China's Bid for Olympics," *New York Times*, July 11, 2001 [OE].
55. Quoted in Steven Mufson, "North Korea, U.S. to Hold Talks Today on Missiles," *Washington Post*, June 13, 2001 [OE] [our emphasis].
56. Quoted in Steven Mufson, "Powell Urges Resumption of N. Korea Talks," *Washington Post*, July 28, 2001 [OE].
57. See Alan Sipress and Steven Mufson, "Powell Takes the Middle Ground," *Washington Post*, August 26, 2001 [OE].
58. Quoted in "European Officials Start Visit in Cuba," *Miami Herald*, August 23, 2001 [OE].
59. Quoted in Anita Snow, "Castro: Cuba Opposes Terrorism, War," *Los Angeles Times*, September 22, 2001 [OE].
60. John Donnelly and Anthony Shadid, " 'Rogue' Nations Furnish Intelligence," *Boston Globe*, September 27, 2001 [OE].
61. See Bill Miller and Walter Pincus, "Defense Analyst Accused of Spying for Cuba," *Washington Post*, September 22, 2001 [OE]; Christopher Marquis, "U.S. Restricts Cuban Diplomats in Capital After Spy Charges," *New York Times*, October 20, 2001 [OE].
62. See "Anti-Terrorism Legislation Threatens to Undo Trade Sanctions Reform Act," *Cuba Trader*, October 1, 2001 [OE]; "White House, Senate Reach Deal to Limit Changes to Trade Sanctions Reform Act," *Cuba Trader*, October 9, 2001 [OE]. In early November, the Senate Agriculture Committee voted to allow private U.S. financing of farm exports to Cuba and later that month four American companies signed the first trade accords with Cuba to supply $20 million worth of food in the

wake of Hurricane Michelle. Although some American commentators speculated that these developments were the beginning of the end of the embargo, White House and Cuban officials concurred that there was no policy shift underway.

63. Email Correspondence, October 2, 2001. Senior official in the Office of Cuban Affairs, Department of State [author's emphasis].

64. Quoted in Kevin Sullivan, "U.S. Is Urged to Remove Cuba from List of Terror Sponsors," *Washington Post*, September 29, 2001 [OE].

65. Quoted in "Sept. 11 Attacks Prompt New Cuba Strategies," *Cuba Trader*, October 1, 2001 [OE].

66. See Susan B. Glasser, "Russia to Dismantle Spy Facility in Cuba," *Washington Post*, October 18, 2001 [OE].

67. Quoted in Patrick E. Tyler, "Russia and the U.S. See a Breakthrough on Divisive Issues," *New York Times*, October 19, 2001 [OE].

68. Tim Johnson, "Cuba Declines U.S. Aid, Wants to Pay For Relief," *Miami Herald*, November 10, 2001 [OE]; "Cuba Opens to American Food Sale," *New York Times*, 17, 2001 [OE].

69. See "Cuba Says Trade Deals 'No Policy Shift' by U.S.," *New York Times*, November 25, 2001 [OE].

70. Quoted in Nancy San Martin, "U.S. Embargo of Cuba Remains Strongly in Place, Official Says," *Miami Herald*, December 6, 2001 [OE] [our emphasis].

71. See Juan O. Tamayo, "Miamian Will Help Oversee Cuba Policy," *Miami Herald*, January 26, 2002 [OE].

72. Quoted in Christoher Marquis, "Bush Hires Hard-Liners to Handle Cuba Policy," *New York Times*, February 3, 2002 [OE].

73. Quoted in Ginger Thompson, "Cuba, Too, Felt the Sept. 11 Shock Waves," *New York Times*, February 7, 2002 [OE].

Index

Index